Pennsylvania
Atlas & Gazetteer™

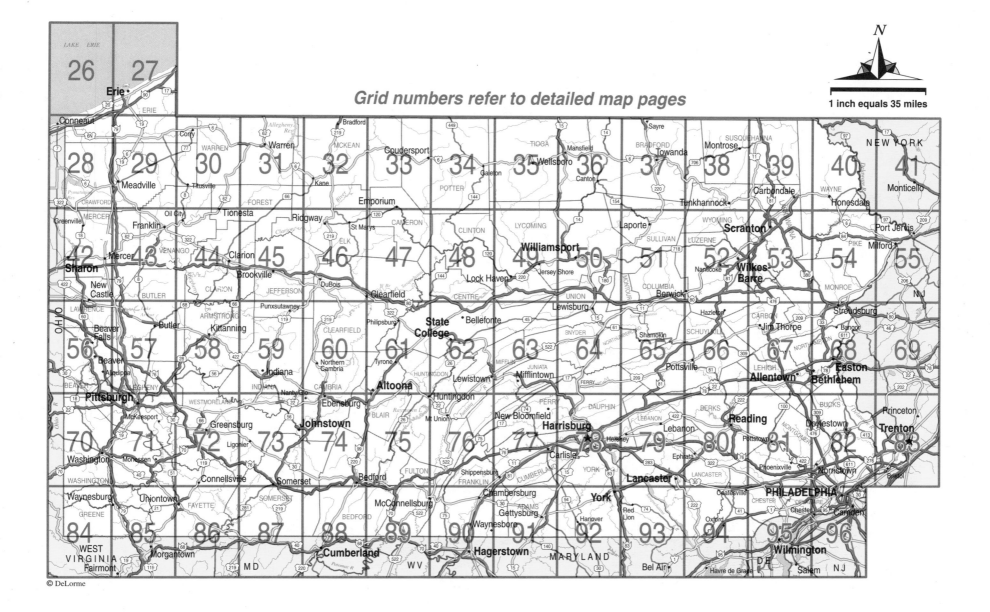

Grid numbers refer to detailed map pages

1 inch equals 35 miles

© DeLorme

Important Notices

DeLorme has made reasonable efforts to provide you with accurate maps and related information, but we cannot exclude the possibility of errors or omissions in sources or of changes in actual conditions. DELORME MAKES NO WARRANTIES OF ANY KIND, EITHER EXPRESS OR IMPLIED, INCLUDING THE WARRANTIES OF MERCHANTABILITY AND FITNESS FOR A PARTICULAR PURPOSE. DELORME SHALL NOT BE LIABLE TO ANY PERSON UNDER ANY LEGAL OR EQUITABLE THEORY FOR DAMAGES ARISING OUT OF THE USE OF THIS PUBLICATION, INCLUDING, WITHOUT LIMITATION, FOR DIRECT, CONSEQUENTIAL OR INCIDENTAL DAMAGES.

Nothing in this publication implies the right to use private property. There may be private inholdings within the boundaries of public reservations. You should respect all landowner restrictions.

Some listings may be seasonal or may have admission fees. Please be sure to confirm this information when making plans.

Safety Information

To avoid accidents, always pay attention to actual road, traffic and weather conditions and do not attempt to read these maps while you are operating a vehicle. Please consult local authorities for the most current information on road and other travel-related conditions.

Do not use this publication for marine or aeronautical navigation, as it does not depict navigation aids, depths, obstacles, landing approaches and other information necessary to performing these functions safely.

EIGHTH EDITION, SECOND PRINTING. Copyright © 2003 DeLorme. All rights reserved.
P.O. Box 298, Yarmouth, Maine 04096   (207) 846-7000   www.delorme.com

Table of Contents

THE ATLAS

THE GAZETTEER

Index

continued on next page

continued on next page

➡ Excursions

BLUE MOUNTAIN & READING RAILROAD – Shoemakersville – (610) 562-2102 – Page 80, A-3 1.5 hour, 29-mile round trip steam railroad excursion drawn by Engine No. 425 or 2102. Over bridges and through small towns and Pennsylvania Dutch farmlands.

CANAL MUSEUM/JOSIAH WHITE – Easton – (610) 515-8000 – Page 68, C-2 Leaves from dock in Hugh Moore Park. 45- to 60-minute ride on the Josiah White, a mule-drawn canal boat. On restored section of Lehigh Canal.

DUMAN LAKE PARK TRAIN – Ebensburg – (814) 948-6247 – Page 60, D-1 Gas-driven model engine runs on 0.5-mile track in Duman Lake Park. Seasonal.

THE DUQUESNE INCLINE – Pittsburgh – (412) 381-1665 – Page 71, A-5 Cable railway in operation since 1877. Original Waiting Rooms have exhibits. Observation Deck at Upper Station with view of Pittsburgh.

EAST BROAD TOP RAILROAD – Orbisonia – (814) 447-3011 – Page 76, C-1 Narrow-gauge line built in 1873, follows 10-mile course through Aughwick Valley. 50-minute round trip. Roundhouse and steam locomotives on display. Registered National Historic Landmark.

FAIRMOUNT PARK TROLLEY – Philadelphia – (215) 925-8687 – Page 96, A-2 Designed to resemble turn-of-20th-century Fairmount Park trolleys. One ticket permits on-and-off all-day travel. Routes pass many of Park's attractions. Seasonal.

GETTYSBURG RAILROAD – Gettysburg – (717) 334-6932 – Page 91, B-7 Existing line used during Civil War. Steam locomotives. Two round trips: Gettysburg to Biglerville (16 miles, 75 minutes), or Gettysburg to Mt. Holly Springs (50 miles, 5 hours). Seasonal.

HIAWATHA – Williamsport – (570) 326-2500 – Page 50, C-1 Narrated paddlewheel excursions along Susquehanna River. Snack bar. Leaves from Susquehanna State Park. Seasonal.

JOHNSTOWN INCLINED PLANE RAILROAD – Johnstown – (814) 536-1816 – Page 73, B-7 Built in 1891 to carry people to safety during flooding. Travels 500 feet up 71.9% grade. Gift shop at upper station.

MILLERSBURG FERRY – Liverpool – (717) 444-3200 – Page 64, D-2 Car and passenger ferry using only two remaining wooden-hulled stern-wheel ferryboats in U.S. Designated State Historic Landmark. Ferries run from North Street, Millersburg, to dock two miles south of Liverpool. Crossing takes 20 minutes. Seasonal.

MONONGAHELA INCLINE – Pittsburgh – (412) 442-2000 – Page 71, A-5 Built in 1870 to connect Pittsburgh with Mt. Washington. Travels 635 feet up 70.9% grade. View of central Pittsburgh skyline. Recently renovated.

MULE BARGE – New Hope – (215) 862-2842 – Page 82, B-4 One-hour excursion on Delaware Canal. Live music on some excursions. Country scenery. Seasonal.

OIL CREEK & TITUSVILLE RAILROAD – Oil City – (814) 676-1733 – Page 44, A-1 Travels round trip of 23 miles through historic Oil Creek Valley. Seasonal with some special trips.

PENNSYLVANIA TROLLEY MUSEUM – Meadowlands – (724) 228-9256 – Page 70, C-3 Follows part of former interurban trolley line between Pittsburgh and Washington. Trolleys, locomotives, and cars on display. Seasonal.

PIONEER TUNNEL COAL MINE AND STEAM LOCOMOTIVE – Ashland – (570) 875-3850 – Page 65, B-7 Two excursions. Tour horizontal-drift coal mine in open cars pulled by battery-operated mine motor. Miner guides. 35 minutes. 30-minute ride on the Henry Clay, a narrow-gauge steam locomotive. Scenic area, mining town, and strip mine.

SHADE GAP ELECTRIC RAILWAY – Rockhill – (814) 447-9576 – Page 76, C-1 Two-mile round trip on restored trolleys follows Blacklog Creek.

STEAMTOWN NATIONAL HISTORIC SITE – Scranton – (570) 340-5200 – Page 53, A-5 Lackawanna Railroad. Two-hour trip through Nay Aug Tunnel and Roaring Brook Gorge. 26 miles. Locomotives and equipment. Seasonal.

STOURBRIDGE LINE RAIL – Honesdale – (570) 253-1960 – Page 40, D-1 50-mile rail trip along Lackawaxen River and Old Delaware and Hudson Canal. Layover in Lackawaxen.

STRASBURG RAILROAD – Strasburg – (717) 687-7522 – Page 94, A-1 Through Lancaster County Amish Country. 45-minute trip on train with coal-burning steam locomotive and coaches over 50 years old. Seasonal. Located next to Railroad Museum of Pennsylvania *(see Historic Sites/Museums)*.

WK&S RAILROAD – Kempton – (610) 756-6469 – Page 66, C-4 Authentic passenger cars pulled by steam-powered locomotive. Picnicking at Furman's Grove. Operating model trains. Gift shops and refreshment stand. Seasonal.

WATER GAP TROLLEY – Delaware Water Gap – (570) 476-9766 – Page 68, A-2 Authentically styled trolleys tour Delaware Water Gap National Recreation Area. Narrated by guides.

✳ Amusements

BLAND PARK – Tipton – (814) 684-3538 – Page 61, C-5 Antique carousel. Miniature steam locomotive. Adult rides and kiddieland. Entertainment, fireworks, sky diving exhibits. Snack stands and chicken barbecue. Shops. Seasonal.

BUSHKILL PARK – Easton – (610) 258-6941 – Page 68, C-1 Antique carousel with hand-carved and painted horses. Whip, Autoscooter, Pretzel Ride, Rocket Ride. Kiddie rides. Arcade, roller rink, game concession. Refreshments, picnic area, shop.

DORNEY PARK AND WILDWATER KINGDOM – Allentown – (610) 395-3724 – Page 67, D-6 Three roller coasters. Wave pool and waterslide. Totspot. Miniature golf. Craftspeople. Stock car racetrack. Food Festival complex. Picnic area. Seasonal.

DUTCH WONDERLAND – 4 mi. E of Lancaster – (717) 291-1888 – Page 80, D-1 Super Slide, miniature railroad, botanical gardens, sternwheel riverboat, miniature auto rides, bumper cars, merry-go-round. Monorail. Diving show. Exhibits and displays. Gift shops, restaurants, refreshment stands.

EAGLE FALLS ADVENTURE PARK – Lancaster – (717) 397-4674 – Page 80, D-1 Four waterslides. Bumper boats. Miniature golf. Snack bar.

HERSHEY'S CHOCOLATE WORLD – Hershey – (717) 534-4900 – Page 79, B-4 Tours of a simulated chocolate-making process, from cocoa tree plantation to chocolate bar. Tropical garden, historical display, shops, and cafe. Visitor center.

HERSHEYPARK – Hershey – (717) 534-3900 – Page 79, B-4 87-acre park features 42 rides in six theme areas: Tudor Square, Rhineland, Deitschplatz, Carrousel Circle, Tower Plaza, Pioneer Frontier. ZooAmerica. Shows and entertainment. Restaurants and refreshment stands.

IDLEWILD PARK – 3 mi. W of Ligonier – (724) 238-3666 – Page 73, B-4 Olde Idlewild with traditional and kiddie rides. Jumpin' Jungle. Story Book Forest. Hootin' Holler. Soak Zone water park with pool and waterslides. Entertainment. Petting zoo.

KENNYWOOD – West Mifflin – (412) 461-0500 – Page 71, A-7 Several roller coasters. Raging Rapids whitewater ride. Paddleboats. Entertainment. Arcades. Refreshment stands and cafeteria.

KNOEBELS AMUSEMENT RESORT – Elysburg – (570) 672-2572 – Page 65, A-5 Jet Star and Phoenix rides. 37 other rides. Miniature golf. Pioneer Railway Train Ride. Bumper cars. Rainbow Castle and Country Bear Show. Refreshment stands, cafeteria, and restaurants. Swimming pool.

MONTAGE – Scranton – (570) 969-7669 – Page 53, B-5 Alpine slide and waterslide. Chairlift rides. Refreshments.

REPTILAND – Allenwood – (570) 538-1869 – Page 50, C-2 Fifty species of snakes, turtles, lizards, alligators, and crocodiles. Handling by staff members with audience participation. Cricket Machine. Gift shop and snack bar. Seasonal.

ROADSIDE AMERICA – Shartlesville – (610) 488-6241 – Page 66, D-2 Indoor miniature village shows rural life over 200 years. Model trains.

SESAME PLACE – Langhorne – (215) 752-7070 – Page 83, C-5 Children's play-and-learn park based on the television show, Sesame Street. Performances by the Sesame Street Muppets. Animal show. Water play. Nets and Climbs. Adult Oasis.

SHAWNEE PLACE – Shawnee-On-Delaware – (570) 421-7231 – Page 54, D-3 Active play park with ball crawl, cable glide, cargo nets, waterslides, pony rides. Refreshments, puppet theater, picnic area, discovery nature trail.

TREXLER-LEHIGH COUNTY GAME PRESERVE – Schnecksville – (610) 799-4171 – Page 67, C-6 1,500-acre animal preserve which visitors drive through to view animals. Miniature farm with petting animals. Nature-study building with displays and films. Refreshments and picnic areas.

WALDAMEER PARK – Erie – (814) 838-3591 – Page 27, D-4 24 rides. Kiddieland. Games and arcade. Shops. Refreshments. Picnic area.

WILLIAMS GROVE PARK – Mechanicsburg – (717) 697-8266 – Page 78, C-1 Rides include Swiss Bobs and Super Water Slide. Fun houses, arcade, shooting gallery. Paddleboats, miniature golf. Refreshments and picnicking.

Spectator Sports

HARRISBURG SENATORS – Harrisburg – (717) 231-4444 – Page 78, B-2 Eastern baseball league, class-AA farm team for Montreal Expos. Plays at City Island Park.

HERSHEY BEARS HOCKEY CLUB – Hershey – (717) 534-3911 – Page 79, B-4 AHL farm team for Philadelphia Flyers.

LADBROOK AT THE MEADOWS – Meadow Lands – (724) 225-9300 – Page 70, C-4 Standardbred harness racing.

LEHIGH VALLEY VELODROME – Trexlertown – (610) 967-7788 – Page 67, D-6 World-class professional and amateur bicycle racing. Site of U.S. National Championship. Open for public use and to observe training during non-race periods.

PENN NATIONAL RACE COURSE – Grantville – (717) 469-2211 – Page 79, A-4 Thoroughbred horse racing.

PETER J. McGOVERN LITTLE LEAGUE MUSEUM – South Williamsport – (570) 326-3607 – Page 50, C-2 Equipment, uniforms, memorabilia, computerized quiz games, and documentary films. Batting and pitching cages with instant replay. Also site of annual Little League World Series at Lamade Stadium.

PHILADELPHIA EAGLES – Philadelphia – (215) 463-5500 – Page 96, A-2 NFL football team. Plays at Veterans Stadium.

PHILADELPHIA FLYERS – Philadelphia – (215) 755-9700 – Page 96, A-2 NHL hockey team. Plays at First Union Center.

PHILADELPHIA PARK – Bensalem – (215) 639-9000 – Page 82, D-4 Thoroughbred horse racing.

PHILADELPHIA PHILLIES – Philadelphia – (215) 463-1000 – Page 96, A-2 National League baseball team. Plays at Veterans Stadium.

PHILADELPHIA 76ERS – Philadelphia – (215) 339-7676 – Page 96, A-2 NBA basketball team. Plays at First Union Center.

PITTSBURGH PENGUINS – Pittsburgh – (412) 642-1800 – Page 71, A-6 NHL hockey team. Plays at Civic Arena.

PITTSBURGH PIRATES – Pittsburgh – (412) 321-2827 – Page 71, A-5 National League baseball team. Plays at PNC Park.

PITTSBURGH STEELERS – Pittsburgh – (412) 323-1200 – Page 71, A-5 NFL football team.

POCONO DOWNS – Wilkes-Barre – (570) 825-6681 – Page 52, B-4 Standardbred harness racing.

POCONO INTERNATIONAL RACEWAY – Long Pond – (570) 646-2300 – Page 53, D-6 Major motor speedway, featuring three 500-mile races annually, including NASCAR Winston Cup stock cars and CART-PPG Indy cars.

READING PHILLIES – Reading – (610) 375-8409 – Page 80, A-3 Eastern baseball league, class-AA farm team for Philadelphia Phillies. Plays at Reading Municipal Stadium.

ROWING/SCULLING – Philadelphia – (215) 542-7844 – Page 96, A-2 High schools, colleges, and clubs participate in rowing races and annual rowing regatta along the Schuylkill River. Watch from grandstands at Fairmount Park's Boat House Row.

Pennsylvania Dutch Country

Pennsylvania Dutch Country offers a glimpse into societies that have maintained rich ethnic, spiritual, and cultural ties to their past. The mostly German (Deutsche) groups who came to this area seeking freedom of religion have retained their habits of work, dress, and belief in simplicity—in sharp contrast to the fast pace of the world around them.

THE AMISH FARM AND HOUSE – 6 mi. E of Lancaster – (717) 394-6185 – Page 80, D-1 Replica of Old Order Amish home and farmstead. 1805 stone house. Operating farm with animals. Annual events. Tours. Gift shop.

AMISH MENNONITE INFORMATION CENTER – Intercourse – (717) 768-0807 – Page 80, D-2 Information on Intercourse area.

THE AMISH VILLAGE – 2 mi. N of Strasburg – (717) 687-8511 – Page 80, D-1 House built in 1840 with authentic furnishings. Smokehouse, blacksmith shop, spring-house. Farm animals. Waterwheel and windmill. One-room schoolhouse.

BIRD-IN-HAND FARMER'S MARKET – Bird-in-Hand – (717) 393-9674 – Page 80, D-1 Meat and farm produce. Baked goods including shoofly pie. Snack counter. Gift shops.

CENTRAL MARKET – Lancaster – (717) 291-4723 – Page 79, D-7 One of oldest covered markets. Fruits, vegetables, cheese, meat, flowers, and baked goods.

HANS HERR HOUSE – Lancaster – (717) 464-4438 – Page 93, A-7 Built 1719. Used as Mennonite meetinghouse. Restored. Outbuildings. Visitors' center. Picnicking.

MENNONITE INFORMATION CENTER – 4.5 mi. E of Lancaster – (717) 299-0954 – Page 80, D-1 Information on Mennonite and Amish cultures. Film. Displays. Hebrew Tabernacle Reproduction. Gift shop. Mennonite guides available for tours of Amish farmlands.

PENNSYLVANIA DUTCH CONVENTION & VISITORS BUREAU VISITORS CENTER – Lancaster – (717) 299-8901 – Page 79, D-7 "Lancaster County: People, Places & Passions" multimedia presentation provides overview of Pennsylvania Dutch Country's attractions. Exhibits. Brochures and maps.

PENNSYLVANIA GERMAN CULTURAL HERITAGE CENTER – Kutztown – (610) 683-1330 – Page 67, D-4 Restored 19th-century farmstead and museum illustrate Pennsylvania German rural life in late 19th and early 20th centuries. 1870 one-room schoolhouse. Genealogical library. Educational and cultural programs.

THE PEOPLE'S PLACE – Intercourse – (717) 768-7171 – Page 80, D-2 Interpretation center tells stories of Amish, Mennonite, and Hutterite people. Three-screen documentary, "Who Are the Amish?" and "Hazel's People," a dramatic film set in Mennonite community. Book and craft shop.

WEAVERTON ONE-ROOM SCHOOLHOUSE – Bird-in-Hand – (717) 768-3976 – Page 80, D-1 Authentic schoolhouse with school session re-created through animated, life-size figures.

Wineries

Wineries listed here are open for tasting and retail sales, although hours and days may vary. While most have winery and/or vineyard tours, calling ahead for an appointment is recommended. Many also have off-premise outlets, including tasting, sales, food, and wine-related displays. In addition, most wineries offer a variety of styles, including wines made from native American, French-American, and European grape varieties, as well as other types of fruit.

ADAMS COUNTY WINERY – Orrtanna – (717) 334-4631 – Page 91, B-6

ALLEGRO VINEYARDS – Brogue – (717) 927-9148 – Page 93, B-6

BROOKMERE FARM VINEYARDS – Belleville – (717) 935-5380 – Page 62, D-3

BUCKINGHAM VALLEY VINEYARDS & WINERY – Buckingham – (215) 794-7188 – Page 82, B-3

CALVARESI WINERY – Bernville – (610) 488-7966 – Page 80, A-2

CHADDSFORD WINERY – Chadds Ford – (610) 388-6221 – Page 95, B-6

CHERRY VALLEY VINEYARDS – Saylorsburg – (570) 992-2255 – Page 68, A-1

CLOVER HILL VINEYARDS & WINERY – Breinigsville – (610) 395-2468 – Page 67, D-5

CONNEAUT CELLARS – Conneaut Lake – (814) 382-3999 – Page 28, D-3

COUNTRY CREEK VINEYARD & WINERY – Telford – (215) 723-6516 – Page 81, B-7

FRANKLIN HILL VINEYARDS – Bangor – (610) 588-8708 – Page 68, B-2

HERITAGE WINE CELLARS – North East – (814) 725-8015 – Page 27, C-7

LANCASTER COUNTY WINERY – Willow Street – (717) 464-3555 – Page 93, A-7

LAPIC WINERY – New Brighton – (724) 846-2031 – Page 56, C-3

MAZZA VINEYARDS – North East – (814) 725-8695 – Page 27, C-7

MOUNT HOPE ESTATE & WINERY – Manheim – (717) 665-7021 – Page 79, C-6

MOUNT NITTANY VINEYARD & WINERY – Linden Hall – (814) 466-6373 – Page 62, B-2

NAYLOR WINE CELLARS – Stewartstown – (717) 993-2431 – Page 93, B-5

NISSLEY VINEYARDS – Bainbridge – (717) 426-3514 – Page 79, D-4

OREGON HILL WINE COMPANY – Morris – (570) 353-2711 – Page 35, D-6

PEACE VALLEY WINERY – Chalfont – (215) 249-9058 – Page 82, B-2

PENN-SHORE VINEYARDS – North East – (814) 725-8688 – Page 27, C-7

PREATE WINERY – Old Forge – (570) 457-1555 – Page 53, B-5

PRESQUE ISLE WINE CELLARS – North East – (814) 725-1314 – Page 27, C-6

Unique Natural Features

ARCHBALD POTHOLE – Archbald Pothole State Park – Page 39, D-6 38 feet deep by 42 feet across. Formed by glacial stream action 15,000 years ago.

BALANCED ROCK – Trough Creek State Park – Page 75, B-6 Appears to be balanced precariously on edge of cliff.

BOULDER FIELD – Hickory Run State Park – Page 53, D-5 Unsorted, loosely packed boulders in flat, 400-foot-by-1,800-foot area. Boulders up to 26 feet long. National Natural Landmark.

BUCK HILL FALLS – Buck Hill Falls – Page 54, C-1 Large waterfalls cascade over sandstone and siltstone rocks.

BUSHKILL FALLS – Bushkill – Page 54, D-3 Eight falls on Little Bushkill and Pond Run Creeks. Highest falls is 100 feet. Shops, refreshments, miniature golf. Picnicking. Fishing. Paddleboats. Seasonal.

CANYON VISTA – Worlds End State Park – Page 51, A-5 View of gorge and mountainous area. Mountain laurel bloom (June) and fall foliage are particularly scenic.

CHINESE WALL (HIGH ROCKS AND BOX-CAR ROCKS) – State Game Lands Number 211 – Page 65, D-5 Outcrop of quartz-pebble conglomerate on Sharp Mountain.

CLARK RUN GORGE – Gallitzin State Forest – Page 73, A-7 In Charles F. Lewis Natural Area. Two-mile trail through gorge. Several small waterfalls and geologic features.

CORAL CAVERNS – Manns Choice – Page 74, D-3 Coral Reef. Fossil wall. Cathedral Room. Stalagmites and stalactites, illuminated by special lighting. Guided tours. Trackless train. Picnicking.

CUCUMBER FALLS – Ohiopyle State Park – Page 86, B-2 On Cucumber Run in Cucumber Ravine. Falls drop about 30 feet. Spring wildflowers and flowering rhododendron.

DEER LEAP, FACTORY, AND FULMER FALLS – Delaware Water Gap National Recreation Area – Page 55, C-4 On Dingmans Creek in Child's Park. Series of highly scenic falls. Trails.

DINGMANS FALLS – Delaware Water Gap National Recreation Area – Page 55, C-4 130-foot-high "stepped" falls. Highest in Pennsylvania.

FRANKFURT MINERAL SPRINGS – Raccoon Creek State Park – Page 51, A-2 In U-shaped grotto formation. Small waterfalls formed from surface creek. Springs are opposite creek emerging from underground. Once mineral springs resort. Trail.

GLENS NATURAL AREA – Ricketts Glen State Park – Page 51, B-7 Twenty-one waterfalls in Y-shaped gorge along two branches of Kitchen Creek. Ganoga Falls is highest at 94 feet. Trails. National Natural Landmark.

HEARTS CONTENT SCENIC AREA – Allegheny National Forest – Page 31, C-4 Virgin forest of 400-year-old white pines and younger hemlocks. Hiking and interpretive trails. National Natural Landmark.

HELL'S HOLLOW FALLS – McConnells Mill State Park – Page 56, A-4 Cascading waterfall along Hell Run in northwest part of park. Wildflowers. Trail.

ICE MINE – Trough Creek State Park – Page 75, B-7 Loose rock mass cooled through opening in hillside releases cold air as outside air begins to warm and forms ice from melted snow water during spring and into summer. Trail.

INDIAN CAVERNS – Spruce Creek – Page 61, C-7 Indian relics. Limestone formations. "Frozen Niagara," flowstone sheet. Lights and walkways. Guided tours. Gift shop.

INDIAN ECHO CAVERNS – Hummelstown – Page 78, B-4 Pillars and pipes. Curtains and cascades of flowstone. Limestone formations. Lights and walkways. Gift shop. Picnicking. Playground.

KELLY'S RUN GORGE – 0.75 mi. N of Holtwood – Page 93, B-7 Shallow, small stream with small cascades and large rocks. Sheer vertical rock walls. Empties into Lake Aldred (Susquehanna River). Ferns and wildflowers. Kelly's Run National Recreational Trail for hiking and horseback riding.

LAUREL CAVERNS – 5 mi. E of Uniontown – Page 86, B-1 2.3 miles of passages; over 4.5 acres. Catacomb-type cave with limestone formation. Guided tour section with lit passages. Self-guided tour through natural, unlit area of cave. Gift shop. Trackless train.

LINCOLN FALLS – Lincoln Falls – Page 37, D-4 On Elk Creek. Waterfalls over red sandstone.

LITTLE FOUR-MILE RUN FALLS – Leonard Harrison State Park – Page 35, C-5 Two waterfalls along Little Four-Mile Run. First along Turkey Path drops 20 feet and second drops 40 feet. Best after heavy rain. Turkey Path is very steep.

MOUNT DAVIS – Forbes State Forest – Page 87, B-5 Highest point in Pennsylvania, at 3,213 feet. Views. Firetower. Trails.

OHIOPYLE FALLS – Ohiopyle State Park – Page 86, B-3 On Youghiogheny River. Falls drop 40 feet over 100 yards. Bordered by Ferncliff Natural Area, a peninsula designated National Natural Landmark.

PENN'S CAVE – 5 mi. E of Centre Hall – Page 62, A-4 Water cavern. Tours by boat. Limestone formations. Picnic area, hiking trails.

PINE CREEK GORGE – Leonard Harrison State Park – Page 35, C-5 "Grand Canyon of Pennsylvania." (Additional overlooks at Colton Point State Park.) 47 miles long. Deepest point is 1,450 feet. Formed by glacial action and water action. 12-mile roadless stretch between Ansonia and Blackwell is National Natural Landmark. Trails. Canoeing and rafting.

PRESQUE ISLE – Presque Isle State Park – Page 27, D-4 3,200-acre peninsula located in Lake Erie. Composed of sand deposits formed by lake currents. National Natural Landmark.

RINGING ROCKS – Pottstown – Page 81, B-6 Field of diabase boulders that produce sounds when struck with hard object.

SHOHOLA FALLS – State Game Lands Number 180 – Page 54, A-4 Series of rapids and falls through 80-foot-high gorge.

SILVERTHREAD FALLS – Delaware Water Gap National Recreation Area – Page 55, C-4 80-foot-high narrow falls in rock fracture.

SLIPPERY ROCK CREEK GORGE – McConnells Mill State Park – Page 56, A-4 Four-mile-long gorge up to 400 feet deep. National Natural Landmark.

Parks/Forests/ Recreation Areas

Ice Sports abbreviations: B = boating; F = fishing; S = skating

Note on camping: Most Pennsylvania state forests allow "primitive" camping. Hikers are free to camp anywhere in the forest, but cannot stay more than one night and must obey any fire restrictions. Check with the forester's office.

NAME, LOCATION, PHONE	ATLAS LOCATION	CAMPSITES	BOATING	FISHING	SWIMMING	HIKING TRAILS (miles)	INTERPRETIVE CENTER	ICE SPORTS	CROSS-COUNTRY SKIING (miles)	SNOWMOBILING (miles)	COMMENTS
Allegheny Island State Park, Oakmont, (724) 865-2131	Page 57, D-7										Undeveloped. No facilities.
Allegheny National Forest, Warren, (814) 723-5150	Page 31, B-7	734	●	●	●	178.5	●	F	54	350	Allegheny River and Reservoir. 18 camping areas.
Archbald Pothole State Park, 9 mi. N of Scranton, (570) 945-3239	Page 39, D-6					2					Archbald Pothole *(see Unique Natural Features.)*
Bald Eagle State Forest, Laurelton, (570) 922-3344	Page 63, B-7			●		58			24	435	Streams, vistas, horse trails.
Bald Eagle State Park, Blanchard, (814) 625-2775	Page 48, D-3	171	●	●	●	8	●	BFS	●		Foster Joseph Sayers Lake. Sledding, 3.5 mi. all-terrain-vehicle trails.
Beltzville State Park, 5 mi. E of Lehighton, (610) 377-0045	Page 67, B-5		●	●	●	15	●	BF	6	5	Beltzville Lake. Sledding.
Bendigo State Park, 4 mi. NE of Johnsonburg, (814) 965-2646	Page 32, D-2			●	●						Sledding and tobogganing.
Benjamin Rush State Park, Philadelphia, (215) 453-5000	Page 82, D-4										Undeveloped. No facilities.
Big Pocono State Park, Tannersville, (570) 894-8336	Page 54, D-1					10					Views. Downhill skiing. 5 mi. horse trails.
Big Spring State Park, 5.5 mi. SW of New Germantown, (717) 776-5272	Page 76, B-3					1			●	●	Big Spring forms Shermans Creek.
Black Moshannon State Park, 9 mi. E of Philipsburg, (814) 342-5960	Page 61, A-7	78	●	●	●	16	●	BFS	12	2	Black Moshannon Lake. Electric motors only.
Blue Knob State Park, Pavia, (814) 276-3576	Page 74, B-3	45		●	●	16	●		4	8	Blue Knob, 3,146-foot-high peak. Downhill skiing.
Buchanan State Forest, McConnellsburg, (717) 485-3148	Page 75, D-6			●		87			5	78	70,500 acres in five sections. Horse trails.
Buchanan's Birthplace State Park, Mercersburg, (717) 485-3948	Page 90, B-1			●							President James Buchanan's birthplace marked by stone pyramid.
Bucktail State Park, Sinnemahoning, (814) 486-3365	Page 33, D-6		●	●							Non-powered boating only. Scenic drive.
Caledonia State Park, Caledonia, (717) 352-2161	Page 91, A-5	184		●	●	10	●		10		Historical center. Golfing. 0.7 mi. bike trails.
Canoe Creek State Park, 7 mi. E of Hollidaysburg, (814) 695-6807	Page 75, A-5		●	●	●	8	●	BFS	5		Canoe Lake. Electric motors only. Sledding. 4.2 mi. horse trails.
Chapman State Park, Clarendon, (814) 723-0250	Page 31, B-5	83	●	●	●	13	●	FS	4.4	2	0.5 mi. bike trails. Lighted sledding and skating. Electric motors only.
Cherry Springs State Park, Galeton, (814) 435-5010	Page 34, C-2	30				1				●	Woodsmen's carnival.
Clear Creek State Forest, Allegheny River Tract, Kennerdell, (814) 226-1901	Page 43, B-7			●		20					6 mi. of Allegheny River frontage.
Clear Creek State Forest, Sigel, (814) 226-1901	Page 45, B-6			●	●	15					Old iron furnace.
Clear Creek State Park, Sigel, (814) 752-2368	Page 45, B-6	53	●	●	●	26	●	S	3		Canoeing on Clarion River. Non-powered boating only.
Codorus State Park, 3 mi. SE of Hanover, (717) 637-2816	Page 92, B-2	198	●	●	●	5	●	BFS	16	●	Lake Marburg. 10-horsepower limit. Sledding. 10 mi. horse trails.
Colonel Denning State Park, 8 mi. N of Newville, (717) 776-5272	Page 77, B-5	52		●	●	18	●	S	1		Trout fishing. Nature activities.
Colton Point State Park, Wellsboro, (570) 724-3061	Page 35, C-5	25		●		4			●	1	Pine Creek Gorge *(see Unique Natural Features).*
Cook Forest State Park, Cooksburg, (814) 744-8407	Page 45, B-5	226	●	●	●	30	●	S	10	20	Sledding. 4.5 mi. horse trails. Non-powered boating only.
Cornplanter State Forest, Tionesta, (814) 723-0262	Page 30, D-3			●		2	●		8		Forest Demonstration Area, Lashure Trail.
Cowans Gap State Park, Richmond Furnace, (717) 485-3948	Page 90, A-1	233	●	●	●	10	●	FS	6.5		Cowans Gap Lake. Electric motors only. Sledding.
Delaware Canal State Park, Bristol to Easton, (610) 982-5560	Page 68, D-3		●	●		60	●	FS	60		Delaware Canal. Electric motors only. National Historic Landmark. 60 mi. bike and 60 mi. horse trails.
Delaware State Forest, 15 mi. N of Stroudsburg, (570) 895-4000	Page 54, D-3		●	●		150		FS	4	128	80,000 acres.
Delaware Water Gap National Recreation Area, Bushkill, (570) 588-2451	Page 54, D-3	125	●	●	●	51	●	FS	5.5		Dingmans Falls Visitor Center. Climbing, waterfalls.
Denton Hill State Park, 11 mi. E of Coudersport, (814) 435-2115	Page 34, B-2			●					2		Downhill skiing. Bowhunting festival.
Elk State Forest, Emporium, (814) 486-3353	Page 33, D-6			●		100			23	91	Elk herd.
Elk State Park, 8 mi. W of Wilcox, (814) 965-2646	Page 32, D-3		●	●				BFS			East Branch Clarion River Lake.
Erie National Wildlife Refuge, Guys Mills, (814) 789-3585	Page 29, C-6			●		●	●		●		Hiking, nature study, exhibits.
Evansburg State Park, Collegeville, (610) 409-1150	Page 81, C-7			●		6	●		7		Mennonite and natural history exhibits. 5 mi. bike and 10 mi. horse trails.
Forbes State Forest, Laughlintown, (724) 238-1200	Page 73, C-5			●		69			40	79	51,700 acres in five divisions.
Fort Washington State Park, Fort Washington, (215) 591-5250	Page 82, C-2			●		5			1.7		Dogwoods and fields. 1 mi. horse trails.
Fowlers Hollow State Park, 7 mi. S of Blain, (717) 776-5272	Page 76, B-4	18		●		6			1	1	Picnic tables. Adjacent to Tuscarora State Forest.
Frances Slocum State Park, Wyoming, (570) 696-3525	Page 52, B-3	100	●	●	●	9	●	FS	●	7	Frances Slocum Lake. Electric motors only. Sledding.
French Creek State Park, 14 mi. SE of Reading, (215) 582-9680	Page 81, C-4	201	●	●	●	38	●	FS	15		Three lakes. Electric motors only. Sledding.
Gallitzin State Forest, 5 mi. E of Windber, (814) 472-1862	Page 74, C-2			●		51			7	21	Charles F. Lewis Natural Area.
Gifford Pinchot State Park, Lewisberry, (717) 432-5011	Page 78, D-2	339	●	●	●	18	●	BFS	8		Pinchot Lake. Electric motors only. Sledding, 2 mi. horse trails.
Gouldsboro State Park, 5 mi. S of Gouldsboro, (570) 894-8336	Page 53, C-7		●	●	●	10		F	●		Gouldsboro Lake. Electric motors only.
Greenwood Furnace State Park, Huntingdon, (814) 667-1800	Page 62, C-2	51		●	●	6	●	FS	4.4	5	Greenwood Lake. Remains of Greenwood Iron Furnace.
Hickory Run State Park, White Haven, (570) 443-0400	Page 53, D-5	381		●	●	45	●	FS	13	20	Boulder Field *(see Unique Natural Features).* Sledding.
Hills Creek State Park, 7 mi. N of Wellsboro, (570) 724-4246	Page 35, B-7	110	●	●	●	5	●	FS	●		Hills Creek Lake. Electric motors only.
Hyner Run State Park, 6 mi. E of Renovo, (570) 923-6000	Page 48, B-3	30		●	●	1			●	1	Within Sproul State Forest. Self-guided nature trail.
Hyner View State Park, Hyner, (570) 923-6000	Page 48, B-4									5	Forest picnic area. Views.
Jacobsburg State Park, Nazareth, (610) 746-2801	Page 68, B-1			●		7.5	●		9		Historic sites. Sledding, 6 mi. horse trails.
Jennings Enviromental Education Center, Slippery Rock, (724) 794-6011	Page 43, D-5					7	●		7.5		Hiking, nature study, programs, exhibits.
John Heinz National Wildlife Refuge, Philadelphia, (215) 365-3118	Page 96, A-1		●	●		10	●				Canoeing. Cusano Enviromental Education Center.
Kettle Creek State Park, 7 mi. N of Westport, (570) 923-6004	Page 48, A-1	71	●	●	●	2	●	FS	1	2	Sledding. Electric motors only.
Keystone State Park, New Derry, (724) 668-2939	Page 72, A-3	100	●	●	●	6	●	FS	3		Keyston Lake. Electric motors only. Sledding, 2 mi. horse trails.
Kings Gap Enviromental Education and Training Center, Carlisle, (717) 486-5031	Page 77, D-6					16	●				Nature study and hiking.
Kinzua Bridge State Park, 4 mi. N of Mt. Jewett, (814) 965-2646	Page 32, B-3			●		1					Kinzua Viaduct *(see Historic Sites/Museums).*
Kooser State Park, Bakersville, (814) 445-8673	Page 73, D-5	47		●	●	1	●		1.5		Playground.
Lackawanna State Forest, 11 mi. N of Scranton, (570) 963-4561	Page 53, C-6			●		23			15	24	Views from Big Pine Hill. Nature trail.
Lackawanna State Park, 10 mi. N of Scranton, (570) 945-3239	Page 39, D-5	96	●	●	●	6	●	FS	2		Lackawanna Lake. Electric motors only. Sledding.
Laurel Hill State Park, 10 mi. W of Somerset, (814) 445-7725	Page 87, A-5	264	●	●	●	12	●	F		10	Laurel Hill Lake. Electric motors only. Self-guided nature trail.
Laurel Mountain State Park, Ligonier, (412) 238-6623	Page 73, C-5								2		Downhill skiing.
Laurel Ridge State Park, Seward to Ohiopyle, (724) 455-3744	Page 86, A-4	●		●		94			55	2	Several sections.
Laurel Summit State Park, 3 mi. S of Rector, (412) 238-6623	Page 73, C-5								●	●	Picnic area.
Lehigh Gorge State Park, Weatherly, (570) 443-0400	Page 67, A-4		●	●		30			15	15	Lehigh River. Whitewater.
Leonard Harrison State Park, 10 mi. W of Wellsboro, (570) 724-3061	Page 35, C-5	30	●	●		2	●				Pine Creek Gorge *(see Unique Natural Features).*
Linn Run State Park, 4 mi. S of Rector, (724) 238-6623	Page 73, C-5			●		5				●	Within Forbes State Forest.
Little Buffalo State Park, Newport, (717) 567-9255	Page 77, A-7		●	●	●	7	●	FS	●		Little Buffalo Lake. Electric motors only. Sledding. Historic sites.
Little Pine State Park, 3 mi. N of Waterville, (570) 753-6000	Page 49, B-6	104	●	●	●	13	●	BFS	4	6	Electric motors only. Sledding.
Locust Lake State Park, Barnesville, (570) 467-2404	Page 66, B-2	282	●	●	●	5	●	FS			Locust Lake. Electric motors only. Woodlands. 1 mi. bike trails.
Lyman Run State Park, 15 mi. E of Coudersport, (814) 435-5010	Page 34, C-2	35				6				4	Picnicing
M.K. Goddard State Park, Sandy Lake, (412) 253-4833	Page 43, A-4		●	●		14	●	BFS	7.6	4	Lake Wilhelm. 10-horsepower limit.
Marsh Creek State Park, Eagle, (610) 458-5119	Page 81, D-5		●	●	●	6		BFS	●		Marsh Creek Lake. Electric motors only. Sledding, covered bridges. 6 mi. horse trails.
McCall Dam State Park, Eastville, (570) 966-1455	Page 49, D-7			●							Picnicking. River fishing.
McConnells Mill State Park, 40 mi. N of Pittsburgh, (724) 368-8091	Page 57, A-4		●	●		11	●				Slipping Rock Creek Gorge. Whitewater, climbing, sledding.
Memorial Lake State Park, 19 mi. NE of Harrisburg, (717) 865-6470	Page 79, A-5		●	●		2		FS	●		Memorial Lake. Electric motors only.
Michaux State Forest, Fayetteville, (717) 352-2211	Page 91, A-5		●	●		65			4	132	Appalachian Trail. All-terrain-vehicle trail. 0.6 mi. bike trails.
Milton State Park, Milton, (570) 988-5557	Page 50, D-3		●	●		1					Island on West Branch of Susquehanna River. 10-horsepower limit. 1 mi. bike trails.
Mont Alto State Park, Mont Alto, (717) 352-2161	Page 91, B-4			●						●	Near Pines State Forest Natural Area.
Moraine State Park, Portersville, (724) 368-8811	Page 57, A-5		●	●	●	27	●	BFS		20	10-horsepower limit. Sledding. 6.8 mi. bike, 3 mi. all-terrain-vehicle, and 7 mi. horse trails.
Moshannon State Forest, Clearfield, (814) 765-0821	Page 46, D-3		●	●		244		F	13	208	Backpacking. Canoeing only
Mt. Pisgah State Park, Troy, (570) 297-2734	Page 37, B-4		●	●	●	10	●	BFS	7.5	8	Stephen Foster Lake. Electric motors only. Sledding, exercise trail.
Nescopeck State Park, White Haven, (570) 297-2734	Page 52, D-4			●				F			Nature Study.
Neshaminy State Park, Croydon, (215) 639-4538	Page 83, D-4		●	●	●	3			●		Boat access to the Delaware River. 1 mi. bike trails.
Nockamixon State Park, 5 mi. E of Quakertown, (215) 529-7300	Page 82, A-2		●	●	●	3	●	BFS	5.3		Nockamixon Lake. 10-horsepower limit. Sledding, 2.8 mi. bike trails. Youth hostels.
Nolde Forest Environmental Education Center, Reading, (610) 796-3699	Page 80, B-3			●		10	●				Environmental education programs. 666 acres.
Ohio River islands National Wildlife Refuge, Midland, (304) 422-0752	Page 56, D-2		●	●	●						Nature study.

Ice Sports abbreviations: B = boating; F = fishing; S = skating

NAME, LOCATION, PHONE	ATLAS LOCATION	CAMPSITES	BOATING	FISHING	SWIMMING	HIKING TRAILS (miles)	INTERPRETIVE CENTER	ICE SPORTS	CROSS-COUNTRY SKIING (miles)	SNOWMOBILING (miles)	COMMENTS
Ohiopyle State Park, Ohiopyle, (412) 329-8591	Page 86, B-3	226	•	•		67	•		29	19	Youghiogheny River Gorge. Whitewater, sledding.
Oil Creek State Park, 4 mi. N of Oil City, (814) 676-5915	Page 30, D-1		•	•		52			20		Oil Creek Gorge. Canoeing. 8.7 mi. bike trails.
Ole Bull State Park, 18 mi. S of Galeton, (814) 435-5000	Page 34, D-3	81	•	•	•	2	•				"The Black Forest."
Parker Dam State Park, 5 mi. S of Penfield, (814) 765-0630	Page 46, C-3	110	•	•	•	4	•	FS	2.7	6	Electric motors only. Backpacking, sledding.
Patterson State Park, Galeton, (814) 435-5010	Page 34, C-1	10				1				•	Susquehannock Trail System.
Penn Roosevelt State Park, 9 mi. S of State College, (814) 667-1800	Page 62, C-3	18	•			1		FS	•	1	Picnic tables. Lake.
Pine Grove Furnace State Park, Laurel, (717) 486-7174	Page 77, D-6	74	•	•	•	2	•	FS	•		Two lakes. Electric motors only. Bicycling.
Poe Paddy State Park, 4 mi. E of Poe Valley, (814) 349-2460	Page 63, B-5	41	•	•		1			0.4		Picnic tables. Fishing in Penn's Creek. Non-powered boating only.
Poe Valley State Park, Coburn, (814) 349-2460	Page 63, B-5	76	•	•	•	6	•	F	2.5	1	Electric motors only. In Bald Eagle State Forest. Winter sports.
Point State Park, Pittsburgh, (724) 471-0235	Page 71, A-5										National Historic Landmark. Views, fountains.
Presque Isle State Park, Erie, (814) 833-7424	Page 27, C-4		•	•	•	19	•	BFS	16		National Natural Landmark.
Prince Gallitzin State Park, Patton, (814) 674-1000	Page 60, C-3	437	•	•	•	10	•	BFS	8	20	Glendale Lake. Sledding. 2 mi. horse trails.
Promised Land State Park, 10 mi. N of Canadensis, (570) 676-3428	Page 54, B-2	480	•	•	•	29	•	FS	1	17	Promised Land and Lower Lakes. Electric motors only. 24.4 mi. horse trails.
Prompton State Park, Prompton, (570) 945-3239	Page 40, D-1		•	•	•						Undeveloped. No facilities.
Prouty Place State Park, Galeton, (814) 435-5010	Page 34, C-1			•							Trout fishing.
Pymatuning State Park, Jamestown, (724) 932-3141	Page 42, A-2	645	•	•	•	2	•	BFS	5	15	Pymatuning Lake. 10-horsepower limit. Sledding.
R.B. Winter State Park, 16 mi. W of Lewisburg, (570) 966-1455	Page 63, A-7	59	•	•	•	6	•	FS	4.3	2	695 acres. Picnic tables. Mountain laurel.
Raccoon Creek State Park, Frankfort Springs, (724) 899-2200	Page 56, D-2	176	•	•	•	13	•	FS	8	8	Wildflower Reserve. Electric motors only. Sledding. 3 mi. horse trails.
Ralph Stover State Park, 2 mi. N of Point Pleasant, (610) 982-5560	Page 82, A-3		•	•		1		FS			Whitewater, 1 mi. bike trails.
Ravensburg State Park, 8 mi. SE of Jersey Shore, (570) 966-1455	Page 49, D-7	21	•	•		1					78 acres, within narrow gorge.
Reeds Gap State Park, 7 mi. E of Millroy, (717) 667-3622	Page 63, C-5	14	•	•	•	5			4		Sledding.
Ricketts Glen State Park, 30 mi. N of Bloomsburg, (570) 477-5675	Page 51, B-7	120	•	•	•	26	•	F	•	18	Electric motors only. Sledding. Glens Natural Area (*see Unique Natural Features*). 5 mi. horse trails.
Ridley Creek State Park, Media, (610) 892-3900	Page 95, A-7			•		12	•		14.8		Sledding. 5 mi. bike and 5 mi. horse trails.
Rothrock State Forest, Petersburg, (814) 643-2340	Page 61, D-7			•		47			38	200	Five state natural areas; virgin timber stands.
Ryerson Station State Park, Wind Ridge, (724) 428-4254	Page 84, A-2	50	•	•	•	10	•	FS	5	6	Electric motors only. Sledding.
S.B. Elliott State Park, 9 mi. N of Clearfield, (814) 765-0630	Page 46, D-3	25				3				•	Within Moshannon State Forest. 1.2 mi. horse trails.
Salt Springs State Park, Dalton, (570) 945-3239	Page 38, A-4			•		2					Deep gorge, Fall Brook, waterfalls.
Samuel S. Lewis State Park, 12 mi. E of York, (717) 432-5011	Page 93, A-5					1	•				Views of Susquehanna River and farmlands.
Sand Bridge State Park, Mifflinburg, (570) 966-1455	Page 63, A-7			•						•	Picnic area and snowmobile trailhead.
Shawnee State Park, Schellsburg, (814) 733-4218	Page 74, D-2	293	•	•	•	12	•	BFS		12	Shawnee Lake. Electric motors only. Sledding.
Shikellamy State Park, Sunbury, (570) 988-5557	Page 64, A-3		•	•		2					Views. 0.7 mi. bike trails.
Sinnemahoning State Park, 5 mi. N of Sinnemahoning, (814) 647-8401	Page 47, A-7	35	•	•		5		FS		5	Sinnemahoning Lake. Electric motors only.
Sizerville State Park, 7 mi. N of Emporium, (814) 486-5605	Page 33, D-6	23		•	•	5	•		•	2	Mountain laurel.
Sproul State Forest, 3 mi. W of Renovo, (570) 923-6011	Page 48, B-2			•		257			14	204	Wilderness trout streams. Horse and all-terrain-vehicle trails.
Susquehanna State Park, Williamsport, (570) 326-2500	Page 50, C-1		•	•							35-mi. view of Susquehanna River. Paddlewheeler Hiawatha (*see Excursions*).
Susquehannock State Forest, Coudersport, (814) 274-3600	Page 33, B-7			•		85			30	230	25 mi. all-terrain-vehicle trails.
Susquehannock State Park, Wakefield, (717) 432-5011	Page 93, B-7			•		4	•				Views of Susquehanna River. Horse trails.
Swatara State Park, Pine Grove, (717) 865-6470	Page 65, D-6		•	•							Non-powered boating only. Undeveloped. No facilities.
Tiadaghton State Forest, South Williamsport, (570) 327-3450	Page 50, B-3		•	•		200			60	302	215,400-acre area in three blocks; canoeing.
Tioga State Forest, Ansonia, (570) 724-2868	Page 35, C-5	30	•	•		34			7	179	Pine Creek Gorge Natural Area (*see Unique Natural Features*). Canoeing.
Tobyhanna State Park, Tobyhanna, (570) 894-8336	Page 53, C-7	140	•	•	•	12		FS	•	5	Tobyhanna Lake. Electric motors only. 4.5 mi. bike trails.
Trough Creek State Park, 16 mi. S of Huntingdon, (814) 658-3847	Page 76, B-4	32	•	•		6			•		"Copperas" rock; Ice Mine and Balanced Rock (*see Unique Natural Features*). Near Raystown Lake.
Tuscarora State Forest, New Germantown, (717) 536-3191	Page 76, B-4			•		49			12	130	Trout streams.
Tuscarora State Park, 6 mi. W of Tamaqua, (570) 467-2404	Page 66, B-2		•	•	•	7	•	FS			Tuscarora Lake. Electric motors only.
Tyler State Park, Newton, (215) 968-2021	Page 82, C-4		•	•		4	•	FS	5.7		Neshaminy Creek. Electric motors only. Sledding. 9 mi. horse and 10.5 mi. bike trails.
Upper Pine Bottom State Park, Waterville, (570) 753-6000	Page 49, B-5			•							In Tiadaghton State Forest.
Warriors Path State Park, Saxton, (814) 658-3847	Page 75, C-5		•	•		3			2		Non-powered boating only. Sledding.
Weiser State Forest, Cressona, (570) 385-7800	Page 64, D-3			•		9			40	40	33-acre island. Hawk migrations.
Whipple Dam State Park, 10 mi. S of State College, (814) 667-1800	Page 62, C-2		•	•	•	1		FS	1.1	4	Electric motors only. Snowmobile trailhead.
White Clay Creek Preserve State Park, Landenberg, (610) 274-2900	Page 95, C-4			•	•	3					Bike trails; day-use park.
Worlds End State Park, Forksville, (570) 924-3287	Page 51, A-5	70	•	•	•	12	•		4	3	Whitewater
Wyoming State Forest, 2 mi. S of Hillsgrove, (570) 387-4255	Page 50, A-4			•		90		F	22	59	High Knob Natural Area. 50-mile horse trail.
Yellow Creek State Park, Brush Valley, (724) 357-7913	Page 59, D-6		•	•	•	5	•	BFS	•	•	10-horsepower limit. Sledding.

🌼 Botanical Gardens

APPLEFORD/PARSONS-BANK ARBORETUM – Villanova – (610) 527-4280 – Page 82, D-1 Small formal gardens. Greenhouse. Woods and informal plantings.

AWBURY ARBORETUM – Philadelphia – (215) 849-2855 – Page 82, D-2 57 acres. Developed by landscape architect William Saunders. Woodlands.

BARNES FOUNDATION ARBORETUM – Merion Station – (610) 667-0290 – Page 82, D-2 Trees, herbs, and flowers. Woodland tract. Lilacs, peonies, dwarf conifers, woody vines. Variety of small gardens.

BARTRAM'S GARDEN – Philadelphia – (215) 729-5281 – Page 96, A-2 Home of John Bartram, colonial botanist. 27 acres of gardens and open fields. 18th-century stone house, barn, and stable. Trails. Museum shop.

BEECHWOOD FARMS NATURE RESERVE – Fox Chapel – (412) 963-6100 – Page 57, D-6 90-acre natural area with herb garden and lawns.

BOWMAN'S HILL STATE WILDFLOWER PRESERVE – Washington Crossing – (215) 862-2924 – Page 82, B-4 In northern section of Washington Crossing Historic Park (*see Historic Sites/ Museums*). 110 acres of woods, meadows, ponds, bogs, and barrens. Native Pennsylvania plants. Penn's Woods. Preserve building with displays and information. Programs, walks, and films.

BRANDYWINE RIVER MUSEUM WILDFLOWER GARDEN – Chadds Ford – (610) 388-2700 – Page 95, B-6 Wildflower plantings with emphasis on color. (*See Art Museums/Science Centers.*)

DELAWARE VALLEY COLLEGE GARDENS – Doylestown – (215) 345-1500 – Page 82, B-2 Greenhouses with orchid collection and labeled tropical plants. Dwarf conifers. Arboretum with labeled trees and shrubs. Nursery Glass House with unusual plants. Herb garden. Hillman Sitting Garden in pink and white.

THE EBENEZER MAXWELL MANSION – Philadelphia – (215) 438-1861 – Page 82, D-2 Victorian house with two gardens. Front garden with rockwork, weeping trees, and mounded berm in style of 1840s and 1850s. Side garden with roses and ribbon garden surrounding fruit trees.

FAIRMONT PARK COMMISSION HORTICULTURE CENTER – Philadelphia – (215) 685-0096 – Page 96, A-2 Greenhouses supply city's plants. Seasonal exhibits. Lectures, demonstrations, workshops. Japanese house and garden.

HARTWOOD – Pittsburgh – (412) 767-9200 – Page 57, D-6 629-acre estate with Tudor Gothic mansion, stable complex, and formal gardens.

HAVERFORD COLLEGE ARBORETUM – Haverford – (610) 896-1100 – Page 82, D-1 400 species of trees and shrubs. Ornamental fruit trees. Duck Pond. Pinetum. Nature walk.

THE HILL-PHYSICK-KEITH HOUSE – Philadelphia – (215) 925-7866 – Page 96, A-2 Home of Dr. Philip Syng Physick, "father of American surgery." 19th-century style garden.

INDEPENDENCE NATIONAL HISTORICAL PARK GARDENS – Philadelphia – (215) 597-8974 – Page 96, A-2 Gardens re-create plantings of colonial Philadelphia. Brochure available at visitor center.

ITALIAN LAKE GARDENS – Harrisburg – (717) 255-3020 – Page 78, B-2 Designed after Italian Renaissance garden.

JENKINS ARBORETUM – Devon – (610) 647-8870 – Page 81, D-7 46 acres. Woodlands developed as arboretum. Azaleas and rhododendrons.

LONGWOOD GARDENS – Kennett Square – (610) 388-1000 – Page 95, B-5 350 acres of country estate gardens with seasonal plants, illuminated fountains, waterlilies. Conservatories with indoor gardens of exotic foliage plants, cacti, flowers, and bonsai.

continued on next page

MALCOLM W. GROSS MEMORIAL ROSE GARDEN – Allentown – (610) 437-7627 – Page 67, D-6 Over 100 varieties of roses. Old-Fashioned Garden has flowerbeds, water lagoons, wishing-well, fountain, and gazebos.

MASONIC HOMES ARBORETUM – Elizabethtown – (717) 367-1121 – Page 79, C-5 6.5-acre formal garden. Trees, roses, chrysanthemums, annual plantings, ornamental shrubs. Paths. Reflecting pool. Fountain.

MONT ALTO ARBORETUM – Mont Alto – (717) 749-3111 – Page 91, B-4 At Pennsylvania State University, Mont Alto Campus. 36 acres with 725 trees and shrubs representing more than 300 species from Asia, Europe, and U.S. Self-guiding trails.

MORRIS ARBORETUM OF THE UNIVERSITY OF PENNSYLVANIA – Philadelphia – (215) 247-5777 – Page 82, D-2 On 175 acres. Formal gardens, natural woodlands with over 3,500 different kinds of trees and shrubs, meadows, streams, and ponds. Azalea Meadow. Magnolia Slope.

THE PENN STATE FLOWER AND VEGETABLE TRIAL GARDENS – University Park – (814) 863-2190 – Page 62, B-2 Established in 1930s to test new plant varieties.

PENNSBURY MANOR – Morrisville – (215) 946-0400 – Page 83, C-5 Re-creation of William Penn's experimental farm and nursery. Kitchen garden, orchards, flower garden.

PENNSYLVANIA HORTICULTURAL SOCIETY – Philadelphia – (215) 988-8800 – Page 96, A-2 Garden in 18th-century style. In Independence National Historical Park *(see Historic Sites/Museums)*. Formal garden. Small orchard, vegetable, and herb gardens.

PETER WENTZ FARMSTEAD – Worcester – (610) 584-5104 – Page 82, C-1 German Kitchen Garden with typical 18th-century plantings and crossed paths.

THE PHILADELPHIA ZOOLOGICAL GARDEN – Philadelphia – (215) 243-1100 – Page 96, A-2 Indigenous plants are used to create natural habitats for animals.

PHIPPS CONSERVATORY – Pittsburgh – (412) 622-6914 – Page 71, A-6 2.5 acres of garden under glass. 13 display rooms. Seasonal flower shows.

THE PHYSIC GARDEN OF THE PENNSYLVANIA HOSPITAL – Philadelphia – (215) 829-3971 – Page 96, A-2 A physic garden was first requested by the physicians of Pennsylvania Hospital in 1774. This garden was finally planted for the Bicentennial. Herbs, wildflowers, shrubs, and trees form typical 18th-century medicinal herb garden.

PITTSBURGH AVIARY – Pittsburgh – (412) 323-7234 – Page 71, A-5 Ecological exhibits and tropical plantings relating to various species of birds inhabiting aviary.

PITTSBURGH CIVIC GARDEN CENTER – Pittsburgh – (412) 441-4442 – Page 71, A-6 Curto Educational Garden, four color and two perennial gardens. Groundcover Garden. Jennie King Mellon Garden, low-maintenance garden with hardy trees and flowering bulbs. Elizabethan Herb Garden with 10 different gardens. Dogwood Garden.

PUBLIC ROSE GARDEN – Bethlehem – (610) 865-7079 – Page 67, D-7 1.5 acres. 40–50 species. Band concerts.

THE SAMUEL POWEL HOUSE – Philadelphia – (215) 627-0364 – Page 96, A-2 Home and gardens date from 1765. Used by Samuel Powel, Philadelphia's mayor from 1775–1776 and 1789–1790.

SCOTT ARBORETUM OF SWARTHMORE COLLEGE – Swarthmore – (610) 328-8025 – Page 96, A-1 Over 5,000 kinds of plants on 110 acres of the campus. Harry Wood Memorial Garden. Various garden settings. Dean Bond Rose Garden. Wister Garden with woodland and rock gardens. James R. Frorer Holly Collection.

STAR ROSE GARDENS – West Grove – (610) 869-2426 – Page 94, B-4 Garden of 5,000 rose plants. 200 varieties. In bloom late May to early October. Adjacent rose fields in bloom at same time.

SWISS PINES – Phoenixville – (610) 933-6916 – Page 81, D-6 Japanese Gardens. Herb Gardens with culinary and aromatic herbs. Rhododendrons and azaleas. Heath and heather. Crab apple grove. Wildflower trail.

TAYLOR MEMORIAL ARBORETUM – Wallingford – (610) 876-2649 – Page 96, B-1 Along Ridley Creek. Unusual trees, hollies, azaleas, and camellias. Hedge demonstration planting. Lectures and courses.

TEMPLE UNIVERSITY AMBLER LANDSCAPE ARBORETUM – Ambler – (215) 283-1292 – Page 82, C-2 Formal flower gardens, Louise Stine Fisher Memorial Garden with dwarf shrubs. Woodland area. Three-acre orchard. Greenhouses.

THE TYLER ARBORETUM – Lima – (610) 566-5431 – Page 95, A-7 Native and exotic trees, shrubs, vines. Asiatic magnolias, cherries, crab apples, and lilacs. North Woods and Rhododendron Hillside. 20 miles of hiking trails.

WILDFLOWER RESERVE – Raccoon Creek State Park – (412) 899-2200 – Page 56, D-3 314 acres. 500 species of flowering plants. Variety of habitats. Hiking trails.

WYCK – Philadelphia – (215) 848-1690 – Page 82, D-2 Home to nine generations of same Quaker family. Garden includes roses, wildflowers, wisteria, shrubs, fruits, and vegetables.

Scenic Drives

CUMBERLAND–PERRY TOUR – Carlisle – 85 miles – Page 77, C-7 Best in autumn as foliage tour. From Carlisle travel south on Rte. 34. Turn right on Pine Rd. to follow Yellow Breeches Creek to Walnut Bottom. Then Rte. 174 through Lees Cross Roads to Rte. 11 in Shippensburg. Right on Rte. 696. Right at Newburg to Rte. 641 towards Newville. From Newville follow Rte. 233 north to Colonel Denning State Park. Continue on Rte. 233 to Rte. 850 east to left on Rte. 34 towards New Bloomfield and site of box huckleberry plant. Return south on Rte. 34 to Carlisle. Farmlands. Falling Springs Lodge. Little Red Schoolhouse.

LEHIGH COUNTY COVERED BRIDGES TOUR – Allentown – 29.9 miles – Page 67, D-7 Start at Bogert's Bridge in Lehigh Parkway at intersection of Oxford Dr. and Fish Hatchery Rd. Take Fish Hatchery Rd. to Rte. 29 (Cedar Crest Blvd.) and turn right. Turn left onto Iron Bridge Rd. and follow to Guth's Bridge. Through Guth's Bridge onto Lapp Rd. Turn left onto River Rd. to Wehr's Bridge. Right on Wehr Mill Rd. Left on Parkland Terrace. Right on Rte. 309. Left on Kernsville Rd. Go 1 mile and turn right on Jordan Rd. to Rex's Bridge. Drive through. Continue 1 mile to "Y" intersection. Go straight on gravel road to Geiger's Bridge. Return back to "Y" and turn right on Jordan Rd. Go 0.2 mile and head straight on dirt road (still Jordan Rd.). Go downhill, bear right. Continue past Trexler-Lehigh County Game Preserve entrance to Schlicher's Bridge. Return to Rte. 309 south to Rte. 222, Hamilton Blvd. exit. Turn left on Hamilton Blvd. back to Allentown.

LONGHOUSE SCENIC DRIVE – Allegheny National Forest – 30 miles – Page 31, B-6 Marked by triangular "scenic drive" signs. Start at Rogertown on forest boundary. Northeast on Rte. 59 along Allegheny River. Turn right at Kinzua Information Center onto Longhouse Scenic Dr. (Forest Rte. 262). At Red Bridge, cross river (Kinzua Bay) and continue along other shore on Rte. 321. At Bradford Ranger Station turn left onto Rte. 59. Continue west back to Kinzua Point.

PINE CREEK GORGE DRIVE – Wellsboro – 57.5 miles – Page 35, C-6 Along Pine Creek Gorge and through Tioga State Forest. Starting from Wellsboro, travel southwest on Rte. 660 to Leonard Harrison State Park (picnicking, overlooks, steep Turkey Path down to Gorge). Travel on Rte. 660 back towards Wellsboro, left on Rte. 362 heading towards Ansonia. Left on Rte. 6. Go 1 mile and turn left on Colton Rd. to Colton Point State Park (overlooks.) Leaving Colton Point State Park, continue on Colton Rd. to left on Painter Leetonia Rd. to left on Bradley Wales Rd. to Bradley Wales Picnic Area. Return back on Bradley Wales Rd. Left on West Rim Rd. to Blackwell. At Blackwell turn left onto Rte. 414. Left at Morris onto Rte. 287 to return to Wellsboro.

VALLEY TOUR – Gettysburg – 36 miles – Page 91, B-7 Marked by "Scenic Valley Tour" signs. Includes Gettysburg National Military Park, orchards, views, and covered bridge. Begin on Springs Ave. Turn left on West Confederate Ave. through the Park. After leaving the Park, travel west on Millerstown Rd., which becomes Pumping Station Rd. Turn right on Camp Gettysburg Rd. which continues as Knoxlyn Rd. Turn left on Knoxlyn–Orrtanna Rd., towards Orrtanna. Right on Orrtanna Rd. After crossing railroad tracks, turn left on Scott School Rd. and right on Bingaman Rd. Turn left at intersection with old Rte. 30 and then continue on Buchanan Valley Rd. (Rte. 234). Take first right on Church Rd., which leads back to Buchanan Valley Rd. (Rte. 234). Travel east on Rte. 234 to Biglerville. Right on South Main St. (Rte. 34), which becomes Biglerville Rd., back to Gettysburg.

Downhill Skiing

ALPINE MOUNTAIN – Analomink – (570) 595-2150 – Page 54, D-2 MOUNTAIN: 2 T-bars, 1 Poma lift, and 1 quad chairlift. VERTICAL DROP: 475 ft. FACILITIES: Snowmaking, ski school, ski shop, rentals, restaurant, lounge, and daycare.

BEAR CREEK SKI AND RECREATION AREA – Macungie – (610) 682-7100 – Page 81, A-6 MOUNTAIN: 2 rope tows, 1 T-bar, and 4 chairlifts. 6 beginners', 5 intermediate, and 2 advanced trails. VERTICAL DROP: 500 ft. FACILITIES: Snowmaking, ski school, ski shop, rentals, night skiing, cafeteria, restaurant, and lounge.

BIG BOULDER SKI AREA – Kidder Township – (570) 722-0101 – Page 53, D-6 MOUNTAIN: 6 double lifts and 1 triple lift. 6 mi. of cross-country trails. 3 beginners', 5 intermediate, and 3 advanced trails. VERTICAL DROP: 475 ft. FACILITIES: Ski school, ski shop, rental equipment, night skiing, cafeteria, restaurant, lounge, bar, snowmaking, daycare, and accommodation at the mountain.

BLUE KNOB RECREATION AREA – Kidder Township (Claysburg) – (814) 239-5111 – Page 74, B-3 MOUNTAIN: 2 double lifts, 2 triple lifts, and 2 platter pull lifts, with combined uphill capacity of 5,400 skiers/hr. 17 mi. of cross-country trails. 20% beginners', 50% intermediate, and 30% advanced trails. VERTICAL DROP: 1,052 ft. FACILITIES: Snowmaking, rentals, ski shop, ski school, night skiing, cafeteria, lounge, daycare, and accommodation at the mountain.

BLUE MOUNTAIN SKI AREA – 7 mi. E of Palmerton – (610) 826-7700 – Page 67, B-6 MOUNTAIN: 1 bar and 3 chairlifts. 33% beginners', 33% intermediate, and 33% advanced trails. VERTICAL DROP: 803 ft. FACILITIES: Snowmaking, ski school, ski shop, rentals, night skiing, cafeteria, restaurant, and lounge.

BOYCE PARK SKI AREA – Pittsburgh – (724) 327-8798 – Page 71, A-7 MOUNTAIN: 1 Poma lift, 1 T-bar, and 2 double lifts. 50% beginners', and 50% intermediate trails. VERTICAL DROP: 180 ft. FACILITIES: Snowmaking, ski school, rentals, night skiing, and cafeteria.

CAMELBACK SKI AREA – Tannersville – (570) 629-1661 – Page 54, D-1 MOUNTAIN: 2 bars and 9 chairlifts. 40% beginners', 40% intermediate, and 20% advanced trails. VERTICAL DROP: 800 ft. FACILITIES: Snowmaking, ski school, ski shop, rentals, night skiing, cafeteria, restaurant, lounge, and daycare.

ELK MOUNTAIN SKI CENTER – 3 mi. S of Union Dale – (570) 679-4400 – Page 39, C-6 MOUNTAIN: 5 chairlifts. 5 beginners', 5 intermediate, and 7 advanced trails. VERTICAL DROP: 1,000 ft. FACILITIES: Snowmaking, ski school, ski shop, rentals, night skiing, cafeteria, restaurant, lounge, and daycare.

FERNWOOD – Bushkill – (570) 588-9500 – Page 54, D-3 MOUNTAIN: 1 rope tow and 1 double chairlift. Beginners' and intermediate trails. 3 cross-country trails. VERTICAL DROP: 225 ft. FACILITIES: Ski school, ski shop, rentals, restaurant, and lounge.

HIDDEN VALLEY RESORT – Somerset – (814) 443-2600 – Page 73, D-4 MOUNTAIN: 1 rope tow, 3 double lifts, and 1 dual triple lift. 22 mi. of cross-country trails. 36% beginners', 36% intermediate, and 28% advanced trails. VERTICAL DROP: 511 ft. FACILITIES: Snowmaking, ski school, ski shop, rentals, night skiing, cafeteria, restaurant, lounge, and daycare.

JACK FROST MOUNTAIN – White Haven – (570) 443-8425 – Page 53, D-5 MOUNTAIN: 7 double lifts, with capacity of 8,700 skiers/hr. 9 mi. of cross-country trails. 4 beginners', 8 intermediate, and 7 advanced trails. VERTICAL DROP: 600 ft. FACILITIES: Snowmaking, ski school, ski shop, rentals, cafeteria, restaurant, lounge, daycare, and accommodation at the mountain.

LAUREL MOUNTAIN SKI RESORT – Boswell – (724) 238-9860 – Page 73, C-5 MOUNTAIN: 1 rope tow, 1 bar, and 1 chairlift. 15 mi. of cross-country trails. 5 beginners', 6 intermediate, and 2 advanced trails. VERTICAL DROP: 900 ft. FACILITIES: Snowmaking, ski school, ski shop, rentals, night skiing, cafeteria, restaurant, and lounge.

MONTAGE – Scranton – (570) 969-7669 – Page 53, B-5 MOUNTAIN: 1 double lift and 4 triple lifts. 20% beginners', 60% intermediate, and 20% advanced trails. VERTICAL DROP: 1,000 ft. FACILITIES: Snowmaking, ski school, ski shop, rentals, night skiing, cafeteria, lounge, and daycare.

MOUNT TONE – Lake Como – (570) 798-2707 – Page 40, B-1 MOUNTAIN: 1 double rope tow, 1 T-bar, 1 mighty mite, and 1 triple chairlift. 7 mi. of cross-country trails. VERTICAL DROP: 450 ft. FACILITIES: Snowmaking, ski school, night skiing, restaurant, and accommodation at the mountain.

MOUNTAIN VIEW – Cambridge Springs – (814) 734-1641 – Page 29, B-5 MOUNTAIN: 3 T-bars. 1 beginners', 8 intermediate, and 2 advanced trails. VERTICAL DROP: 350 ft. FACILITIES: Snowmaking, ski school, ski shop, rentals, night skiing, and cafeteria.

SAW CREEK – Bushkill – (570) 588-9266 – Page 54, C-3 MOUNTAIN: 1 double chairlift. VERTICAL DROP: 300 ft. FACILITIES: Snowmaking, ski school, ski shop, rentals, restaurant, lounge, and accommodation at the mountain.

SEVEN SPRINGS MOUNTAIN RESORT – Champion – (814) 352-7777 – Page 73, D-4 MOUNTAIN: 8 rope tows, 2 double lifts, 7 triple lifts, 2 quad lifts. 14 beginners', 11 intermediate, and 5 advanced trails. VERTICAL DROP: 750 ft. FACILITIES: Snowmaking, ski school, ski shop, rentals, night skiing, snowboarding, cafeteria, restaurant, lounge, daycare, and accommodations.

SHAWNEE MOUNTAIN – Shawnee-on-Delaware – (570) 421-7231 – Page 54, D-3 MOUNTAIN: 7 double lifts, 1 triple lift, 9 quad lifts. 2 mi. of cross-country trails. 7 beginners', 8 intermediate, and 5 advanced trails. VERTICAL DROP: 700 ft. FACILITIES: Snowmaking, ski school, ski shop, rentals, night skiing, cafeteria, restaurant, lounge, daycare, and accommodation at the mountain.

SKI BIG BEAR – Lackawaxen – (570) 685-1400 – Page 40, D-3 MOUNTAIN: 1 bar and 1 double chairlift. 5 mi. of cross-country trails. 4 beginners', 4 intermediate, and 2 advanced trails. VERTICAL DROP: 650 ft. FACILITIES: Snowmaking, ski school, ski shop, rentals, night skiing, cafeteria, restaurant, and lounge.

SKI DENTON – Coudersport – (814) 435-2115 – Page 34, B-2 MOUNTAIN: 3 Poma lifts and 1 chairlift with combined uphill capacity of 3,150 skiers/hr. Cross-country ski trails. 33% beginners', 33% intermediate, and 33% advanced trails. VERTICAL DROP: 600 ft. FACILITIES: Snowmaking, ski school, ski shop, rentals, cafeteria, lounge, and accommodation at the mountain.

SKI LIBERTY – Fairfield – (717) 642-8282 – Page 91, B-6 MOUNTAIN: 1 bar and 4 chairlifts, with combined uphill capacity of 6,800 skiers/hr. 5 beginners', 5 intermediate, and 4 advanced trails. VERTICAL DROP: 606 ft. FACILITIES: Snowmaking, ski school, ski shop, rentals, night skiing, cafeteria, restaurant, lounge, and daycare.

SKI ROUNDTOP – Lewisberry – (717) 432-9631 – Page 78, D-2 MOUNTAIN: 2 J-bars, 5 chairlifts, and 1 triple lift. 30% beginners', 40% intermediate, and 30% advanced trails. VERTICAL DROP: 600 ft. FACILITIES: Snowmaking, ski school, ski shop, rentals, night skiing, cafeteria, and daycare.

SKI SAWMILL – Morris – (570) 353-7521 – Page 35, D-6 MOUNTAIN: 3 T-bars and 1 chairlift. 35% beginners', 35% intermediate, and 30% advanced trails. VERTICAL DROP: 500 ft. FACILITIES: Snowmaking, ski school, ski shop, rentals, night skiing, cafeteria, restaurant, lounge, and daycare.

SPLIT ROCK – Lake Harmony – (570) 772-9111 – Page 53, D-6 MOUNTAIN: 1 T-bar and 1 double lift. 1 mi. of cross-country trails. 4 beginners', 1 intermediate, and 1 advanced trail. VERTICAL DROP: 250 ft. FACILITIES: Snowmaking, ski school, ski shop, rentals, cafeteria, restaurant, and lounge.

TANGLWOOD – Tafton – (570) 226-7669 – Page 54, A-2 MOUNTAIN: 1 beginners' rope tow, 2 T-bars, and 2 double chairlifts. Cross-country trails. VERTICAL DROP: 415 ft. FACILITIES: Snowmaking, ski school, rentals, night skiing, cafeteria, restaurant, lounge, and daycare.

TUSSEY MOUNTAIN SKI RESORT – Boalsburg – (814) 466-6266 – Page 62, B-2 MOUNTAIN: 2 bars and 1 chairlift. 2 beginners', 4 intermediate, and 2 advanced trails. VERTICAL DROP: 550 ft. FACILITIES: Snowmaking, ski school, ski shop, rentals, night skiing, cafeteria, restaurant, lounge, and daycare.

Canoe Trips

Pennsylvania has thousands of miles of navigable water. Some rivers, like the Delaware, the Allegheny, and the Youghiogheny, are navigable for most of their length. Listed below are selected canoe trips. Since water levels and river conditions change seasonally, it is advisable to check ahead with local officials when planning a trip.

ALLEGHENY RIVER – Franklin – Page 43, A-7 – 42 miles Put-in below U.S. Rte. 322 bridge in Franklin. Stop overnight at Kennerdell. Take-out at Route 208 bridge above Emlenton. Gorge and valley scenery. Suitable for novices. Class I–II.

CLARION RIVER – Ridgway – Page 46, A-2 – 36 miles Put-in at Rte. 949 bridge in Ridgway. Smooth but swift, flows through scenic wooded gorge. Camping possible along riversides. Take-out at Rte. 899 bridge in Clarington. Class I–II.

DELAWARE RIVER – Hancock – Page 40, A-1 – 31 miles Put-in at Balls Eddy access, two miles above Hancock on Pennsylvania side of West Branch of Delaware River. Take-out at Callicoon bridge (fourth bridge encountered) on New York side. Very heavily used. Class I.

JUNIATA RIVER – Lewistown – Page 62, D-4 – 30 miles Put-in at Rte. 103 bridge (Memorial Bridge) in Lewistown. Clear, quiet river leads down through high ridges. Take-out at Rte. 17 bridge in Millerstown (fourth bridge encountered). Class I.

LITTLE SCHUYLKILL RIVER – Hecla – Page 66, C-3 – 13 miles Put-in at highway bridge in Hecla. Views of Hawk Mountain, with hawk migrations. Take-out in Port Clinton just south of Rte. 61 bridge, at confluence of rivers. Class I–II.

LOYALSOCK CREEK – Forksville – Page 51, A-5 – 36 miles Numerous other access points along Rte. 87, including bridges at Barbours and Loyalsockville. Mild rapids; dam, three miles below Forksville should be scouted before going through. Take-out in Montoursville. Class I–II.

PINE CREEK – Blackwell – Page 35, D-5 – 11 miles Put-in at Blackwell access area south of Pine Creek Bridge. Pine Creek flows through "Grand Canyon of Pennsylvania," and is very popular canoeing stream. Fast water. Camping possible along river (ask permission). Take-out at Slate Run access area on left, north of Slate Run Bridge. Class I–II.

RED BANK CREEK – New Bethlehem – Page 44, D-4 – 21.5 miles Put-in below dam at bridge where Rtes. 28 and 66 cross Red Bank Creek. River access at Climax for shorter trips. Take-out in Rimer. Class I.

SUSQUEHANNA RIVER – Sunbury – Page 64, B-3 – 37 miles Put-in below inflatable dam south of highway bridge between Sunbury and Shamokin Dam. Campsites throughout. Susquehanna is broad, slow-moving river, with motorboats allowed in lower section. McKee Half Falls 18 miles below Sunbury; easily run. Take-out in Halifax. Class I.

SUSQUEHANNA RIVER, WEST BRANCH – Renovo – Page 48, B-3 – 30 miles Put-in at Rte. 144 bridge in Renovo. River runs through scenic canyon, widens to narrow valley. Take-out in Lock Haven at ramp below Jay Street bridge. Class I.

FOR EXPERIENCED CANOEISTS

PINE CREEK – Ansonia – Page 35, C-5 – 19 miles Put-in at Big Meadows access area off Rte. 6 in Ansonia. Popular with whitewater enthusiasts. Follows deep gorge known as "Grand Canyon of Pennsylvania." Take-out at Blackwell access area along Rte. 414, just south of Pine Creek Bridge. Class III.

YOUGHIOGHENY RIVER – Ohiopyle – Page 86, B-3 – 19.6 miles One of most famous whitewater trips in Appalachians. Put-in at Ohiopyle, below falls. Rapids throughout. Open canoes suitable only if designed for whitewater. Take-out at waterworks on left, 0.25 mile past footbridge and 100 yards above dam in South Connellsville. Class I–IV.

Hiking

APPALACHIAN TRAIL – Delaware Water Gap to border at Pen Mar, Maryland – 222 miles – Page 68, A-2 White rectangular blazes and diamond-shaped metal markers. Shelters and cabins. Passes through Michaux State Forest, Caledonia State Park, Pine Grove Furnace State Park, Swatara State Park, and National Park lands. Day and overnight hikes possible using side trails. A National Scenic Trail. Guidebook available from: The Appalachian Trail Conference, P.O. Box 807, Harper's Ferry, WV 25425.

BEAR RUN NATURE RESERVE LOOP – 4 mi. N of Ohiopyle – 7 miles – Page 86, A3 Start at Bear Run Center. Cross Rte. 381. Follow Peninsula Trail along Youghiogheny River Gorge. Continue on Laurel Run Trail along Laurel Run for 2.3 miles. Head south on difficult Tulip Tree Trail for 1 mile to Rhododendron Trail for 1 mile. Turn right onto Tree Trail to return to Bear Run Center. Campsites available for backpackers.

BRUCE LAKE NATURAL AREA – Delaware State Forest – 5 miles – Page 54, B-2 Bruce Lake Rd. from Rte. 390 to East Branch Bruce Lake Trail to Bruce Lake Trail to Rock Oak Ridge Trail to Brown Trail and return on Bruce Lake Rd. Lake and bog in roadless natural area.

DINGMANS FALLS TRAIL – Delaware Water Gap National Recreation Area – 0.75 mile – Page 54, C-4 Starts at Delaware Water Gap National Recreation Area. Visitors Center at Dingmans Falls. Silverthread Falls (80 feet), and Dingmans Falls (130 feet), along Dingmans Creek. Bridges across stream. Rhododendron grove.

HORSESHOE TRAIL – Valley Forge to 12 mi. N of Hershey – 120 miles – Page 81, D-7 Also used for horseback riding. Main trail has yellow blazes, side trails have white. Start at Woolman Memorial Marker on south bank Valley Creek at intersection of Rtes. 252 and 23. Trail passes through Hopewell Furnace National Historic Site and French Creek State Park. Contact Range Control Officer at (717) 861-2152, before entering Fort Indiantown Gap National Guard Training Center. Connects with Appalachian Trail on Sharp Mountain. For more information contact: Horseshoe Trail Club, c/o Warwick Park, RD 2, Pottstown, PA 19464.

LOYALSOCK TRAIL – 10 mi. N of Montoursville to Ringdale – 58 miles – Page 50, B-2 Marked by red metal discs with letters "LT." Sidetrails have yellow discs marked "X." Footpaths, old logging roads, abandoned railroad grades. Mountain ridges and streams. Elevations from 665 feet to 2,140 feet. Camping in Tiadaghton and Wyoming State Forests and Worlds End State Park. Guide available from: The Alpine Club of Williamsport, P.O. Box 501, Williamsport, PA 17703.

MIDDLE CREEK WILDLIFE MANAGEMENT AREA – Kleinfeltersville – 6.5 miles – Page 79, B-7 Forms loop. East side of Millstone Trail to Horseshoe connector to right on Horseshoe Trail to left on Elder Run Trail to left on Middle Creek Trail to right on Horseshoe Trail to Millstone Connector. Return to parking lot on west side of Millstone Trail. Vista, old quarry, wildlife.

NORTH COUNTRY NATIONAL SCENIC TRAIL – Allegheny National Forest – 119 miles (incomplete) – Page 31, A-7 Trail was authorized by Congress in 1980. When complete, will stretch from New York to North Dakota. Currently six segments of trail in Pennsylvania. Largest segment in Allegheny National Forest, runs south from New York border near Willow Bay to Tionesta Natural Area, east towards Dunham Mills, and south to join Baker Trail. Other segments in Clear Creek State Forest, Cook Forest State Park, Jennings Environmental Education Center, Moraine State Park, and McConnells Mill State Park. For more information write: North Country National Scenic Trail, National Park Service, 1709 Jackson St., Omaha, NE 68102.

NORTH LOOKOUT TRAIL/HAWK MOUNTAIN SANCTUARY – 8 mi. W of Kempton – 1.2 miles – Page 66, C-3 Admission passes from visitors center. Moderately steep. 0.75 mile to North Lookout. Express Trail is shorter alternate. Migrating hawks in fall. View of River of Rocks.

POTOMAC HERITAGE NATIONAL SCENIC TRAIL – Ohiopyle to Seward – 70 miles (incomplete) – Page 86, B-3 Trail is incomplete. When finished will parallel both sides of mouth of Potomac River in Maryland and Virginia to join up and then run to Conemaugh Gorge. At present, only segment in Pennsylvania follows course of Laurel Highlands Trail, from Ohiopyle through Ohiopyle State Park, Laurel Ridge State Park, Laurel Hill State Park, Laurel Mountain State Park, north to Seward. For further information write: Potomac Heritage National Scenic Trail, National Park Service, 1100 Ohio Drive SW, Washington, D.C. 20242.

QUEBEC RUN WILD AREA LOOP – Forbes State Forest – 6 miles – Page 86, B-1 Park in area near Skyline Dr. Start on Hess Trail to east. As Hess Trail heads north continue east on West Rd. to Brocker Trail to Tebolt Trail to parking area. Steep areas. Forest and streams.

WARRIOR TRAIL – Greensboro to West Virginia border – 45 miles – Page 85, B-6 Trail follows 5,000-year-old Indian path, which parallels Mason-Dixon Line. Aluminum bands mark trees along trail, with "Warrior Trail" carved into round posts marking each mile. Three shelters. Rolling hills. May be hiked in sections. More information from: Warrior Trail Assoc., RD 1, Box 35, Spraggs, PA 15362.

Covered Bridges

More covered bridges exist in the United States than anywhere else in the world, and there are more in Pennsylvania than in any other state. The styles of bridges vary enormously, but they have one thing in common—they are all picturesque remnants of a vanished age.

The use of wood in bridge-building has been with us since ancient times. Only with the invention of the truss system, however, did wood come into its own. By using variations on interlocking triangles of timber, great spans could be achieved.

Wooden bridges were cheaper to build than stone or iron, and thus were ideally suited to meeting the needs of small communities. As they evolved, they were roofed over to protect the trusses from weathering.

There were around 1,500 covered bridges in Pennsylvania during their peak. There are now around 160 left. Luckily, interest in them has been growing rapidly, and there are many people now working to preserve them.

This Atlas locates nearly all of the covered bridges with the corresponding symbol on the map. A short list of a few of the more interesting covered bridges follows.

ACADEMIA/POMEROY BRIDGE, Page 77, A-5, at 270 feet, is the longest in the state.

FORKSVILLE BRIDGE, Page 51, A-5, located in a beautiful setting, has a single span of 146 feet.

GUDGEONVILLE BRIDGE, Page 28, A-3, boasts a spectacular setting.

JACKSON'S MILL BRIDGE, Page 94, A-2, is in the Amish country.

McCONNELL'S MILL BRIDGE, Page 57, A-4, set in a state park, is in excellent condition.

PLEASANTVILLE BRIDGE, Page 81, A-5, is an attractive bridge in a rural setting.

RISHEL BRIDGE, Page 64, A-3, is arguably the oldest bridge in the state.

THOMAS MILL BRIDGE, Page 82, D-2, located in the heart of Philadelphia, is one of the oldest and largest of the Howe Truss bridges.

WAGGONER MILL BRIDGE, Page 77, B-6, is in a beautiful setting with a gristmill nearby.

While these are some of the most attractive, each bridge in Pennsylvania may be said to have a charm of its own.

⛺ Campgrounds

To locate campgrounds in this Atlas, look on the appropriate map for the campground symbol and corresponding four-digit number. Members of the Pennsylvania Campground Owners Association (PCOA) are listed here.

NUMBER, NAME, LOCATION, PHONE	CAMPSITES	ELECTRIC	WATER	SEWER	SNACK BAR	LP GAS	LAUNDRY	DUMP STATION	BOAT RENTAL	SWIMMING	FISHING	HUNTING	BARRIER-FREE ACCESS	ATLAS LOCATION
2009 Appalachian Campsites, Shartlesville, (800) 424-5746	300	285	285	270		●	●			●	●			Page 66, D-2
2018 Bake Oven Campground, Ashfield, (570) 386-2911	120	120	120	90			●			●	●			Page 67, B-4
2021 Bald Eagle Campsite, 4 mi. N of Tyrone, (814) 684-3485	50	50									●			Page 61, C-6
2024 Beach Comber, Erie, (814) 833-4560	200	200	200	150	●	●	●		●	●	●			Page 27, D-4
2027 Beacon Camping, Intercourse, (717) 768-8775	46	46	46	30	●	●	●			●				Page 80, D-2
2030 Bear Run Campground, Portersville, (724) 368-3564	220	180	180	130	●	●	●		●	●				Page 57, A-4
2036 Beechwood Campground, Coatesville, (610) 384-1457	300	165	165	125	●	●	●	●		●				Page 81, D-4
2039 Bellefonte/State College KOA, Bellefonte, (814) 355-7912	130	94	94	52	●	●	●			●	●			Page 62, A-3
2042 Benner's Meadow Run Camping and Cabins, Farmington, (724) 329-4097	200	114	118	118	●	●	●			●	●			Page 86, B-2
2045 Berry Patch Campground, Honey Brook, (610) 273-3720	140	120	120	81		●	●			●	●			Page 80, D-3
2048 Birchview Farm Campground, Coatesville, (610) 384-0500	200	200	200	170	●	●	●	●		●	●			Page 66, D-3
2051 Blue Rocks Family Campground, Lenhartsville, (610) 756-6366	200	150	140	42	●	●	●			●	●			Page 80, D-4
2054 Brandywine Meadows Family Campground, Honey Brook, (610) 273-9753	166	166	166	10	●	●	●			●				Page 29, D-5
2057 Brookdale Family Campground, Meadville, (814) 789-3251	135	128	128	37	●	●	●	●		●	●			Page 36, B-1
2060 Bucktail Camping Resort, Mansfield, (570) 662-2923	125	125	100	10		●	●			●	●		●	Page 57, B-6
2063 Buttercup Campground, Renfrew, (724) 789-9340	250	250	250	250	●	●				●	●			Page 65, C-6
2065 Camp-A-While, Hegins, (570) 682-8696	58	33	33	33		●				●	●			Page 35, C-5
2067 Canyon Country Campground, Wellsboro, (570) 724-3818	60	44	31	14				●						Page 77, C-7
2069 Carlisle Campground, Carlisle, (717) 249-4563	100	80	80	50	●	●	●			●				Page 27, D-4
2072 Cassidy's Presque Isle Trailer Park & Campground, Erie, (814) 833-6035	40	40	26	12			●							Page 66, D-2
2078 Christmas Pines Campground, Auburn, (570) 366-8866	92	92	92			●	●			●	●			Page 80, B-1
2081 Cocalico Creek Campground, Denver, (717) 336-2014	124	120	120	118			●			●	●			Page 68, D-2
2084 Colonial Woods Family Camping Resort, Upper Black Eddy, (610) 847-5808	235	235	235		●	●	●			●				Page 57, A-4
2090 Cooper's Lake Campground, Slippery Rock, (724) 368-8710	96	82	72	23			●			●				Page 52, D-2
2091 Council Cup Campground, Wapwallopen, (570) 379-2566	241	141	141	69		●	●			●	●	●		Page 80, D-1
2092 Country Acres Family Campground, Gordonville, (717) 687-8014	59	44	49	22		●				●				Page 80, D-2
2093 Country Haven Campsite, New Holland, (717) 354-7926	55	55	55	52	●	●				●				Page 54, D-2
2099 Cranberry Run Campground, Analomink, (570) 421-1462	109	66	66	66	●	●					●			Page 28, C-2
2102 Crystal Spring Campground, Linesville, (814) 683-5885	250	250	250	250				●		●	●	●		Page 38, C-2
2106 Day's End Campground, Meshoppen, (570) 965-2144	45	45	45					●	●					Page 54, D-3
2108 Delaware Water Gap KOA Kampground, East Stroudsburg, (570) 223-8000	170	115	115		●	●	●			●				Page 67, B-6
2117 Don Laine Campground, Palmerton, (610) 381-3381	150	150	150	117		●	●			●				Page 68, B-3
2120 Driftstone On The Delaware, Mt. Bethel, (570) 897-6859	190	183	190		●	●	●	●		●	●			Page 91, B-7
2123 Drummer Boy Camping Resort, 1.5 mi. E of Gettysburg, (717) 334-3277	300	240	240	70	●	●	●			●	●			Page 80, C-2
2126 Dutch Cousins Campsite, Denver, (717) 336-6911	72	68	68	7		●	●		●					Page 80, B-1
2128 Eagles Peak Family Camping Resort, Robesonia, (610) 589-4800	270	235	235	137	●	●	●			●	●	●		Page 27, C-7
2135 Family Affair Campground, North East, (814) 725-8112	250	200	200			●	●			●	●			Page 64, A-3
2136 Fantasy Island Campground, Sunbury, (570) 286-1307	84	84	84			●			●	●	●			Page 42, A-3
2138 Farma Travel Trailer Park, Greenville, (724) 253-4535	300	300	300	290		●	●			●	●			Page 53, D-6
2140 Fern Ridge Campground, Blakeslee, (570) 646-2267	110	72	72		●	●	●			●				Page 64, A-2
2141 Ferryboat Campsites, Liverpool, (717) 444-3200	285	285	285	285	●	●				●	●		●	Page 80, D-1
2144 Flory's Campground and Cottages, Ronks, (717) 687-6670	71	71	71	71		●				●				Page 62, A-3
2147 Fort Bellefonte Campground, Bellefonte, (814) 355-9820	100	70	70	37		●				●	●	●		Page 54, D-3
2150 Foxwood Family Campgrounds, East Stroudsburg, (570) 421-1424	250	200	200	125		●	●			●	●			Page 74, D-3
2156 Friendship Village Camp and RV Park, Bedford, (814) 623-1677	155	135	135	91	●	●	●			●	●			Page 44, C-1
2159 Gaslight Campground, Emlenton, (724) 867-6981	125	125	84	65	●	●	●			●				Page 91, B-6
2161 Gettysburg Campground, Gettysburg, (717) 334-3304	260	238	238	90	●	●	●			●	●			Page 91, B-6
2162 Gettysburg KOA Kampground, Gettysburg, (717) 642-5713	99	83	83	39	●	●	●			●				Page 43, A-4
2163 Goddard Park Vacationland Campground, Sandy Lake, (412) 253-4645	580	522	522	484	●					●				Page 91, B-6
2164 Granite Hill Campground, Gettysburg, (717) 642-8749	300	300	300	100	●	●	●			●	●			Page 63, B-7
2165 Gray Squirrel Campsites, Beaverton, (570) 837-0333	260	260	260	100	●	●	●			●				Page 49, B-6
2171 Happy Acres Campground, Waterville, (570) 753-8221	150	125	100	75		●	●				●			Page 30, A-2
2174 Harecreek Campground, Corry, (814) 664-9684	80	80	80	80		●	●			●				Page 78, C-3
2177 Harrisburg East Campground, Harrisburg, (717) 939-4331	75	59	59	44	●	●	●			●				Page 53, C-7
2180 Hemlock Campground & Cottages, Tobyhanna, (570) 894-4388	75	71	71	60	●	●	●			●				Page 78, B-4
2183 Hershey High Meadow Camp, Hershey, (717) 566-0902	290	117	117	87	●	●	●			●				Page 79, A-6
2186 Hershey/Jonestown KOA Kampground, Jonestown, (717) 865-2526	127	106	103	66	●	●	●			●				Page 80, D-3
2189 Hidden Acres Campground, Coatesville, (610) 857-3990	200	200	200	45		●	●	●		●				Page 64, A-1
2192 Hidden Valley Camping Resort, 9 mi. W of Lewisburg, (570) 966-1330	344	330	330	150	●	●	●	●		●				Page 26, D-4
2198 Hills Family Campground, Fairview, (814) 833-3272	108	108	108	88						●				Page 57, D-5
2200 Indian Brave Campground, Harmony, (724) 452-9204	170	170	170	170						●				Page 65, A-6
2201 Indian Head Campground, Bloomsburg, (570) 784-6150	180	180	180		●			●	●	●	●			Page 92, A-4
2204 Indian Rock Campground, York, (717) 741-1764	40	40	40	35						●				Page 67, B-4
2207 Jim Thorpe Camping Resort, Jim Thorpe, (570) 325-2644	200	125	125	40	●	●	●			●	●			Page 42, C-4
2208 Junction 19–80 Campground, Mercer, (724) 748-4174	150	140	140	86		●	●			●				Page 45, B-4
2209 Kalyumet Campground, Lucinda, (814) 744-9622	180	150	150					●		●				Page 39, D-7
2210 Keen Lake Camping Cottage Resort, Waymart, (570) 488-6161	300	260	260	200	●	●	●		●	●	●			Page 54, C-4
2213 Ken's Woods Campground, Bushkill, (570) 588-6381	150	100	100	26	●	●	●			●	●	●		Page 34, C-4
2216 Kenshire Kampsite, Gaines, (814) 435-6764	100	80	70			●	●			●				Page 65, A-5
2222 Knoebels Amusement Resort and Campground, Elysburg, (570) 672-9555	500	450			●					●				Page 43, C-6
2225 Kozy Rest Kampground, Harrisville, (724) 735-2417	125	125	125	125			●			●		●		Page 80, C-3
2234 Lake In Wood Campground, Narvon, (717) 445-5525	250	250	250	200	●	●	●			●				Page 75, B-6
2237 Lake Raystown Resort, Entriken, (814) 658-3500	272	250	250		●	●	●		●	●	●			Page 79, A-5
2246 Lickdale Campground, Jonestown, (717) 865-6411	50	50	50	17	●	●				●				Page 64, B-2
2249 Little Mexico Campground, Winfield, (570) 374-9742	200	200	200	30		●	●	●		●	●			Page 45, A-5
2251 Loleta Road Runner, Marienville, (814) 927-6649	55	55	55	25	●	●				●	●			Page 72, C-5
2253 Madison/New Stanton KOA, Ruffs Dale, (724) 722-4444	100	95	95	54	●	●	●			●				Page 64, D-2
2255 Mahantongo Campground, Dalmatia, (570) 758-3101	34	34	34	14						●	●			Page 28, C-2
2257 Mallards Landing Family Campground, Linesville, (814) 683-5870	92	64	64	25		●					●	●		Page 43, C-4
2261 Mercer–Grove City KOA, 5 mi. S of Mercer, (724) 748-3160	177	169	169	65	●	●	●	●		●				Page 80, D-1
2264 Mill Bridge Village and Camp Resort, Strasburg, (717) 687-8181	100	100	100	70		●	●			●				Page 77, D-7
2270 Mountain Creek Campground, Gardners, (717) 486-7681	115	105	105		●	●	●			●	●			

CAMPGROUNDS, *continued*

NUMBER, NAME, LOCATION, PHONE	CAMPSITES	ELECTRIC	WATER	SEWER	SNACK BAR	LP GAS	LAUNDRY	DUMP STATION	BOAT RENTAL	SWIMMING	FISHING	HUNTING	BARRIER-FREE ACCESS	ATLAS LOCATION
2271 Mountain Pines Camping Resort, Champion, (724) 455-3300	950	950	950	900	●		●		●	●				Page 72, D-4
2273 Mountain Springs Camping Resort, Shartlesville, (610) 488-6859	300	260	260	30		●	●	●	●	●	●			Page 66, D-2
2276 Mountain Vista Campground, East Stroudsburg, (570) 223-0111	180	180	180	50	●		●		●	●				Page 54, D-2
2287 Mt. Pocono Campground, Mt. Pocono, (570) 839-7573	155	105	105	75	●	●	●	●		●				Page 54, C-1
2296 Nittany Mountain Campground, New Columbia, (570) 568-5541	320	320	320	18	●	●	●	●	●	●	●			Page 50, D-2
2299 Oak Creek Campground, 1.5 mi. E of Bowmansville, (717) 445-6161	311	292	292	136	●	●	●	●		●				Page 80, C-3
2305 Oil Creek Camp Resort, 4 mi. S of Titusville, (814) 827-1023	99	36	36	45		●			●				●	Page 30, D-1
2308 Old Mill Stream Camping Manor, 4 mi. E of Lancaster, (717) 299-2314	240	220	220		●	●	●	●		●				Page 80, D-1
2317 Otter Lake Camp–Resort, East Stroudsburg, (570) 223-0123	300	300	300	100	●	●	●	●	●	●	●			Page 54, C-2
2342 Paradise Camp Resort, Nescopeck, (570) 379-3729	15	15	15	15	●		●	●	●	●	●			Page 52, D-2
2345 Pennsylvania Dutch Campsite, Shartlesville, (610) 488-6268	250	250	250	12	●	●	●	●		●				Page 66, D-1
2348 Pequea Creek Campground, Pequea, (717) 284-4587	84	82	75			●		●	●		●			Page 93, A-7
2351 Philadelphia/West Chester KOA, Unionville, (610) 486-0447	110	80	78	42	●	●	●	●		●				Page 95, A-5
2354 Pinch Pond Family Campground, Manheim, (717) 665-7640	150	75	75	75		●	●	●		●	●			Page 79, C-6
2357 Pine Cradle Lake, Rome, (570) 247-2424	90	85	85	55		●	●	●	●	●	●			Page 37, A-7
2360 Pine Hill Campground, Kutztown, (610) 285-6776	125	125	125	125	●		●	●		●				Page 67, D-4
2362 Piney Meadows Park, Limestone, (814) 764-5381	45	45	45	10				●		●				Page 44, C-4
2364 Pioneer Campground, Laporte, (570) 946-9971	91	66	66		●	●	●	●	●	●	●	●	●	Page 51, A-5
2366 Pioneer Park Campground, Somerset, (814) 445-6348	192	192	192	185	●		●	●	●	●				Page 73, D-5
2369 Pittsburgh North Campground, Cranberry Township, (724) 776-1150	110	110	110	90	●		●	●		●				Page 57, C-5
2372 Plantation Park Campers Association, Mercer, (724) 662-4110	675	675	675	675	●	●	●	●		●				Page 42, C-4
2375 Pleasant Hills Resort Campground, Hesston, (814) 658-3986	120	91	91	45	●		●	●	●	●				Page 75, A-7
2378 Pocono Vacation Park, Stroudsburg, (570) 421-8049	200	200	200	200	●		●			●				Page 68, A-2
2381 Prospect Valley Farm, Columbia, (717) 684-8893	95	54	54	24	●		●	●		●				Page 79, D-6
2384 Quakerwoods Campground, Quakertown, (215) 536-1984	185	170	170	100	●		●	●		●				Page 81, A-7
2390 Red Oak Campground, Russell, (814) 757-8507	210	208	210	145	●		●	●		●	●	●		Page 31, A-7
2391 Red Ridge Lake Campground, Zion Grove, (570) 384-4760	150	130	130	25	●		●		●	●				Page 66, A-1
2392 Red Run Campground, New Holland, (717) 445-4526	115	115	115	18	●		●	●		●				Page 80, C-2
2393 Ridge Run Campground, Elizabethtown, (717) 367-3454	137	120	120	90	●	●	●	●		●				Page 79, C-5
2396 River Beach Campsites, 3 mi. N of Milford, (800) 356-2852	160	57	22		●		●	●	●		●		●	Page 55, B-5
2397 River's Edge Family Campground, Connellsville, (724) 628-4880	90	65	65	65	●		●	●		●				Page 72, D-1
2399 Riverfront Campground, Duncannon, (717) 834-5252	55	35	35	35				●	●		●			Page 78, A-1
2402 Riverside Acres Campground, Towanda, (570) 265-3235	41	35	35	12		●		●			●			Page 37, B-7
2405 Roamers Retreat Campground, Kinzer, (717) 442-4287	110	110	110	100	●	●		●		●				Page 94, A-2
2408 Robin Hill Camping Resort, Lenhartsville, (610) 756-6117	270	256	256	135	●	●	●	●		●			●	Page 66, D-4
2409 Rocky Springs Campground, Mercer, (724) 662-4415	81	81	81	68	●		●	●		●				Page 42, C-3
2411 Rose Point Park Campground, New Castle, (724) 924-2415	143	133	133	120	●		●	●		●				Page 57, A-4
2414 Rosemount Camping, Tamaqua, (570) 668-2580	200	200	200	145	●		●	●		●				Page 66, C-2
2415 Rustic Meadows Camping & Golf Resort, Elizabethtown, (717) 367-7718	121	108	108	55	●	●	●	●		●				Page 79, C-4
2417 Sacony Park Campsites, Kutztown, (610) 683-3939	115	100	100			●		●		●				Page 66, D-4
2420 Sandy Valley Campground, White Haven, (570) 636-0770	98	98	98		●	●	●	●		●				Page 52, D-4
2423 Scarlett Knob Campground, 2.5 mi. N of Ohiopyle, (724) 329-5200	110	18	18					●						Page 86, A-3
2424 Scenic View Campground, Tioga, (570) 835-5863	160	90	90	50	●		●	●		●				Page 35, A-7
2425 Schlegel's Grove & Campsites, Bechtelsville, (610) 367-8576	147	140	140							●				Page 81, B-6
2426 Scottyland Camping Resort, Rockwood, (814) 926-3200	710	557	557	536	●	●	●	●		●				Page 87, A-4
2427 Seven Mountains Campground, Spring Mills, (814) 346-1910	70	70	70	17			●	●						Page 62, B-4
2429 Shady Acres Campground, Portland, (570) 897-6230	110	93	91			●	●	●		●				Page 68, A-2
2430 Shady Grove Campground, Adamstown, (717) 484-4225	90	84	84	84			●	●	●	●				Page 80, C-2
2432 Shady Oaks Campground, Newmanstown, (717) 949-3177	85	80	80	60	●	●		●		●				Page 80, B-1
2434 Shangri-La By The Lake, Jamestown, (724) 932-5044	250	50	50	150			●		●		●		●	Page 28, D-2
2436 Shangri-La On The Creek, Milton, (570) 524-4561	167	138	138	29			●	●		●	●			Page 64, A-3
2438 Shawnee Sleepy Hollow, Schellsburg, (814) 733-4380	75	53	70				●	●						Page 74, D-3
2440 Sheshequin Campground, Trout Run, (570) 995-9230	120	111	111				●	●			●			Page 50, A-2
2442 Shore Forest Manor Campground, Hop Bottom, (570) 289-4666	160	160	160	120	●	●	●	●		●				Page 39, C-4
2444 Sill's Family Campground, Adamstown, (717) 484-4806	125	115	115	110		●		●		●				Page 80, C-2
2446 Slippery Rock Campground Association, Slippery Rock, (724) 794-4868	112	98	98		●	●	●	●		●				Page 43, D-5
2448 Slumber Valley Farms Campground, Meshoppen, (570) 833-5208	100	60	60	20			●	●		●				Page 38, D-2
2450 Spring Gulch Resort Campground, New Holland, (800) 255-5744	400	400	400	300	●	●	●	●		●	●			Page 80, D-2
2452 Starlite Camping Resort, Stevens, (717) 733-9655	215	215	215	90	●		●	●		●				Page 80, B-1
2454 Sun Valley Campground, 1 mi. E of Bowmansville, (717) 445-6262	265	258	261	200	●	●	●	●		●				Page 80, C-3
2456 Sunrise Lake Family Campground, Nicholson, (570) 942-6421	108	38	108	38		●		●		●				Page 39, D-4
2459 Sunset Vue Campground, Smethport, (814) 887-2527	70	70	70					●						Page 33, B-4
2462 Susquehanna Campground, Jersey Shore, (570) 398-0462	190	130	160	39		●		●		●				Page 49, C-7
2463 Tall Oaks Campground, Farmington, (724) 329-4777	104	12	12				●			●				Page 86, B-2
2467 Thousand Trails, Hershey Preserve, Lebanon, (717) 867-5515	232	232	232	232	●	●	●	●		●				Page 79, B-5
2470 Tucquan Park Family Campground, Holtwood, (717) 284-2156	125	91	91	81		●		●		●				Page 93, B-7
2474 Twin Bridge Meadow Family Campground, 5 mi. W of Chambersburg, (717) 369-2216	120	120	120					●		●				Page 90, A-3
2480 Twin Streams Campground, 12 mi. S of Wellsboro, (570) 353-7251	85	70	70	43		●		●		●				Page 35, D-6
2486 Valleyview Farm & Campground, Waymart, (570) 448-2268	50	50	50	21		●		●		●				Page 39, C-7
2487 Virginia's Beach Campground, North Springfield, (814) 922-3261	140	110	110	90				●		●				Page 26, D-2
2489 W. T. Family Camping, Blakeslee, (570) 646-9255	100	80	80	60	●		●	●		●				Page 53, D-6
2490 Warwick Woods Campground, St. Peters, (610) 286-9655	225	200	200	20	●	●	●	●		●				Page 81, C-4
2498 Wheel-In Campground, Shelocta, (724) 354-3693	99	99	99	8				●		●				Page 58, C-4
2502 Whispering Pines Family Campground, Washington, (724) 222-9830	44	9	20	10		●				●				Page 70, C-3
2504 White Oak Campground, Strausburg, (717) 687-6207	145	135	135	75	●									Page 94, A-1
2507 Wild Gypsy Rose, McElhattan, (570) 769-6445	40	40	40											Page 50, A-2
2510 Wolf's Camping Resort, Knox, (814) 797-1103	667	642	642	627	●	●	●	●	●	●				Page 44, C-4
2515 Woodland Campground, Woodland, (800) 589-1674	70	60	65			●	●	●		●	●			Page 47, D-5
2519 Woodland Campsites, Somerset, (814) 445-8860	125	105	105	70		●		●		●				Page 73, D-6
2521 Yogi Bear's Camp Resort of North Washington, West Sunbury, (724) 894-2421	100	85	85	45	●	●	●	●		●				Page 43, D-7
2523 Yogi Bear's Jellystone Park, Mill Run, (724) 455-2929	150	94	82	70	●	●	●	●		●	●			Page 86, A-3
2525 Yogi-on-the-River Campground, 2 mi. N of Northumberland, (570) 473-8021	123	123	123	6	●	●	●	●		●				Page 64, A-3

Bicycle Routes

ATLANTIC COAST BICYCLE ROUTE – Delaware Water Gap – 184 miles – Page 68, A-2 Bar Harbor, Maine, to Ft. Myers Beach, Florida. Pennsylvania section traverses southeastern part of state with spur into Philadelphia. Follows rural roads where possible. Flat to hilly terrain. For more information write: Adventure Cycling Association, P.O. Box 8308, Missoula, MT 59807.

DELAWARE RIVER BIKE TRIP – Riverton – 19 miles – Page 68, B-3 Loop trip. From Riverton turn left on River Rd. Right at Hemlock Dr. Continue along Delaware River to Portland. Left on State St. Left on Jacoby Creek Rd. Left on Potomac St. Left on Sunrise Blvd. Right on Belvidere Corner Rd. Left at Hemlock Dr. Return to Riverton on River Rd. Rolling hills and some steep terrain. Farmlands, river, canoe rentals.

GETTYSBURG NATIONAL MILITARY PARK – Gettysburg – 14.5 miles – Page 91, B-7 Loop follows same route as Park auto tour over gentle terrain with slight grades. On internal park roads with short segments on highways with adequate shoulders. Start at Cyclorama and Visitor Center where a map is available. Passes many points of interest in the Park. Shorter bike trips have been designated within the Park.

HARRISBURG BIKEWAY – Harrisburg – 18 miles – Page 78, B-2 Loop. Flat with several short grades. Marked by bike route signs. Shared roads with 3.5 miles of separate Riverfront Park Bike Path along Susquehanna River. Begins and ends at City Island Park. Crosses Walnut St. Bridge. Some areas with heavy traffic. Reservoir Park, Wildwood Park, Governor's Mansion.

LEHIGH CANAL – Allentown – 4.2 miles – Page 67, D-7 Along Lehigh Canal Towpath from Lehigh Canal Park, Albert St. Ends in Bethlehem. No traffic and easy terrain along towpath. Unpaved, compressed earth and gravel in parts. Possible side trips to Keck Park in Allentown or through historic areas of Bethlehem.

NORTHERN TIER BICYCLE ROUTE – 1 mi. W of West Springfield – 46 miles – Page 28, A-1 Anacortes, Washington, to Bar Harbor, Maine. Pennsylvania portion travels along Lake Erie. Flat terrain. For more information write: Adventure Cycling Association, P.O. Box 8308, Missoula, MT 59807.

OIL CREEK STATE PARK BIKE TRAIL – 5 mi. N of Oil City – 10 miles – Page 30, D-1 Paved trail from Petroleum Center (bicycle rentals available) to Drake Well Park and Museum with exhibits on history of early oil days. Terrain is flat.

PITTSBURGH BIKEWAY – Pittsburgh – 16.5 miles – Page 71, A-6 Two possible routes from Highland Park Reservoir to Carnegie Institute. Bikeway is along separate bike lane or shared lane on city streets. Bikeway signs. Parks and recreation facilities, Pittsburgh Zoo, Phipps Conservatory, Carnegie Mellon and Pittsburgh Universities.

STRUBLE HIKING AND BIKING TRAIL – Downingtown – 15 miles – Page 81, D-5 Flat, paved trail follows East Branch of Brandywine Creek. Start off Rte. 282 on Norwood Rd. Through Lyndell, Cornog, and Glenmore.

UNION CANAL TOWPATH TRAIL – E of Reading – 4.5 miles – Page 80, B-3 Flat with several short grades. In Tulpehocken Creek Valley Park. Along historic Union Canal. Stonecliffe Recreation Area (formerly Gring's Limestone Quarry). Kissinger Homestead and Blacksmith Shop. Several locks. Gring's Mill and Homestead. Berks County Heritage and Wertz's Covered Bridge.

Historic Sites/Museums

ALLEGHENY PORTAGE RAILROAD NATIONAL HISTORIC SITE – 2 mi. E of Cresson – (814) 886-8176 – Page 74, A-3 Remaining structures of portage railroad, in operation from 1833–1857. Used to bring canal boats over Allegheny Mountains. Hiking, picnicking, tours by costumed guides.

THE ANTHRACITE MUSEUM OF ASHLAND – Ashland – (570) 875-4708 – Page 65, B-7 Formation, mining, and processing of anthracite. Tool and machine exhibits, models, photographs.

THE ANTHRACITE MUSEUM OF SCRANTON – Scranton – (570) 963-4804 – Page 53, A-5 Silk manufacturing and coal mining exhibits. Antique and classic vehicles.

BAKER MANSION – Altoona – (814) 942-3916 – Page 75, A-4 Thirty-five-room Greek Revival mansion built from 1844–1848. Period furnishings, Abraham Lincoln materials. Minerals, guns, and Indian artifacts.

BOYERTOWN MUSEUM OF HISTORIC VEHICLES – Boyertown – (610) 367-2090 – Page 81, B-5 18th- to 20th-century vehicles include automobiles, buggies, sleighs, horseless carriages, and tools used by workers who crafted the vehicles. Other antiques also on display.

BRANDYWINE BATTLEFIELD PARK – Chadds Ford – (610) 459-3342 – Page 95, B-6 Site of Revolutionary War battle. Restored farmhouses, headquarters of Washington and LaFayette. Visitor center with interpretive displays. Picnic tables.

BUSHY RUN BATTLEFIELD – Jeannette – (724) 527-5584 – Page 72, B-2 Site of strategic 1763 battle between British and Indian forces during Pontiac's War. Visitor center, picnicking, trails.

CAMBRIA COUNTY HISTORICAL SOCIETY MUSEUM – Ebensburg – (814) 472-6674 – Page 74, A-2 Varied collection of historic artifacts including a 13-star handsewn flag, dolls, furniture, lamps, lanterns, and a Seth Thomas clock. Also Textile Room and Military Room.

CANAL MUSEUM AND HUGH MOORE PARK – Easton – (610) 250-6700 – Page 68, C-2 Focus on historic canals and their contribution to industrial development of U.S. Models, dioramas, photographs, documents, and artifacts. Audio-visual programs. Mule-drawn canal boat *(see Excursions)*.

THE CASHIER'S HOUSE – Erie – (814) 454-1813 – Page 27, C-5 Built in 1839 for cashier of United Bank office. Period furnishings. Listed on National Register of Historic Places.

CENTRE COUNTY LIBRARY AND HISTORICAL MUSEUM – Bellefonte – (814) 355-1516 – Page 62, A-2 Local history emphasis. Furniture, china, clothing, artifacts, and documents. Pennsylvania Room. Spangler Genealogical Collection.

COLUMBUS FAMILY CHAPEL, BOAL MANSION AND MUSEUM – Boalsburg – (814) 466-6210 – Page 62, B-2 16th-century chapel originally owned by Columbus family, now held by descendants, the Boal family. Contains heirlooms, woodcarvings, and church relics. Boal Mansion. Museum.

CORNWALL IRON FURNACE – Cornwall – (717) 272-9711 – Page 79, B-6 Furnace operated from 1742–1883. Preserved along with related structures and buildings. Visitor center with exhibits.

CUMBERLAND COUNTY HISTORICAL SOCIETY & HAMILTON LIBRARY – Carlisle – (717) 249-7610 – Page 77, C-7 Woodcarvings, furniture, memorabilia from Carlisle Indian School, antique printing press.

DANIEL BOONE HOMESTEAD – Birdsboro – (610) 582-4900 – Page 81, B-4 Mid-18th-century farmhouse built on foundations of Daniel Boone's log cabin birthplace. Farm buildings.

DRAKE WELL MUSEUM – Titusville – (814) 827-2797 – Page 30, D-1 Site of first oil well ever drilled. Replica of engine shed and derrick. Museum.

ECKLEY MINERS' VILLAGE – 9 mi. E of Hazleton – (570) 636-2070 – Page 66, A-4 19th-century mining town. Visitor center with orientation slide show and exhibits. Picnic area.

EDGAR ALLEN POE NATIONAL HISTORIC SITE – Philadelphia – (215) 597-8780 – Page 96, A-2 One of Edgar Allen Poe's Philadelphia homes. Visitor center with exhibits and audio-visual program. Guided tours.

18TH-CENTURY INDUSTRIAL AREA – Bethlehem – (610) 691-0603 – Page 67, D-7 Moravian heritage. Tool exhibits, craft demonstrations, tours of restored buildings by costumed guides.

EISENHOWER NATIONAL HISTORIC SITE – Gettysburg – (717) 334-1124 – Page 91, B-6 Mamie and Dwight Eisenhower's retirement home. Adjacent to Gettysburg battlefield. (Tour tickets obtained from visitor center in Electric Map Building on Business Rte. 15.)

EPHRATA CLOISTER – Ephrata – (717) 733-6600 – Page 80, C-1 One of first communal societies in America, founded in 1732 by Conrad Biessel, a German Pietist mystic. Restored buildings include Saal (chapel), Saron (sisters' house), Biessel's log home, and Academy.

ERIE HISTORICAL MUSEUM – Erie – (814) 453-5811 – Page 27, C-5 Museum in Romanesque-style house. Regional history. Multimedia presentation on Battle of Lake Erie.

FALLINGWATER – Bear Run Nature Reserve – (724) 329-8501 – Page 86, A-3 Frank Lloyd Wright's most famous private house. Dramatic cantilevered design makes it one of finest examples of modern architecture. Donated to Western Pennsylvania Conservancy in 1963 by owners, the Kaufmanns.

FIREMAN'S HALL – Philadelphia – (215) 923-1438 – Page 96, A-2 1876 fire house. Story of firefighting from earliest days. Graphic and sound exhibits, memorabilia, equipment, film.

FORT BEDFORD PARK AND MUSEUM – Bedford – (814) 623-8891 – Page 74, D-3 Museum housed in blockhouse structure, containing large-scale model of Old Fort Bedford, implements of early settlers and Indians, old rifles, and vehicles.

FORT HUNTER MANSION AND PARK – Harrisburg – (717) 599-5751 – Page 78, B-2 Federal-style mansion built by Archibald McAllister in 1814. Costumes, furniture, tools, firearms, and toys. Other old buildings on grounds not open to public. Picnicking, play area, trail.

FORT NECESSITY NATIONAL BATTLEFIELD – Farmington – (724) 329-5512 – Page 86, B-2 Reconstruction of stockade, storehouse and entrenchments. Audio-visual room with slide show. Exhibit area tells of archaeological study which "rediscovered" fort. Picnicking.

FORT PITT MUSEUM – Pittsburgh – (412) 281-9284 – Page 71, A-5 Tells story of Fort Pitt, which defended Britain's position at the Forks of the Ohio against French. Dioramas, exhibits, models, reconstructed rooms. Live reenactments during summer.

FORT ROBERDEAU – Altoona – (814) 695-5541 – Page 61, D-5 Built during American Revolution to protect lead miners from attack. Fort was reconstructed on original site. Interpretive programs and reenactments. Rock and mineral museum. Picnicking. Nature trails.

GERMANTOWN HISTORICAL SOCIETY MUSEUM COMPLEX – Philadelphia – (215) 844-0514 – Page 82, D-2 Five museums tell story of Germantown's past. Conyngham-Hacker House, with orientation center and displays of decorative arts; Von Trott Annex with agricultural and domestic tools, three sleighs, and firefighting memorabilia; Clark-Watson House with period costumes; Howell House with toys and quilts; and Baynton House, containing library and archives.

GETTYSBURG NATIONAL MILITARY PARK AND CEMETERY – Gettysburg – (717) 334-1124 – Page 91, B-7 Site of Civil War battle. Interpretive programs. Visitor center with exhibits and "Electric Map." Cyclorama Center with exhibits and short film. Trails and auto tour.

GRAEME PARK – Horsham – (215) 343-0965 – Page 82, C-2 Built in 1721–1722 by Provincial Governor William Keith.

HERSHEY MUSEUM OF AMERICAN LIFE – Hershey – (717) 534-3439 – Page 79, B-4 Collections of organs and music boxes, English 18th- and 19th-century china, fire engines, and Indian lore. Costumes, Pennsylvania German crafts, rifles, and civil war guns. Participatory exhibits.

HISTORIC FALLSINGTON – Fallsington – (215) 295-6567 – Page 83, C-5 Four restored buildings open for tours. Moon-Williamson House, a late 17th-century Swedish-style log house; the Tavern, first operated in 1799; Burgess-Lippincott House, a late-Georgian early-Federal style home; and Schoolmaster's House, built in 1758. Slide show. Seasonal.

HISTORIC HANNA'S TOWN – N of Greensburg – (724) 836-1800 – Page 72, B-2 Reconstruction of Robert Hanna's house, one-room jail, and stockade. Archaeological excavations. Costumed guides. Demonstrations. Seasonal.

THE HISTORICAL SOCIETY OF DAUPHIN COUNTY – Harrisburg – (717) 233-3462 – Page 78, B-2 Museum in historic house, built by Harrisburg founder. Decorative arts and local history. Changing exhibits.

HOPE LODGE – Fort Washington – (215) 646-1595 – Page 82, D-2 Original, mid-1700s Georgian mansion, used as field headquarters by Surgeon General in the Revolution. Furnished with collections of Philadelphia furniture, fine art, and early Chinese porcelain ware.

HOPEWELL FURNACE NATIONAL HISTORIC SITE – 5 mi. S of Birdsboro – (610) 582-8773 – Page 81, C-4 Restoration and reconstruction of the anthracite furnace, related machinery, structures, and buildings of ironmaking village of 1771–1883.

HORSESHOE CURVE – Altoona – (814) 943-8151 – Page 74, A-4 Built in 1854, one of largest engineering projects undertaken at that time. Made practical rail route through Alleghenies possible.

INDEPENDENCE NATIONAL HISTORICAL PARK – Philadelphia – (215) 597-8974 – Page 96, A-2 Independence Hall, open by tour only. Carpenter's Hall, meeting place of First Continental Congress. Liberty Bell Pavilion, new location of Liberty Bell. Many other historical sites of Colonial, Revolutionary, and Federal-periods within park and neighboring area. Visitor center with exhibits, schedules of daily events, 20-minute film "Independence" by John Huston. Guided and self-guided tours.

JACOBSBURG ENVIRONMENTAL EDUCATION CENTER – Nazareth – (610) 746-2801 – Page 68, B-1 Remains of 18th-century industrial village of Jacobsburg. Benade House (Henry Forge), Henry Homestead, springhouse, bakery. Old foundations of Jacobsburg Tavern and other buildings. Self-guided tours. Call for times when Benade House and Henry Homestead are open to public.

JOHNSTOWN FLOOD MUSEUM – Johnstown – (814) 539-1889 – Page 73, B-7 Local history museum with emphasis on flood of 1889. Photographs and artifacts related to flood and Johnstown history. Changing exhibits.

JOHNSTOWN FLOOD NATIONAL MEMORIAL – Saint Michael – (814) 495-5718 – Page 74, B-1 Remains of old South Fork Dam, which broke in 1889 causing Johnstown flood. Visitor center with model of dam. Self-guided trail and auto tour around former lake bed. Picnic area.

KINZUA VIADUCT – Kinzua Bridge State Park – (814) 965-2646 – Page 32, B-3 Second highest bridge of type on North American Continent. Built of iron in 1882, was rebuilt to same dimensions in steel in 1900. 301 feet high and 2,110 feet long. On National Register of Historic Places.

LANDIS VALLEY MUSEUM – 4.5 miles NE of Lancaster – (717) 569-0401 – Page 79, D-7 Rural life of southeastern Pennsylvania from colonial days through 19th century. 22 buildings include 1780 Log House; Henry Landis House, 1870; Schoolhouse; Federal-style farmhouses. Displays and exhibits. Demonstrations by costumed workers. Visitor center.

LIBERTY BELL SHRINE – Allentown – (610) 435-4232 – Page 67, D-7 Liberty Bell hidden here from September 1777 until June 1778. Full-size replica of bell; mural depicts story of Liberty Bell's trip to Allentown; "Portrait of Freedom" painting collection; displays of colonial and post-colonial objects including flags, maps, guns, uniforms, 1790 clock, and furniture.

LYCOMING COUNTY HISTORICAL MUSEUM – Williamsport – (570) 326-3326 – Page 50, C-1 Shempp Toy Train Collection. Lumbering exhibits. 1870 "Millionaire Row" Victorian Parlor. Indian and frontier exhibits.

MERCER MUSEUM OF THE BUCKS COUNTY HISTORICAL SOCIETY – Doylestown – (215) 345-0210 – Page 82, B-2 Housed in 1913 concrete structure, designated National Historic Landmark. Extensive collection of pre-industrial American tools and products. Folk art.

MORAVIAN MUSEUM – Bethlehem – (610) 867-0173 – Page 67, D-7 Housed in Gemein Haus built 1741. Articles reflecting life of early Moravians. Furniture, clocks, musical instruments, religious articles, seminary art, and needlework. Guided tours.

MORTON HOMESTEAD – Prospect Park – (610) 583-7221 – Page 96, A-1 Pre-1700 example of Finnish-Scandinavian log construction. Visitor center. Special exhibits and seasonal programs. Demonstration Garden. Picnicking.

MUSEUM OF INDIAN CULTURE – Allentown – (610) 797-2121 – Page 67, D-6 Collection of Indian artifacts dating from 12,000 B.C. Also settlers' artifacts. Slide show. Focus on history and culture of Lenni Lenape people and local history.

OLD BEDFORD VILLAGE – 1 mi. N of Bedford – (814) 623-1156 – Page 74, D-3 Reconstructed village of period from 1750–1850. Craftsmen and interpreters in colonial costume. Craft demonstrations. Working farm. Special events. Refreshments. Picnic area.

OLD ECONOMY VILLAGE – Ambridge – (724) 266-4500 – Page 56, D-4 Third home of Harmonists, a German Pietist group who lived in a Christian communal society, specializing in manufacturing. Lived in Economy from 1824–1905. 17 fully restored buildings on two blocks of village.

PENNSYLVANIA LUMBER MUSEUM – 10 mi. E of Coudersport – (814) 435-2652 – Page 34, B-2 Exhibits of Pennsylvania's lumbering and logging days. Tools, logging locomotive, logging camp, and sawmill.

PENNSYLVANIA MILITARY MUSEUM – Boalsburg – (814) 466-6263 – Page 62, B-2 History of Pennsylvania's military participation. Weapons and uniforms. Dioramas, maps, photographs, reproduced section of WWI battlefield, 28th Division Shrine.

RAILROAD MUSEUM OF PENNSYLVANIA – Strasburg – (717) 687-8628 – Page 94, A-1 History of railroading in Pennsylvania. Locomotives, railroad cars, paraphernalia, models, tools.

RAILROADERS MEMORIAL MUSEUM – Altoona – (814) 946-1047 – Page 61, D-4 Collections and exhibits relating to Pennsylvania's "Golden Age of Railroading." Mural, locomotives, railroad cars, operating model railroad, models.

THE SCRANTON IRON FURNACES – Scranton – (570) 963-4804 – Page 53, A-5 Four remaining stone smokestacks of anthracite-burning blast furnaces of Lackawanna Iron and Coal Company.

SLATEFORD FARM – Slateford – (570) 897-6566 – Page 68, A-3 In Delaware Water Gap National Recreation Area. 10-room house of 19th-century farm family. Site of early slate quarry. Seasonal tours and demonstrations.

STATE MUSEUM OF PENNSYLVANIA – Harrisburg – (717) 787-4978 – Page 78, B-2 Exhibits on history, geology, industry, technology, and arts of Pennsylvania. State documents including original charter granted to William Penn. Planetarium, changing exhibits.

STEAMTOWN NATIONAL HISTORIC SITE – Scranton – (570) 340-5200 – Page 53 , A-5 Collection of over 100 historic railroad cars and locomotives. *(See Excursions.)*

SWIGART MUSEUM – Huntingdon – (814) 643-3000 – Page 76, A-1 40 vintage steam, gas and electric automobiles. Automobile name and license plates. Accessories. Collections of antique toys, trains, dolls, and clothing.

THOMAS NEWCOMEN LIBRARY AND MUSEUM – Exton – (610) 363-6600 – Page 81, D-5 Steam engines, electrically operated scale models of steam engines, steam technology, and history. 2,700 volumes on early steam. 19th-century pamphlets and trade catalogs.

TIOGA POINT MUSEUM – Athens – (570) 888-7225 – Page 37, A-5 Collections on Indian lore, geology, local and natural history. Rare books, documents, costumes. Railroad and canal history; also Revolutionary and Civil War materials. Guided tours by appointment.

U.S. BRIG NIAGARA – Erie – (814) 871-4596 – Page 27, C-5 Built in 1812, one of three surviving ships of period. Used by Admiral Perry to defeat British fleet on Great Lakes.

U.S. MINT – Philadelphia – (215) 408-0114 – Page 96, A-2 Authorized by Congress in 1792. Self-guided tours. Viewing of actual coin production. Exhibits.

UNION CITY AREA HISTORICAL MUSEUM – Union City – (814) 438-2151 – Page 29 A-7 Variety of exhibits and displays show history of Union City area from settlement in 1797.

VALLEY FORGE NATIONAL HISTORIC PARK – Valley Forge – (610) 783-1077 – Page 81, D-7 Site of Continental Army's encampment during winter of 1777–1778. Reconstructed huts, memorials, markers, monuments. Washington and other officers' quarters. National Memorial Arch. Visitor center with film and exhibits. Interpreters in period costumes. Hiking, biking, riding. Picnicking. Fishing in Valley Creek. Boat ramp.

VENANGO COUNTY HISTORICAL SOCIETY – Franklin – (814) 437-2275 – Page 43, A-7 Changing exhibits relating to Venango County's past. Library.

WASHINGTON CROSSING HISTORIC PARK – 1.5 mi. SE of New Hope – (215) 493-4076 – Page 83, B-5 Composed of two sites where Washington's troops crossed Delaware River on December 25, 1776. Restored buildings. Memorial Building and visitor center with copy of Emanuel Leutze's painting "Washington Crossing the Delaware," film, and exhibits. Seasonal interpretive programs.

WRIGHT'S FERRY MANSION – Columbia – (717) 684-4325 – Page 79, D-5 Restored 1738 stone home built for Susanna Wright, a literary Quaker. Furnished with pieces and accessories 1700–1750. Seasonal.

Art Museums/Science Centers

ACADEMY OF NATURAL SCIENCES OF PHILADELPHIA – Philadelphia – (215) 299-1000 – Page 96, A-2 Discovering Dinosaurs, an exploration of dinosaurs with research into their behavior and extinction. North American, Asian, and African Halls with native animals in natural settings. Egyptian Mummy Exhibit. Gem and crystal exhibit. Hall of Endangered Species. OUTSIDE-IN, the children's nature museum with participatory exhibits. Other exhibits, classes, and special programs.

ALLENTOWN ART MUSEUM – Allentown – (610) 432-4333 – Page 67, D-7 Collections include textiles; Renaissance and Baroque paintings of Italy, Holland, Germany; 19th- and 20th-century American paintings; decorative arts and sculpture. Changing exhibits. Special programs. Children's programs.

ANNIE S. KEMERER MUSEUM – Bethlehem – (610) 868-6868 – Page 67, D-7 Collections of decorative art, largely regional. 18th- and 19th-century furniture. Glass, ceramics, clocks. Temporary exhibits change monthly.

ASSOCIATED ARTISTS OF PITTSBURGH GALLERY – Pittsburgh – (412) 263-2710 – Page 71, A-6 All media exhibits of regional artists. Also exhibits at Carnegie Museum of Art.

BRANDYWINE RIVER MUSEUM – Chadds Ford – (610) 388-7601 – Page 95, A-6 In restored gristmill with new wing. Art of Brandywine Region and American illustration. Wyeth family paintings. Special exhibitions. Craft fairs.

BUTEN MUSEUM – Merion – (610) 664-6601 – Page 82, D-2 Ceramics museum. Collection of 10,000 pieces of Wedgewood dating from mid-18th century to present. Temporary exhibits. Educational programs.

THE CARNEGIE – Pittsburgh – (412) 622-3131 – Page 71, A-6 Cultural complex including museums, library, and concert hall. Carnegie Museum of Natural History highlights include Dinosaur Hall, arctic life exhibit, and display of minerals and gems. Carnegie Museum of Art features masterpieces from French Impressionists to contemporary works.

CARNEGIE SCIENCE CENTER – Pittsburgh – (412) 237-3400 – Page 71, A-5 Participatory exhibits on science and technology. Subjects include computers, light and energy, movement, laserium and planetarium shows, robots. Special programs, exhibits, classes.

DREXEL UNIVERSITY ART MUSEUM – Philadelphia – (215) 895-2424 – Page 96, A-2 Selections on display in permanent gallery include 19th-century Academic paintings, works of Barbizon School, decorative arts, sculpture, costumes, porcelain, glass. Changing exhibits.

ERIE ART MUSEUM – Erie – (814) 459-5477 – Page 27, C-5 Painting, sculpture, drawings, graphics. American ceramics and contemporary photography. Annual juried exhibitions. Films and performances.

EVERHART MUSEUM OF NATURAL HISTORY, SCIENCE AND ART – Scranton – (570) 346-7186 – Page 53, A-5 Permanent collections include American art, folk art, Dorflinger glass, Oriental art, and primitive art. Bird collection. Earth sciences and ecology. Changing exhibits in arts and sciences.

FISHER COLLECTION – Philadelphia – (215) 925-2178 – Page 96, A-2 17th- and 18th-century works include Dutch and Flemish oil paintings, engravings, and etchings with emphasis on alchemy and scientific themes.

FRANKLIN INSTITUTE SCIENCE MUSEUM AND PLANETARIUM – Philadelphia – (215) 448-1200 – Page 96, A-2 Aviation, meteorology, astronomy and space exploration, physics, marine and naval science, transportation. Hands-on exhibits, live museum demonstrations. Planetarium. Ben Franklin National Memorial.

THE FRANKLIN MINT MUSEUM – Franklin Center – (610) 459-6168 – Page 95, A-7 Collections of world's largest private mint (founded 1964). Jewelry, porcelain, dolls, reproduction furniture, books. Self-guided tour.

THE FRICK ART MUSEUM – Pittsburgh – (412) 371-0600 – Page 71, A-6 13th- to 18th-century paintings and decorative arts. Temporary and traveling exhibits. Concerts and lectures.

THE FROST ENTOMOLOGICAL MUSEUM – University Park – (814) 863-2865 – Page 62, B-2 At Pennsylvania State University. Exhibits of preserved specimens, photographs, and models of insects. Seasonal exhibits with live insects.

GOLDIE PALEY GALLERY AT MOORE COLLEGE – Philadelphia – (215) 568-4515 – Page 96, A-2 Changing exhibits focus on contemporary art, graphic design, and architecture. Lectures and gallery talks.

HERITAGE CENTER OF LANCASTER COUNTY – Lancaster – (717) 299-6440 – Page 79, D-7 Decorative arts. Pieces produced by early Lancaster County craftspeople. Furniture, quilts, silver, folk art, clocks, and Pennsylvania long rifles.

HUNT INSTITUTE FOR BOTANICAL DOCUMENTATION – Pittsburgh – (412) 268-2434 – Page 71, A-6 Changing exhibits on botanical art and illustration. 30,000 watercolors, drawings, and prints; 27,000 volumes.

INSTITUTE OF CONTEMPORARY ART OF THE UNIVERSITY OF PENNSYLVANIA – Philadelphia – (215) 898-7108 – Page 96, A-2 Exhibitions of contemporary art with emphasis on new art. Programs for children, performances, concerts, and lectures.

LA SALLE COLLEGE ART MUSEUM – Philadelphia – (215) 951-1221 – Page 82, D-2 Permanent exhibit with paintings and drawings in many major styles and themes of Western art. Temporary shows.

LEHIGH UNIVERSITY ART GALLERIES – Bethlehem – (610) 758-3615 – Page 67, D-7 20 exhibits per year focus on contemporary architecture, graphics, and photography. Sculpture garden. Lectures.

THE MERRICK ART GALLERY – New Brighton – (724) 846-1130 – Page 56, C-3 Founded in 1880. Collections of European and American 18th- and 19th-century paintings. Manuscripts. Mineral collection. Library. Guided tours, changing temporary exhibits.

MUSEUM OF ART, PENNSYLVANIA STATE UNIVERSITY – University Park – (814) 865-7672 – Page 62, B-2 Three galleries with changing exhibitions of historic, contemporary, and architectural exhibits. Gallery talks. Lecture and film series.

MUTTER MUSEUM, COLLEGE OF PHYSICIANS OF PHILADELPHIA – Philadelphia – (215) 563-3737 – Page 96, A-2 Exhibits from permanent collections include anatomical and pathological specimens, and memorabilia of famous physicians and scientists. Medical history. Herb garden.

NORMAN ROCKWELL MUSEUM – Philadelphia – (215) 922-4345 – Page 96, A-2 *Saturday Evening Post* covers, "The American Family" drawings, advertisements, prints, collotypes, lithographs, and sketches. Life-size replica of Norman Rockwell's studio. Slide show.

THE NORTH MUSEUM OF FRANKLIN AND MARSHALL COLLEGE – Lancaster – (717) 291-3941 – Page 79, D-7 Natural history exhibits on Indians, wildlife, rocks and minerals, fossils, and birds. Planetarium with shows. 18th- and 19th-century furniture. Discovery Room. Changing exhibits.

PENNSYLVANIA ACADEMY OF FINE ARTS – Philadelphia – (215) 972-7600 – Page 96, A-2 Changing exhibits from American Art collection. Special exhibits on historic and contemporary American Art. Concert and film series. Lectures.

THE PHILADELPHIA ART ALLIANCE – Philadelphia – (215) 545-4302 – Page 96, A-2 Exhibits in sculpture, prints, industrial design, architecture, painting, jewelry, glass, wood, metals, and other crafts. Lectures, demonstrations, performances.

PHILADELPHIA MUSEUM OF ART – Philadelphia – (215) 763-8100 – Page 96, A-2 Changing exhibits in Print Gallery. American paintings and decorative arts. Near and Far Eastern rugs. European paintings from Renaissance to 19th century. Armor and arms collection in Great Stair Hall.

PLEASE TOUCH MUSEUM – Philadelphia – (215) 963-0667 – Page 96, A-2 Museum designed for children up to age seven. Arts, sciences, technology, natural sciences, and cultural subjects presented in participatory exhibits. Special exhibits. Performances and workshops.

READING PLANETARIUM – Reading – (610) 371-5850 – Page 80, B-3 Changing multimedia planetarium shows. Model of moon shows features and Apollo landings. Model of Telstar. Meteorites.

READING PUBLIC MUSEUM AND ART GALLERY – Reading – (610) 371-5850 – Page 80, B-3 Art gallery emphasizes contemporary American Art. Nature museum. Indian artifacts.

RODIN MUSEUM – Philadelphia – (215) 763-8100 – Page 96, A-2 Sculpture and drawings of Auguste Rodin.

THE ROSENBACH MUSEUM AND LIBRARY – Philadelphia – (215) 732-1600 – Page 96, A-2 English, French, and American furniture. 18th-century silver. 18th- and 19th-century English and French drawings and prints. Drawings and watercolors by children's book illustrator Maurice Sendak. Literature collections. Changing exhibits.

SORDONI ART GALLERY – Wilkes-Barre – (570) 824-4651 – Page 52, C-3 At Wilkes College. 19th- and 20th-century American art. Changing exhibits.

SOUTHERN ALLEGHENIES MUSEUM OF ART – Loretto – (814) 472-6400 – Page 60, D-2 Selections from permanent collection of American paintings and graphics and works by prominent living Pennsylvania artists. Changing exhibits in various disciplines of contemporary and historical American art.

THE UNIVERSITY MUSEUM – Philadelphia – (215) 898-4000 – Page 96, A-2 At University of Pennsylvania. Archaeological and anthropological exhibits. Results of 300 expeditions in 33 countries.

THE UNIVERSITY OF THE ARTS – Philadelphia – (215) 717-6000 – Page 96, A-2 Contemporary art. Student, alumni, faculty, and departmental shows. Exhibitions of works by present day artists.

WAGNER FREE INSTITUTE OF SCIENCE – Philadelphia – (215) 763-6529 – Page 96, A-2 Natural history museum with over 100,000 specimens.

THE WESTMORELAND COUNTY MUSEUM OF ART – Greensburg – (724) 837-1500 – Page 72, B-2 18th-century rooms with English and European paintings and decorative arts. American collection of paintings, sculpture, watercolors, drawings, prints, and decorative arts. Antique toy collection shown during Christmas season.

WOODMERE ART MUSEUM – Philadelphia – (215) 247-0476 – Page 82, D-2 Exhibitions of works by Delaware Valley artists and selections from permanent collections of fine and decorative arts from 18th and 19th centuries.

Golf Courses

To locate golf courses in this Atlas, look on the appropriate map for the golf symbol and corresponding four-digit number.

3007 **Allentown**, Allentown, Page 67, D-6
3010 **Appledale Public**, Ebensburg, Page 74, A-2
3013 **Armitage**, Mechanicsburg, Page 78, C-2
3016 **Arrowhead**, Douglassville, Page 81, B-4
3019 **Aubrey's**, Butler, Page 57, A-6
3025 **Birchwood**, Transfer, Page 42, B-2
3031 **Black Hawk**, Beaver Falls, Page 56, B-2
3034 **Blackwood**, Douglassville, Page 81, C-5
3037 **Blue Mountain**, Saylorsburg, Page 68, A-1
3040 **Blue Mountain View**, Fredericksburg, Page 79, A-6
3043 **Blueberry Hill**, Russell, Page 31, A-6
3046 **Bon Air**, Coraopolis, Page 71, A-4
3049 **Borland's Par 3**, New Wilmington, Page 42, D-3
3058 **Briarwood**, York, Page 92, A-3
3064 **Buck Hill**, Buck Hill Falls, Page 54, C-1
3067 **Bucknell University**, Lewisburg, Page 64, A-2
3070 **Buffalo**, Sarver, Page 58, C-1
3076 **Bush's**, Snydersville, Page 68, A-1
3079 **Butler's Public**, Elizabeth Township, Page 71, B-7
3082 **Butter Valley**, Barto, Page 81, A-6
3085 **Cabin Greens**, Freeport, Page 58, C-2
3088 **Cable Hollow**, Akeley, Page 31, A-6
3091 **Caledonia**, Fayetteville, Page 91, A-5
3094 **Cambrian Hills**, Hastings, Page 60, C-2
3095 **Carmichaels**, Carmichaels, Page 85, A-6
3097 **Carroll Valley Resort**, Carroll Valley, Fairfield, Page 91, B-5
3100 **Carter Heights**, Corry, Page 30, A-1
3103 **Castle Hills**, New Castle, Page 42, D-3
3106 **Cedarbrook**, Belle Vernon, Page 71, C-7
3109 **Center Square**, Center Point, Page 82, C-1
3112 **Champion Lakes**, Bolivar, Page 73, B-5
3118 **Cherokee**, Danville, Page 65, A-5
3121 **Cherry Hills Inn**, McDonald, Page 70, B-3
3124 **Cherry Valley**, Stroudsburg, Page 68, A-2
3130 **Chestnut Ridge**, Blairsville, Page 73, A-5
3133 **Chetremon**, Cherry Tree, Page 60, B-1
3136 **Chippewa**, Bentleyville, Page 71, C-5
3142 **Cliff Park Inn**, Milford, Page 55, B-5
3145 **Cloverleaf**, Delmont, Page 72, A-2
3148 **Colonial Crest**, Lewisburg, Page 64, A-2
3151 **Colonial**, Uniontown, Page 85, A-7
3154 **Conley's**, Butler, Page 57, B-6
3157 **Conocodell**, Fayetteville, Page 91, A-4
3160 **Cool Creek**, Wrightsville, Page 79, D-5
3166 **Corey Creek**, Mansfield, Page 36, B-1
3169 **Country Club of Hershey**, Hershey, Page 79, B-5
3172 **Crafton Public**, Pittsburgh, Page 71, A-5
3175 **Cricket Hill**, Hawley, Page 40, D-2
3178 **Cross Creek Resort**, Titusville, Page 30, D-1
3180 **Culbertson Hills**, Edinboro, Page 29, A-4
3181 **Cumberland**, Carlisle, Page 77, C-6
3184 **Del-Mar**, Ellwood City, Page 56, A-3
3187 **Double Dam**, Claysville, Page 70, D-2
3189 **Down River**, Everett, Page 75, D-5
3190 **Downing**, Erie, Page 27, C-6
3193 **Downington**, Downington, Page 81, D-5
3196 **Edgewood Pines**, Edgewood, Page 52, D-3
3202 **Elk Forest Resort**, Waymart, Page 40, D-1
3205 **Elk Valley**, Girard, Page 28, A-4
3208 **Erie**, Erie, Page 27, D-5
3214 **Evergreen**, Mastersonville, Page 79, C-6
3217 **Evergreen Park**, Analomink, Page 54, D-2
3220 **Exeter Public**, Reading, Page 80, B-4
3223 **Fairview**, Quentin, Page 79, B-6
3226 **Fallen Timber**, Midway, Page 70, A-3
3229 **Fernwood**, Bushkill, Page 54, D-3
3232 **Flying Hills**, Cumru Township, Page 80, B-3
3233 **Four Seasons**, Landisville, Page 79, D-6
3234 **Fox Hollow**, Quakertown, Page 81, A-7
3235 **Fox Run**, Beaver Falls, Page 56, B-3
3238 **Foxburg**, Foxburg, Page 44, C-1
3241 **Franklin Park**, Pittsburgh, Page 57, D-5
3244 **Freeport Mills**, Lebanon, Page 79, A-6
3247 **Galen Hall**, Wernersville, Page 80, B-2
3253 **General Washington Recreation Center**, Audubon, Page 81, C-7
3256 **Gilbertsville**, Pottstown, Page 81, B-6
3259 **Glen Brook**, Stroudsburg, Page 68, A-2
3262 **Golf Hollow**, Southampton, Page 82, C-3
3268 **Gospel Hill**, Erie, Page 27, C-6
3271 **Grand View**, York, Page 92, A-3
3274 **Grandview**, Curwensville, Page 60, A-3
3277 **Green Acres**, Bernville, Page 80, A-2
3280 **Green Acres**, Titusville, Page 29, C-7
3283 **Green Hills**, Birdsboro, Page 80, C-3
3286 **Green Meadows**, Volant, Page 43, D-4
3289 **Green Meadows**, Erie, Page 27, C-6
3292 **Green Pond**, Bethlehem, Page 68, C-1
3295 **Green Valley**, Pittsburgh, Page 57, D-5
3298 **Greenwood**, Altoona, Page 61, D-5
3301 **Hailwood**, Meadville, Page 29, C-4
3304 **Happy Valley**, Exeter, Page 52, B-4
3307 **Hartmann's Deep Valley**, Harmony, Page 57, B-5
3310 **Hartstown**, Hartstown, Page 28, D-2
3313 **Hawk Valley Public**, Denver, Page 80, C-2
3316 **Hawthorne Valley**, Ohioville, Page 56, C-2
3322 **Hi Level**, Kossuth, Page 44, B-2
3324 **Hickory Valley**, Gilbertsville, Page 81, B-6
3328 **Hidden Springs**, Horsham, Page 82, C-2
3331 **Hidden Valley**, Pittsburgh, Page 71, B-5
3334 **Hidden Valley**, Pine Grove, Page 65, D-7
3337 **Hiland Public**, Butler, Page 57, A-7
3340 **Holiday Acres**, Edinboro, Page 29, A-4
3343 **Homestead**, Carbondale, Page 39, D-6
3346 **Honey Run**, York, Page 92, A-3
3349 **Host Farm Resort**, Lancaster, Page 80, D-1
3352 **Hotel Hershey**, Hershey, Page 79, B-4
3361 **Ingleside**, Thorndale, Page 81, D-4
3364 **Iron Masters**, Roaring Springs, Page 75, B-4
3367 **Iron Wood**, Conneaut Lake, Page 28, C-3
3373 **Jackson Valley**, Warren, Page 31, A-4
3375 **Jean's Run**, Muhlenberg, Page 52, C-1
3376 **Jefferson**, Jeffersonville, Page 81, C-7
3379 **Jepko's Three Ponds**, Elysburg, Page 64, B-5
3381 **Johnstown Municipal**, Johnstown, Page 73, B-7
3384 **Joseph Martin**, Erie, Page 27, D-5
3387 **Kimberton**, Phoenixville, Page 81, C-6
3390 **King's Mountain Resort**, Rockwood, Page 86, A-4
3393 **Krendale**, Butler, Page 57, A-6
3396 **Lake Arthur**, Butler, Page 57, A-6
3399 **Lakeland**, Fleetville, Page 39, D-5
3402 **Lakelawn Park**, Irwin, Page 72, B-1
3405 **Lakevue North**, Butler, Page 57, B-6
3408 **Laurel Grove Inn**, Canadensis, Page 54, C-1
3411 **Lawrence Park**, Erie, Page 27, C-5
3414 **Lebanon Valley**, Myerstown, Page 79, A-7
3420 **Lenape Heights**, Ford City, Page 58, C-2
3423 **Limerick**, Limerick, Page 81, C-6
3426 **Linden Hall**, Dawson, Page 72, D-1
3429 **Lindenwood**, McMurray, Page 71, B-4
3432 **Little Creek**, Spring Grove, Page 92, A-3
3435 **Loch Nairn**, Toughkenamon, Page 95, B-4
3438 **Locust Valley**, Coopersburg, Page 81, A-7
3444 **Lost Creek**, Oakland Mills, Page 63, D-6
3447 **Maggi's 84**, Canonsburg, Page 71, C-4
3453 **Manada**, Grantville, Page 79, A-4
3456 **Manor**, Sinking Springs, Page 80, B-2
3459 **Manor Valley**, Export, Page 72, A-1
3462 **Mar-Jon**, Moscow, Page 53, A-6
3465 **Marada**, Clinton, Page 70, A-3
3471 **Mayfield**, Clarion, Page 44, C-3
3474 **Meadow Brook**, Phoenixville, Page 81, D-6
3477 **Meadow Lane**, Indiana, Page 59, C-6
3480 **Meadowink**, Murrysville, Page 72, A-1
3483 **Mercer Public**, Mercer, Page 42, B-3
3486 **Mermaid Swim & Golf Club**, Blue Bell, Page 82, C-1
3489 **Middlecreek**, Rockwood, Page 87, A-5
3492 **Mill Race**, Benton, Page 51, C-7
3495 **Mohawk Trails**, New Castle, Page 42, D-2
3498 **Monroe Valley**, Jonestown, Page 79, A-6
3501 **Montgomeryville**, Montgomeryville, Page 82, B-2
3507 **The Mountain Laurel Resort**, White Haven, Page 53, D-4
3510 **Mt. Odin Park Municipal**, Greensburg, Page 72, B-2
3514 **Mt. Pocono**, Mt. Pocono, Page 54, C-1
3516 **Mulberry Hill**, East Huntingdon, Page 72, C-2
3519 **Murrysville**, Murrysville, Page 72, A-1
3525 **North Hills Municipal**, Corry, Page 30, A-1
3528 **North Park**, Allison Park, Page 57, D-5
3531 **Northampton Valley**, Richboro, Page 82, C-4
3534 **Norvelt**, Norvelt, Page 72, C-3
3537 **Oakbrook**, Stoystown, Page 73, C-6
3540 **Oakland Beach**, Conneaut Lake, Page 28, C-3
3543 **Oakmont East**, Oakmont, Page 57, D-7
3546 **Ohio View Public**, Industry, Page 56, C-2
3549 **Over Lake**, Girard, Page 28, A-3
3552 **Overlook**, Lancaster, Page 79, D-7
3555 **Park**, Conneaut Lake, Page 28, C-3
3561 **Penn National**, Fayetteville, Page 91, A-4
3564 **Pennsburg**, Pennsburg, Page 81, A-7
3567 **Pennsylvania State University**, State College, Page 62, B-2
3570 **Perry**, Shoemakersville, Page 66, D-3
3573 **Pine Acres**, Bradford, Page 32, B-2
3576 **Pine Grove Public**, Grove City, Page 43, C-5
3579 **Pine Hills**, Taylor, Page 53, A-5
3585 **Pinecrest**, Brookville, Page 45, C-5
3588 **Pinehill**, Greenville, Page 42, A-3
3591 **Piney Run**, Garrett, Page 87, A-6
3594 **Pittsburg-North**, Gibsonia, Page 57, C-6
3597 **Plantation Inn**, Mechanicsburg, Page 78, C-2
3600 **Pleasant Hill**, Fleetwood, Page 80, A-4
3603 **Pleasant Valley**, Connellsville, Page 72, D-2
3606 **Pleasant Valley**, Stewartstown, Page 93, B-5
3609 **Pleasant Valley**, Vintondale, Page 73, A-7
3612 **Pleasure**, Edinboro, Page 29, A-4
3621 **Pocono Manor**, Pocono Manor, Page 54, D-1
3627 **Ponderosa Golflands**, Frankfort Springs, Page 70, A-2
3636 **Ranch View**, Washington, Page 70, C-4
3639 **Rich Maiden**, Fleetwood, Page 80, A-4
3645 **Richland Greens**, Johnstown, Page 74, B-1
3648 **Ridgeview**, Ligonier, Page 73, B-5
3650 **Rittswood**, Valencia, Page 57, C-6
3651 **River Ridge**, Franklin, Page 43, A-7
3654 **Riverside**, Cambridge Springs, Page 29, B-5
3657 **Riverview**, Elizabeth, Page 71, C-6
3663 **Rohanna's**, Waynesburg, Page 85, A-5
3666 **Rolling Acre Pitch and Putt**, York, Page 93, A-4
3669 **Rolling Fields**, Murrysville, Page 58, D-1
3672 **Rolling Green**, Eighty Four, Page 71, C-5
3675 **Rolling Hills**, Pulaski, Page 42, D-2
3678 **Rolling Meadows**, Mowry, Page 65, B-6
3681 **Rolling Acres**, Beaver Falls, Page 56, C-2
3684 **Rolling Turf**, Schwenksville, Page 81, B-7
3687 **Rose Ridge**, Allison Park, Page 57, D-6
3690 **Saint Jude**, Chicora, Page 58, A-1
3693 **Sauers**, Erie, Page 27, D-5
3696 **Scally's**, Coraopolis, Page 71, A-4
3702 **Scranton Municipal**, Lake Ariel, Page 53, A-6
3705 **Seven Springs**, Elizabeth Township, Page 71, C-7
3711 **Seven Springs Resort**, Champion, Page 73, D-4
3714 **Shadow Brook**, Tunkhannock, Page 38, D-3
3717 **Shamrock Public**, Slippery Rock, Page 43, D-5
3720 **Shawnee Inn**, Shawnee-on-Delaware, Page 54, D-3
3723 **Silver Spring**, Mechanicsburg, Page 78, B-1
3726 **Skippack**, Skippack, Page 81, C-7
3729 **Sleepy Hollow**, Franklin, Page 43, A-6
3732 **Somerton Springs**, Feasterville, Page 82, C-3
3735 **South Hills**, Hanover, Page 92, B-2
3738 **South Park**, Library, Page 71, B-6
3741 **South Woods**, McKean, Page 29, A-5
3744 **Speer Public**, Franklin, Page 43, A-7
3747 **Sportsman's**, Harrisburg, Page 78, B-3
3749 **Spring Mill**, Ivyland, Page 82, C-3
3750 **Springdale**, Uniontown, Page 85, A-7
3753 **Springfield**, Springfield, Page 96, A-1
3756 **Springside Par 3**, Reinholds, Page 80, B-2
3759 **Standing Stone**, Huntingdon, Page 62, D-1
3762 **Statler's Par 3**, Greensburg, Page 72, B-3
3765 **Stonecrest**, Wampum, Page 56, B-3
3768 **Stop & Sock**, New Brighton, Page 56, B-3
3771 **Stoughton Acres**, Butler, Page 57, A-6
3774 **Strickland's Wiscasset**, Mount Pocono, Page 54, D-1
3777 **Sugarloaf**, Rock Glen, Page 66, A-1
3780 **Summit**, Cresson, Page 74, A-3
3783 **Suncrest**, Butler, Page 57, B-6
3786 **Sunset**, Middletown, Page 78, C-4
3789 **Sweet Valley**, Sweet Valley, Page 52, B-2
3792 **Tam-O-Shanter**, West Middlesex, Page 42, C-2
3795 **Tamiment Resort**, Tamiment, Page 54, C-3
3798 **Tanglewood**, Pulaski, Page 42, D-2
3804 **Tanglewood Manor**, Quarryville, Page 94, B-1
3810 **Timberlink**, Ligonier, Page 73, B-4
3811 **Toftrees**, State College, Page 62, B-1
3814 **Towanda**, Towanda, Page 37, B-6
3817 **Tree Top**, Manheim, Page 79, C-6
3823 **Turbot Hills**, Milton, Page 50, D-3
3826 **Twin Lake Par 3**, Kittanning, Page 58, B-2
3829 **Twin Lakes**, Allentown, Page 67, C-6
3832 **Twin Lakes**, Mainland, Page 82, C-1
3835 **Twin Oaks**, Orange, Page 52, A-3
3838 **Twin Ponds**, Gilbertsville, Page 81, B-6
3841 **Twin Woods**, Hatfield, Page 82, B-1

Fishing

Note on trout: The Pennsylvania Fish Commission stocks 5,000 miles of streams and 7,000 acres of lakes with more than five million trout each year, using a mix of brown, rainbow, and brook varieties.

LAKES

Allegheny Reservoir – Page 31, A-7 largemouth and smallmouth bass, muskellunge, northern pike, walleye

Alvin R. Bush Dam – Page 48, B-1 largemouth and smallmouth bass, trout, bullheads, panfish

Belmont Lake – Page 39, B-7 largemouth and smallmouth bass, pickerel, muskellunge, walleye, panfish

Beltzville Lake – Page 67, B-6 largemouth and smallmouth bass, pickerel, tiger muskellunge, walleye, channel catfish, panfish

Blue Marsh Lake – Page 80, A-2 largemouth bass, crappies

Bradys Lake – Page 53, C-6 largemouth bass, pickerel, panfish

Briar Creek Park Lake – Page 51, D-7 largemouth bass, walleye, muskellunge, pickerel, channel catfish, panfish

Bruce Lake – Page 54, B-2 largemouth and smallmouth bass, walleye, muskellunge, pickerel, panfish

Canoe Lake – Page 75, A-5 trout, largemouth bass, walleye, pickerel, muskellunge, panfish

Chapman Lake – Page 39, D-6 trout, largemouth and smallmouth bass, panfish

Clarence E. Walker Dam – Page 63, B-7 largemouth bass, muskellunge, walleye, northern pike, panfish

Conemaugh River Lake – Page 73, A-4 suckers, catfish, perch

Conneaut Lake – Page 28, D-3 muskellunge, northern pike, largemouth and smallmouth bass, panfish

Conowingo Reservoir – Page 93, B-7 smallmouth bass, walleye, hybrid striped bass, crappies

Cowanesque Lake – Page 35, A-7 largemouth bass, muskellunge, walleye, channel catfish, black crappies

Cowans Gap Lake – Page 76, D-1 trout

Crooked Creek Lake – Page 58, C-2 largemouth bass, crappies, bluegills, walleye

Curwensville Lake - Page 60, A-3 largemouth and smallmouth bass, northern pike, panfish, pickerel, walleye

Donegal Lake – Page 73, C-4 rainbow and brook trout, largemouth and smallmouth bass, muskellunge, walleye, catfish, panfish

Duck Harbor Pond – Page 40, B-2 trout, largemouth and smallmouth bass, pickerel, walleye, panfish

East Branch Clarion River Lake – Page 32, D-3 trout, muskellunge, bullheads, panfish

Edinboro Lake – Page 29, A-4 largemouth bass, muskellunge, yellow perch, crappies, carp, bluegills

Foster Joseph Sayers Dam (Blanchard Lake) – Page 48, D-3 largemouth and smallmouth bass, northern pike, walleye, muskellunge, pickerel, panfish

Frances Slocum State Park – Page 52, B-3 largemouth and smallmouth bass, muskellunge, walleye, pickerel, crappies

Francis E. Walter Dam/Reservoir – Page 53, D-5 rainbow and brook trout, largemouth and smallmouth bass, pickerel, muskellunge, yellow perch

Glendale Lake – Page 60, C-3 Amur pike, northern pike, walleye, muskellunge (including tiger muskellunge), largemouth bass, bowfin, panfish

Gouldsboro Lake – Page 53, C-7 largemouth bass, muskellunge, walleye, panfish

Green Lane Reservoir – Page 81, A-6 northern pike, crappies

Harveys Lake – Page 52, B-2 trout, largemouth and smallmouth bass, perch, pickerel, smelts

High Point Lake – Page 87, B-5 muskellunge, walleye, northern pike, smallmouth bass, panfish

Hills Creek Lake – Page 35, B-7 largemouth and smallmouth bass, muskellunge, walleye, pickerel, panfish

Hunters Lake – Page 51, A-5 trout, largemouth bass, pickerel, walleye, panfish

Keystone Lake – Page 72, B-3 brook and rainbow trout, panfish, largemouth and smallmouth bass, crappies, muskellunge, walleye

Keystone Lake (Plum Creek Reservoir) – Page 59, C-4 largemouth and smallmouth bass, walleye, channel catfish, crappies, bluegills, lake and brook trout, muskellunge

Kinzua Dam/Allegheny Reservoir – Page 31, B-7 smallmouth bass, walleye, northern pike, muskellunge, brown and rainbow trout, crappies, yellow perch

Lake Aldred – Page 93, A-6 smallmouth bass, walleye, hybrid striped bass, crappies

Lake Arthur – Page 57, A-5 largemouth bass, muskellunge, northern pike, walleye, channel catfish, crappies

Lake Carey – Page 38, D-3 rainbow and brook trout, largemouth bass, pickerel, walleye, perch, bluegills, crappies

Lake Chillisquaque – Page 51, D-4 largemouth and smallmouth bass, muskellunge, northern pike, pickerel, walleye

Lake Erie – Page 26, D-3 trout, coho and chinook salmon, walleye

Lake Galena – Page 82, B-2 largemouth and smallmouth bass, panfish

Lake Gordon – Page 88, B-2 walleye, largemouth bass, muskellunge, pickerel, panfish

Lake Jean – Page 51, B-7 largemouth and smallmouth bass, muskellunge, walleye, panfish

Lake Koon – Page 88, B-2 largemouth bass, panfish

Lake Marburg – Page 92, B-2 trout, largemouth bass, muskellunge, northern pike, walleye, panfish

Lake Ontelaunee – Page 80, A-3 largemouth and smallmouth bass, northern pike, muskellunge, walleye, panfish

Lake Redman – Page 92, A-4 largemouth and smallmouth bass, muskellunge, northern pike, panfish

Lake Somerset – Page 73, D-6 muskellunge, northern pike, walleye, largemouth bass, panfish

Lake Wallenpaupack – Page 54, A-2 trout, largemouth and smallmouth bass, walleye, muskellunge, pickerel, striped bass, panfish

Lake Wilhelm – Page 43, A-5 largemouth and smallmouth bass, muskellunge, northern pike, walleye, panfish

Lake Williams – Page 92, A-4 largemouth and smallmouth bass, panfish

Lake Winola – Page 38, D-4 palomino, rainbow, brown, and brook trout; largemouth bass, walleye, bluegills, perch

Laurel Hill Lake – Page 73, D-5 largemouth bass, rainbow trout

Laurel Lake – Page 77, D-6 trout, pickerel, perch, sunfish

Leaser Lake – Page 66, C-4 trout, largemouth and smallmouth bass, walleye, muskellunge, pickerel, panfish

Letterkenny Reservoir – Page 76, D-3 trout, largemouth and smallmouth bass

Lily Lake – Page 52, C-2 largemouth and smallmouth bass, pickerel, northern pike, panfish

Little Buffalo State Park Lake – Page 77, A-7 trout, largemouth and smallmouth bass, muskellunge, northern pike, pickerel, crappies

Little Pine Dam – Page 49, B-6 trout, largemouth bass, pickerel, panfish

Locust Lake – Page 66, B-2 trout, largemouth and smallmouth bass, pickerel, panfish

Lower Twin Lake – Page 72, B-3 rainbow and brook trout, crappies

Loyalhanna Lake – Page 72, A-3 largemouth and smallmouth bass, sunshine bass, muskellunge, walleye, crappies, bullheads

Mahoning Creek Lake – Page 59, A-4 largemouth and smallmouth bass, northern pike, walleye, muskellunge, crappies

Marsh Creek Lake – Page 81, D-5 channel catfish, panfish

Mauch Chunk Lake – Page 66, B-4 largemouth and smallmouth bass, pickerel, muskellunge, walleye, channel catfish, panfish

Meadow Grounds Lake – Page 89, A-7 largemouth and smallmouth bass, pickerel

Memorial Lake – Page 79, A-5 largemouth bass, yellow perch, catfish, crappies

Merli-Sarnoski Park Lake – Page 39, D-6 trout, pickerel, bluegills

Middle Creek Lake (Snyder County) – Page 64, B-2 largemouth bass, pickerel, muskellunge, panfish

Middle Creek Waterfowl Management Area Lake – Page 80, B-1 largemouth and smallmouth bass, pickerel, panfish

Minsi Lake – Page 68, A-2 pickerel, walleye, panfish

Muddy Run Lake – Page 93, B-7 largemouth and smallmouth bass, walleye, northern pike, catfish, panfish

Nockamixon State Park Lake – Page 82, A-2 largemouth and smallmouth bass, pickerel, walleye, tiger muskellunge, panfish

Octoraro Lake – Page 94, B-2 muskellunge, northern pike, largemouth and smallmouth bass, walleye, panfish

Opossum Lake – Page 77, C-6 trout, largemouth and smallmouth bass, muskellunge, crappies

Oxbow Lake – Page 38, D-3 rainbow, palomino, brook, and brown trout; largemouth bass, perch, bluegills

Pecks Pond – Page 54, B-3 largemouth and smallmouth bass, pickerel, panfish

Pinchot Lake (Conewago Lake) – Page 78, D-2 muskellunge, northern pike, largemouth and smallmouth bass, pickerel, panfish

Presque Isle Bay, Lake Erie – Page 27, C-5 panfish, largemouth and smallmouth bass, muskellunge, coho salmon

Prompton Reservoir – Page 40, D-1 largemouth and smallmouth bass, pickerel, walleye, muskellunge, panfish

Pymatuning Lake – Page 28, C-1 walleye, crappies, largemouth bass, white bass, muskellunge

Quaker Lake – Page 38, A-3 trout, perch, pickerel, bluegills

Raystown Lake – Page 75, B-7 largemouth bass, rock and striped bass, trout, northern pike, walleye, panfish, muskellunge

Rose Valley Lake – Page 50, A-2 largemouth bass, pickerel, walleye, muskellunge, panfish

Shawnee Lake – Page 74, D-2 muskellunge, northern pike, walleye, largemouth bass, panfish

Shenango River Lake – Page 42, B-2 largemouth and smallmouth bass, northern pike, muskellunge, panfish, walleye

Shohola Lake – Page 54, A-4 largemouth bass, pickerel, panfish

Speedwell Forge Lake – Page 79, C-7 largemouth bass

Springton Reservoir – Page 95, A-7 largemouth bass, crappies, bluegills, muskellunge

Stevens Lake – Page 38, D-3 largemouth bass, pickerel, bullheads, panfish

Struble Lake – Page 80, D-4 panfish

Sweet Arrow Lake – Page 65, D-7 largemouth bass, crappies

Sylvan Lake – Page 52, B-1 largemouth and smallmouth bass, bluegills, walleye

Tamarack Lake – Page 29, D-5 largemouth bass, muskellunge, walleye, crappies, bullheads, bluegills

Tioga Hammond Lake – Page 35, A-7 largemouth bass, muskellunge, walleye, black crappies

Tionesta Lake – Page 44, A-3 muskellunge, smallmouth bass, panfish

Tobyhanna Lake – Page 53, C-7 largemouth and smallmouth bass, pickerel, panfish

Tuscarora Lake – Page 66, B-2 trout, walleye, crappies

Union City Lake – Page 29, A-6 trout

Upper Twin Lake – Page 72, B-3 rainbow and brook trout, largemouth and smallmouth bass, catfish, crappies

Upper Woods Pond – Page 40, B-1 trout, kokanee salmon

Woodcock Creek Lake – Page 29, C-5 trout, muskellunge, largemouth and smallmouth bass, walleye, panfish

Youghiogheny River Lake – Page 86, B-4 northern pike, walleye, trout, largemouth and smallmouth bass, panfish

STREAMS

Allegheny River – Page 44, D-1 smallmouth bass, northern pike, muskellunge, walleye, channel catfish

Clarion River, Clarion County – Page 44, C-3 smallmouth bass, northern pike, muskellunge, walleye, channel catfish

Delaware River, Delaware County – Page 96, B-1 bullheads, channel catfish, white perch, eels, largemouth bass, striped bass, carp

Delaware River, Monroe County – Page 54, D-3 suckers, shad, walleye, muskellunge

Delaware River, Northampton County – Page 68, B-2 channel and white catfish, white suckers, shad, smallmouth bass, muskellunge, walleye

Delaware River, Philadelphia County – Page 82, D-3 channel catfish, bullheads, white perch, eels, carp, striped bass, shad, herring, largemouth bass

Delaware River, Pike County – Page 55, B-6 shad, smallmouth bass, rainbow and brown trout

Delaware River, Wayne County – Page 40, C-3 shad, smallmouth bass, walleye, trout

Red Bank Creek – Page 45, D-4 smallmouth bass, northern pike, muskellunge, walleye

TROUT STREAMS

All streams listed below contain trout. Only other species have been listed.

Allegheny River – Page 33, B-6 largemouth and smallmouth bass, muskellunge, panfish

Big Bushkill Creek – Page 54, D-3

Bowmans Creek – Page 52, A-2 largemouth and smallmouth bass, panfish

Bushkill Creek – Page 68, C-2 panfish

Chest Creek – Page 60, B-2 largemouth and smallmouth bass, panfish

Clarion River, West Branch – Page 32, D-2

Clarks Creek – Page 78, A-3 pickerel

Clover Creek – Page 75, B-5 panfish

continued on next page

FISHING, *continued*

Conewago Creek – Page 91, A-7   largemouth and smallmouth bass, panfish

Conneaut Creek – Page 28, B-2   largemouth and smallmouth bass, panfish

Deep Creek – Page 65, C-6

Falling Springs Branch (Creek) – Page 90, A-4   panfish

Fishing Creek – Page 51, D-6   largemouth and smallmouth bass, pickerel, panfish

French Creek – Page 81, C-5   panfish

French Creek, South Branch – Page 30, A-1   largemouth and smallmouth bass, panfish

Hammer Creek – Page 79, C-7

Harvey(s) Creek – Page 52, C-2

Juniata River, Raystown Branch – Page 74, D-3   largemouth and smallmouth bass, muskellunge, pickerel, walleye, panfish

Kettle Creek – Page 34, D-3   largemouth and smallmouth bass, panfish

Kinzua Creek, South Branch – Page 32, C-1

Lackawaxen River – Page 54, A-3   largemouth and smallmouth bass, pickerel, panfish

Laurel Hill Creek – Page 73, D-5

Laurel Run – Page 77, B-4   panfish

Leatherwood Creek – Page 44, D-4

Lehigh River – Page 53, C-6   panfish

Little Lehigh Creek (River) – Page 67, D-6   panfish

Little Loyalsock Creek – Page 37, D-6   largemouth and smallmouth bass

Little Pine Creek – Page 49, A-6

Little Shenango River – Page 42, A-3   pickerel, panfish

Loyalsock Creek – Page 50, B-2   largemouth and smallmouth bass, panfish

Monocacy Creek – Page 68, C-1   panfish

Muddy Creek – Page 93, B-7

Octoraro Creek, West Branch – Page 94, A-2   largemouth and smallmouth bass, panfish

Oil Creek – Page 30, D-1   muskellunge, walleye, panfish

Oil Creek – Page 29, C-7   largemouth and smallmouth bass, northern pike, panfish

Penns Creek – Page 63, B-7   largemouth and smallmouth bass, muskellunge, pike, panfish

Pine Creek – Page 35, D-5   largemouth and smallmouth bass, pickerel

Pine Creek – Page 49, B-6

Pine Creek, West Branch – Page 35, C-5

Potato Creek – Page 33, B-4   largemouth and smallmouth bass, muskellunge, walleye, panfish

Red Bank Creek – Page 45, C-6   largemouth and smallmouth bass, northern pike, panfish

Red Bank Creek, North Fork – Page 45, C-6   panfish

Ridley Creek – Page 95, A-7   largemouth and smallmouth bass, panfish

Schrader Creek – Page 37, C-5

Shenango River – Page 42, B-2   largemouth and smallmouth bass, northern pike, striped bass, walleye, panfish

Shohola Creek – Page 54, B-3   largemouth and smallmouth bass, pickerel, panfish

Sinnemahoning Creek, East Fork – Page 34, D-1

Skippack Creek – Page 81, C-7   largemouth and smallmouth bass, panfish

Snake Creek – Page 38, A-4   panfish

Spring Creek – Page 45, A-7   largemouth and smallmouth bass, panfish

Tionesta Creek – Page 31, D-5   largemouth and smallmouth bass, muskellunge, panfish

Tionesta Creek, East Branch – Page 31, C-7

Unami Creek – Page 81, B-7   largemouth and smallmouth bass, muskellunge, pickerel

Wissahickon Creek – Page 82, C-2   largemouth and smallmouth bass, panfish

Woodcock Creek – Page 29, C-5   largemouth and smallmouth bass, panfish

Yellow Breeches Creek – Page 77, C-7   largemouth and smallmouth bass, panfish

Yellow Creek – Page 75, C-5   panfish

Hunting

To locate hunting areas in this Atlas, look on the appropriate map for the hunting symbol and State Game Lands (SGL) number (e.g., SGL 12). More hunting information and State Game Lands maps are available from Pennsylvania Game Commission, 2001 Elmerton Avenue, Harrisburg 17110-9797; or call (717) 787-4250.

SGL NUMBER, LOCATION		ATLAS LOCATION	ACREAGE	SPECIES
12	Canton	Page 36, D-3	24,479	bear, deer, turkey
13	Sonestown	Page 51, B-5	49,528	deer, grouse, turkey
14	Howard Siding	Page 47, A-5	13,875	bear, deer, turkey
24	Newmansville	Page 44, A-4	8,389	bear, deer, turkey
25	Johnsonburg	Page 46, A-2	24,010	bear, deer, turkey
26	Beaverdale	Page 74, B-2	11,976	deer, grouse, squirrel, turkey
28	Hallton	Page 45, A-7	9,848	bear, deer, turkey
29	Warren	Page 31, C-4	9,363	bear, deer, turkey
30	Norwich	Page 33, C-5	11,572	bear, deer, turkey
31	East Branch	Page 45, D-6	5,176	deer, squirrel, turkey
33	Philipsburg	Page 61, B-6	16,580	bear, deer, turkey
34	Medix Run	Page 47, C-5	8,800	bear, deer, turkey
35	Hallstead	Page 39, A-5	7,771	deer, grouse, raccoon
36	Monroeton	Page 37, C-5	18,929	bear, deer, turkey
37	Hammond	Page 35, B-7	13,233	deer, grouse, squirrel, turkey
38	Tannersville	Page 53, D-7	5,488	bear, deer, grouse
39	Pearl	Page 43, B-6	9,809	deer, grouse, squirrel
40	White Haven	Page 53, D-5	6,119	deer, grouse, turkey
41	Bakers Summit	Page 75, B-4	2,627	deer, grouse, rabbit, squirrel
42	New Florence	Page 73, B-6	14,618	deer, grouse, squirrel, turkey
43	Warwick	Page 81, C-4	2,300	deer, grouse, squirrel
44	Portland Mills	Page 46, B-1	24,529	bear, deer, turkey
45	Van	Page 44, B-1	5,170	deer, grouse, squirrel
46	Hopeland	Page 79, B-7	6,228	deer, pheasant, squirrel
47	Oil City	Page 44, A-2	2,216	deer, squirrel
48	Gravel Pit	Page 88, A-2	10,807	deer, grouse, rabbit, turkey
49	Amaranth	Page 89, B-5	6,310	deer, grouse, squirrel, turkey
50	Somerset	Page 87, A-6	3,158	deer, grouse
51	Deer Lake	Page 86, B-2	16,139	deer, grouse, squirrel
52	Morgantown	Page 80, C-3	2,443	deer, grouse, pheasant, squirrel
53	McConnellsburg	Page 89, A-7	5928	deer, grouse, turkey
54	Brockway	Page 46, B-1	23,132	bear, deer, turkey
55	Orangeville	Page 51, D-7	2,474	deer, grouse
56	Uhlerstown	Page 68, D-3	1,737	deer, grouse, rabbit
57	Noxen	Page 52, A-2	44,493	bear, deer, turkey
58	Catawissa	Page 65, A-6	12,646	deer, grouse, squirrel
59	Roulette	Page 33, B-6	7,004	deer, grouse, turkey
60	Sandy Ridge	Page 61, B-6	7,240	bear, deer, turkey
61	Port Allegany	Page 33, B-5	9,228	bear, deer, turkey
62	Mt. Jewett	Page 32, B-2	1,334	deer, rabbit
63	Shippenville	Page 44, C-3	3,413	deer, squirrel, turkey
64	West Pike	Page 34, B-3	8,021	bear, deer, turkey
65	Crystal Spring	Page 89, A-6	6,073	deer, grouse, turkey
66	McCarroll Corner	Page 51, A-7	8,144	deer, grouse, turkey
67	Broad Top City	Page 75, C-6	5,724	deer, grouse, turkey
68	Cedar Run	Page 35, D-5	3,397	bear, deer, turkey
69	Guys Mills	Page 29, C-6	4,496	ducks, grouse, pheasant
70	Stevens Point	Page 39, A-6	6,363	deer, grouse, rabbit
71	Mapleton Depot	Page 76, B-1	4,122	deer, squirrel, turkey
72	Clarion	Page 44, C-3	2,025	deer, grouse, squirrel
73	Martinsburg	Page 75, B-5	20,817	deer, grouse, squirrel, turkey
74	Strattanville	Page 45, C-4	6,500	bear, deer, turkey
75	English Center	Page 49, A-6	27,400	bear, deer, turkey
76	Upper Strasburg	Page 76, D-3	4,324	deer, squirrel, turkey
77	Clear Run	Page 46, C-1	3,038	bear, deer, rabbit, squirrel
78	Bigler	Page 61, A-5	721	bear, deer, turkey
79	Belsano	Page 59, D-7	8,609	deer, grouse, squirrel
80	Rock	Page 65, D-7	10,600	deer, grouse, squirrel, turkey
81	Meadow Gap	Page 76, C-1	3,533	deer, grouse, turkey
82	Wittenberg	Page 87, B-7	6,708	deer, grouse, squirrel
83	York Furnace	Page 93, B-6	768	deer, pheasant, rabbit
84	Gowen City	Page 65, C-5	8,892	deer, grouse, squirrel
85	Jervis Corners	Page 29, B-6	115	ducks, pheasant, rabbit
86	Cobham	Page 30, C-4	14,227	deer, squirrel, turkey
87	Irishtown	Page 60, A-2	1,124	deer, grouse, turkey
88	Ickesburg	Page 77, A-5	6,930	deer, grouse, turkey
89	Farrandville	Page 49, C-4	10,571	bear, deer, turkey
90	Goshen	Page 47, D-4	3,958	bear, deer, turkey
91	Pleasant View Summit	Page 53, C-5	15,900	bear, deer, grouse
92	Howard	Page 48, D-3	5,171	deer, squirrel, turkey
93	Sabula	Page 46, C-2	4,876	bear, deer, turkey
94	Lecontes Mills	Page 47, C-5	2,108	bear, deer, turkey
95	Annandale	Page 43, D-6	9,045	deer, pheasant, rabbit
96	Dempseytown	Page 29, D-7	4,973	deer, grouse, rabbit, squirrel
97	Rainsburg	Page 88, B-3	7,312	deer, grouse, squirrel, turkey
98	Blue Ball	Page 61, A-5	1,172	deer, rabbit, turkey
99	Three Springs	Page 76, B-1	3,296	deer, squirrel, turkey
100	Cherry Run	Page 48, D-1	19,372	bear, deer, turkey
101	Tracy	Page 28, B-2	4,706	grouse, rabbit, woodcock
102	Union City	Page 29, A-7	384	deer, grouse, squirrel
103	Gum Stump	Page 62, A-2	8,994	deer, grouse, turkey
104	Hyndman	Page 88, B-2	8,182	deer, grouse, squirrel, turkey
105	Somerville	Page 58, A-2	2,613	deer, fox, grouse, muskrat, raccoon
106	Eckville/Kepner	Page 66, C-3	9,374	deer, grouse, rabbit, squirrel, turkey
107	Wagner	Page 63, C-5	6,561	deer, grouse, turkey
108	Frugality	Page 60, C-4	20,252	deer, grouse, rabbit
109	Waterford	Page 29, A-6	1,639	ducks, pheasant, rabbit
110	Summit Station	Page 66, D-1	10,093	deer, grouse, rabbit, turkey
111	Ursina	Page 86, A-4	10,520	deer, grouse,
112	Center Union	Page 62, D-1	5,770	deer, grouse, turkey
113	Strodes Mills	Page 62, D-3	534	deer, grouse, squirrel
114	Cogan House	Page 49, A-7	2,881	bear, deer, turkey
115	Danville	Page 65, A-4	1,243	deer, grouse, rabbit
116	Shohola	Page 54, A-4	3,024	bear, deer, grouse
117	Burgettstown	Page 70, A-2	2,932	pheasant, rabbit
118	Williamsburg	Page 75, A-6	6,029	deer, squirrel, turkey
119	Ochre Mill	Page 53, C-4	7,949	bear, deer, grouse
120	Irvona	Page 60, B-3	3,426	deer, grouse, rabbit
121	New Grenada	Page 75, C-7	2,207	deer, grouse, squirrel
122	Tyronville	Page 29, C-7	2,649	ducks, pheasant, rabbit
123	Checkerville	Page 36, A-3	1,607	grouse, rabbit, waterfowl
124	Cove Gap	Page 90, B-1	6,835	deer, squirrel, turkey
126	Duboistown	Page 50, C-1	652	deer, rabbit, squirrel
127	Tobyhanna	Page 53, C-7	25,527	bear, deer, grouse
128	Amaranth	Page 89, B-6	1,695	deer, grouse, turkey
129	Lake Harmony	Page 53, D-6	3,518	bear, deer, grouse
130	Sandy Lake	Page 43, B-5	3,094	deer, pheasant, rabbit
131	Birmingham	Page 61, C-6	309	deer, squirrel
132	Hegins	Page 65, C-6	1,247	deer, grouse, squirrel, turkey
133	Calvert	Page 50, A-2	2,521	deer, squirrel, turkey
134	Proctor	Page 50, A-3	6,722	bear, deer, turkey
135	Gouldsboro	Page 53, C-6	3,430	bear, deer, grouse
136	Kirkwood	Page 94, B-2	91	deer, rabbit, squirrel
137	South Bethlehem	Page 58, A-4	929	rabbit, squirrel
138	Elliotsville	Page 86, B-1	2,919	deer, grouse, turkey
139	Perkasie	Page 82, A-1	261	deer, rabbit
140	Friendsville	Page 38, A-2	1,244	deer, grouse, rabbit
141	Jim Thorpe	Page 67, A-4	17,048	deer, grouse, turkey
142	New Albany	Page 37, D-7	369	deer, grouse, rabbit
143	Garland	Page 30, B-3	8,177	deer, grouse, squirrel

SGL NUMBER, LOCATION	ATLAS LOCATION	ACREAGE	SPECIES
144 Concord Corners	Page 30, B-1	422	grouse, rabbit
145 Colebrook	Page 79, C-5	2,793	grouse, pheasant, rabbit, squirrel
146 New Richmond	Page 29, C-6	526	grouse, pheasant, rabbit
147 Martinsburg	Page 75, B-5	6,074	deer, grouse, rabbit, turkey
148 Possum Hollow	Page 56, B-3	369	pheasant, rabbit, squirrel
149 White Haven	Page 53, D-4	1,334	deer, grouse, squirrel
150 Pulaski	Page 42, D-2	505	pheasant, rabbit, squirrel
151 Brent	Page 43, D-4	1,108	fox squirrel, grouse, rabbit
152 Crossingville	Page 28, B-4	499	deer, grouse, rabbit
153 Bolivar/Robinson	Page 73, A-5	2,927	deer, grouse, squirrel
154 Wheelock	Page 30, A-1	1,415	pheasant, rabbit, woodcock
155 Phillipsville	Page 27, D-7	391	pheasant, rabbit, woodcock
156 Poplar Grove	Page 79, C-7	4,537	deer, pheasant, squirrel
157 Harrow	Page 82, A-2	2,010	deer, rabbit, squirrel
158 Blandburg	Page 61, C-4	15,632	deer, grouse, squirrel
159 Rileyville	Page 40, C-1	9,368	deer, grouse, turkey
160 Pine Grove	Page 65, D-7	245	pheasant, rabbit, squirrel
161 West Greene	Page 27, D-6	235	pheasant, rabbit, squirrel
162 Wattsburg	Page 29, A-7	354	pheasant, rabbit, woodcock
163 Colt Station	Page 27, C-7	332	pheasant, rabbit, woodcock
164 Carbon Center	Page 57, A-7	456	grouse, rabbit, squirrel
165 Trevorton	Page 65, B-4	1,190	deer, grouse, rabbit
166 Canoe Creek	Page 61, D-6	10,440	deer, grouse, squirrel, turkey
167 Union City	Page 29, A-7	627	pheasant, rabbit, woodcock
168 Katellen	Page 68, B-1	5,644	deer, grouse, rabbit
169 Green Spring	Page 77, C-5	2,440	pheasant, quail, rabbit
170 Keystone	Page 78, B-1	9,054	deer, grouse, squirrel
171 Thompsontown	Page 63, D-7	1,087	deer, grouse, squirrel
172 Wyalusing	Page 37, C-7	722	deer, grouse, squirrel
173 Ohioville	Page 56, C-2	1,063	pheasant, rabbit, squirrel
174 McGees Mills	Page 60, A-1	3,161	deer, grouse
175 New Milford	Page 39, A-5	736	deer, grouse, squirrel
176 Marysville	Page 62, B-1	6,956	deer, grouse, rabbit, turkey
178 New Castle	Page 42, D-3	164	pheasant, rabbit, squirrel
179 New Freeport	Page 84, B-3	5,325	grouse, fox, squirrel, woodchuck
180 Greeley	Page 54, B-3	11,372	deer, grouse, turkey
181 Kyleville	Page 93, B-7	563	deer, grouse, pheasant, rabbit
182 Kutztown	Page 67, D-4	273	deer, quail, rabbit
183 Wilsonville	Page 54, A-2	2,778	deer, grouse, turkey
184 Dysart	Page 60, D-3	4,298	deer, grouse, squirrel
185 Spruce	Page 60, C-1	630	deer, grouse, squirrel
186 Snydersville	Page 68, A-1	967	grouse, rabbit, squirrel
187 Reilly	Page 52, D-3	8,186	deer, rabbit, woodcock
188 Beavertown	Page 63, B-7	1,636	deer, pheasant, rabbit
189 Harshaville	Page 56, D-3	415	grouse, rabbit, squirrel
190 Waterford	Page 29, A-6	327	pheasant, rabbit, woodcock
191 Little Hope	Page 27, D-7	1,224	pheasant, rabbit, woodcock
192 Phelps Corners	Page 29, A-5	333	pheasant, rabbit, woodcock
193 Winfield	Page 64, A-2	323	deer, rabbit, squirrel
194 Meiserville	Page 64, C-2	721	deer, pheasant, rabbit
195 Big Run	Page 60, A-1	1,294	deer, squirrel, turkey
196 Trumbauersville	Page 82, A-1	358	deer, pheasant, rabbit
197 Columbus	Page 30, A-2	1,556	deer, ducks, rabbit
198 Newry	Page 74, A-4	6,950	deer, grouse, squirrel
199 Riceville	Page 29, B-7	1,132	grouse, pheasant, rabbit
200 New Richmond	Page 29, C-6	154	grouse, rabbit, squirrel
201 Mifflinburg	Page 64, A-1	269	deer, pheasant, rabbit
202 New Richmond	Page 29, B-7	507	grouse, rabbit, squirrel
203 Bradford Woods	Page 57, C-5	1,246	grouse, rabbit, squirrel
204 Coneville	Page 33, A-7	4,029	deer, grouse, squirrel, turkey
205 Schnecksville	Page 67, C-5	1,303	pheasant, quail, rabbit
206 Sweet Valley	Page 52, B-1	1,525	deer, grouse, turkey
207 Sugar Notch	Page 52, C-3	1,400	deer, grouse, turkey
208 Gaines	Page 35, C-4	8,862	bear, deer, turkey
209 Pond Eddy	Page 55, A-5	4,391	bear, deer, grouse
210 Lykens	Page 65, D-4	11,124	deer, grouse, turkey
211 Manada Gap/Green Point	Page 65, D-5	44,343	deer, grouse, turkey
212 Selinsgrove	Page 64, B-3	513	deer, pheasant, rabbit
213 Geneva	Page 28, D-4	5,555	ducks, pheasant, rabbit
214 Hartstown	Page 28, D-3	5,399	ducks, geese, rabbit
215 Reeds Gap	Page 76, A-3	1,263	deer, grouse, rabbit
216 Harlansburg	Page 42, D-4	487	ducks, pheasant, rabbit
217 Slatedale	Page 67, B-6	6,173	deer, grouse, turkey
218 Bogus Corners	Page 27, D-6	1,344	ducks, pheasant, rabbit
219 Warren Center	Page 38, A-1	5,619	deer, grouse, rabbit
220 Reinholds	Page 80, B-2	96	pheasant, rabbit
221 Cresco	Page 54, C-1	4,618	deer, grouse, turkey
222 New Ringgold	Page 66, C-2	865	deer, rabbit, squirrel
223 Fordyce	Page 85, B-5	7,202	rabbit, squirrel
224 Hunlock Creek	Page 52, C-2	481	grouse, rabbit
225 Cocalico	Page 80, B-1	297	deer, squirrel, turkey
226 Millville	Page 51, D-5	4,335	deer, pheasant, rabbit
227 Barnesville	Page 66, B-2	1,505	deer, pheasant, quail, rabbit, turkey
228 Central City	Page 74, D-2	3,461	deer, grouse
229 Tremont	Page 65, D-6	2,891	grouse, rabbit, turkey
230 Carlisle Springs	Page 77, B-7	1,083	pheasant, quail, rabbit
231 Boynton	Page 87, B-6	429	deer, grouse
232 Dunsfort	Page 70, C-2	1,188	fox, gray squirrel, rabbit, woodchuck
233 Herndon	Page 64, C-3	382	Waterfowl Refuge
234 Linfield	Page 81, C-6	158	pheasant, rabbit
235 Ft. Loudon	Page 90, A-1	6,277	deer, squirrel, turkey
236 Herrick Center	Page 39, B-6	2,010	rabbit, waterfowl
237 Rummerfield	Page 37, C-7	161	waterfowl, woodcock
238 Adah/Gates	Page 85, A-6	663	pheasant, rabbit
239 Greens Landing	Page 37, A-5	671	rabbit, waterfowl
242 Rossville	Page 78, D-2	1,516	deer, grouse, pheasant, rabbit
243 Franklintown	Page 78, D-1	1,059	grouse, squirrel, woodcock
244 O'Donnell	Page 45, D-7	4,868	deer, grouse, turkey
245 Claysville	Page 70, D-2	3,653	rabbit, squirrel
246 Middletown	Page 79, C-4	424	deer, grouse
247 Ford City/Kittanning	Page 58, B-2	452	pheasant, rabbit, turkey
248 Upper Two Lick	Page 59, D-6	829	deer, grouse, rabbit
249 Heidlersburg	Page 92, A-1	1,942	pheasant, rabbit, squirrel
250 Wyalusing	Page 37, C-7	444	rabbit, waterfowl
251 Shade Gap	Page 76, C-2	4,221	deer, squirrel, turkey
252 Allenwood	Page 50, C-2	3,018	deer, grouse, rabbit, waterfowl
253 Plummer	Page 44, A-1	665	deer, grouse, rabbit
254 Halifax/New Buffalo	Page 78, A-2	907	deer, rabbit, waterfowl
255 Beech Creek	Page 49, D-4	2,276	bear, deer, turkey
256 New Bloomfield	Page 77, A-7	1,223	deer, grouse, rabbit, squirrel, turkey
257 Tamaqua	Page 66, B-3	3,417	deer, pheasant, quail, rabbit
258 Paxton/Liverpool	Page 64, D-2	797	deer, grouse, quail, rabbit, waterfowl
259 Cowansville	Page 58, A-1	351	deer, rabbit, squirrel, turkey
260 Shickshinny	Page 52, C-1	3,061	deer, grouse, rabbit, squirrel
261 Hopewell	Page 75, D-6	3,248	deer, grouse, rabbit, squirrel
262 Hillsdale	Page 59, B-7	443	deer, grouse, rabbit, raccoon, woodchuck
263 Corry	Page 30, A-2	668	deer, rabbit
264 S of Gratz	Page 64, D-3	8,826	deer, grouse, rabbit, turkey
265 Flat Rock	Page 86, B-3	380	deer, grouse, rabbit
267 Wopsononock	Page 60, D-4	1,041	deer, grouse, squirrel, turkey
268 Draper	Page 35, D-6	2,394	deer, rabbit, turkey
269 Mosiertown	Page 28, B-4	590	ducks, pheasant, rabbit
270 Sheakleyville	Page 43, A-4	2,026	deer, dove, pheasant, rabbit, woodcock
271 Listonburg	Page 87, B-4	1,856	deer, grouse, rabbit
272 Newton Station	Page 30, C-2	189	deer, rabbit, squirrel
273 Waterman	Page 59, D-6	963	deer, rabbit, squirrel
274 Vinemont	Page 80, B-2	334	deer, pheasant, rabbit
275 Highspire	Page 78, C-3	1	waterfowl
276 Hesbon	Page 73, A-6	3,942	deer, rabbit, squirrel
277 Cambridge Springs	Page 29, B-5	972	ducks, pheasant, rabbit
278 Tyrone	Page 61, C-6	1,947	deer, grouse, rabbit, squirrel, woodcock
279 Cresson	Page 74, A-3	461	deer, rabbit, squirrel
280 Mt. Pleasant	Page 80, A-2	2,631	ducks, pheasant, rabbit
281 Newport	Page 78, A-1	1,554	deer, rabbit
282 Akeley	Page 31, A-5	434	deer, rabbit, squirrel
283 Cooksburg	Page 45, B-5	6,564	deer, rabbit, squirrel
284 Leesburg	Page 42, C-4	1,373	deer, pheasant, rabbit
285 Cannelton	Page 56, B-2	2,149	ducks, rabbit, woodcock
286 Schuylkill Haven	Page 66, C-1	478	deer, ducks, rabbit
287 Templeton	Page 58, A-3	1,167	pheasant, rabbit, squirrel
288 Martic Forge	Page 93, A-7	89	pheasant, rabbit, woodcock
289 Burlington	Page 37, B-4	1,547	deer, grouse, squirrel, turkey
290 Haldeman Island	Page 78, A-1	963	deer, pheasant, rabbit
291 2 mi. S of Cory	Page 30, A-2	1,193	deer, grouse, squirrel, turkey
292 Oliver Mills	Page 52, C-4	624	deer, grouse, rabbit, squirrel, turkey
293 Swissmont	Page 46, A-4	2,284	bear, deer, turkey
294 5 mi. N of Mercer	Page 42, B-4	417	deer, furbearers, grouse, rabbit
295 Tylersville	Page 63, A-5	12,860	bear, deer, turkey
296 Jacobs Creek	Page 72, D-1	2,022	deer, grouse, squirrel, turkey
297 5 mi. N of Marianna	Page 71, D-4	631	deer, fox, grouse, muskrat, raccoon
298 Warrensville	Page 50, B-2	1,140	bear, deer, grouse, squirrel, turkey
299 Sherman	Page 39, A-7	1,054	bear, deer, raccoon, squirrel
300 Carbondale	Page 33, A-4	5,506	bear, grouse, rabbit, squirrel, turkey
301 Coryville	Page 33, A-4	842	bear, deer, grouse, rabbit, turkey
302 Nebo	Page 84, A-2	915	deer, fox, grouse, raccoon, woodchuck
303 Jefferson	Page 70, B-2	221	deer, fox, grouse, raccoon
304 Nichola	Page 58, A-1	457	deer, grouse, squirrel
305 Boiling Springs	Page 78, D-1	730	deer, grouse, squirrel
306 Corry	Page 30, A-2	892	deer, ducks, grouse, squirrel
307 Jermyn	Page 39, D-6	1,053	deer, grouse, squirrel
308 Lofty	Page 66, B-2	1,068	deer, squirrel
309 Tidioute	Page 30, C-3	975	deer, turkey
310 Maplewood	Page 53, A-7	1,120	deer, ducks, grouse
311 Benezette	Page 47, B-5	1,730	deer, elk
312 Gouldsboro	Page 53, B-7	3,912	deer, ducks, grouse
313 Wellsboro	Page 35, B-6	140	ducks
314 Conneaut	Page 28, A-1	3,131	deer, ducks, grouse
315 Dale	Page 81, A-6	305	deer, grouse, squirrel
316 Masthope	Page 40, D-3	2,715	deer, squirrel, turkey
317 Hartleton	Page 63, A-7	688	deer, grouse, rabbit, squirrel, turkey, waterfowl
318 Pocono Pines	Page 53, D-6	854	bear, deer, grouse, turkey

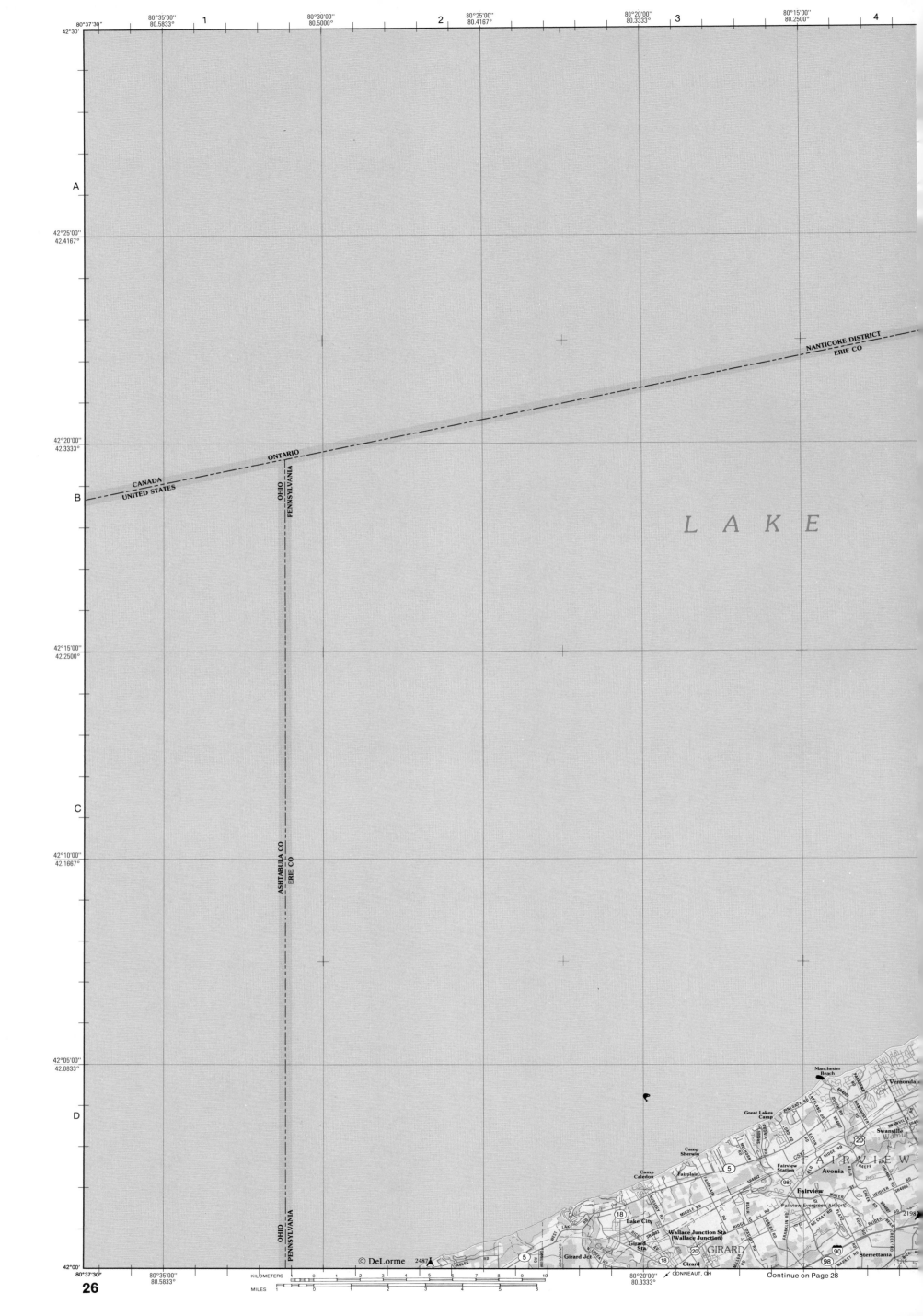

1   80°35'00"
80.5833°

80°30'00"
80.5000°

2   80°25'00"
80.4167°

80°20'00"
80.3333°

3   80°15'00"
80.2500°

4

A

42°25'00"
42.4167°

NANTICOKE DISTRICT
ERIE CO

42°20'00"
42.3333°

ONTARIO

CANADA
UNITED STATES

B

OHIO
PENNSYLVANIA

L A K E

42°15'00"
42.2500°

C

ASHTABULA CO
ERIE CO

42°10'00"
42.1667°

Manchester
Beach

Vernondale

42°05'00"
42.0833°

D

Great Lakes
Camp

Swanville

Camp
Sherwin

F A I R V I E W

Fairview
Station

Avonia

Camp
Caledon

Fairplain

Fairview

Fairview Evergreen Airport

OHIO
PENNSYLVANIA

Lake City

Lake

MIDDLE RD

2198

© DeLorme

2487

Wallace Junction Sta
(Wallace Junction)

Girard
Sta.

GIRARD

Girard Jct

Girard

Sterrettania

80°37'30"
42°00'

26

80°35'00"
80.5833°

KILOMETERS

MILES

80°20'00"
80.3333°

CONNEAUT, OH

Continue on Page 28

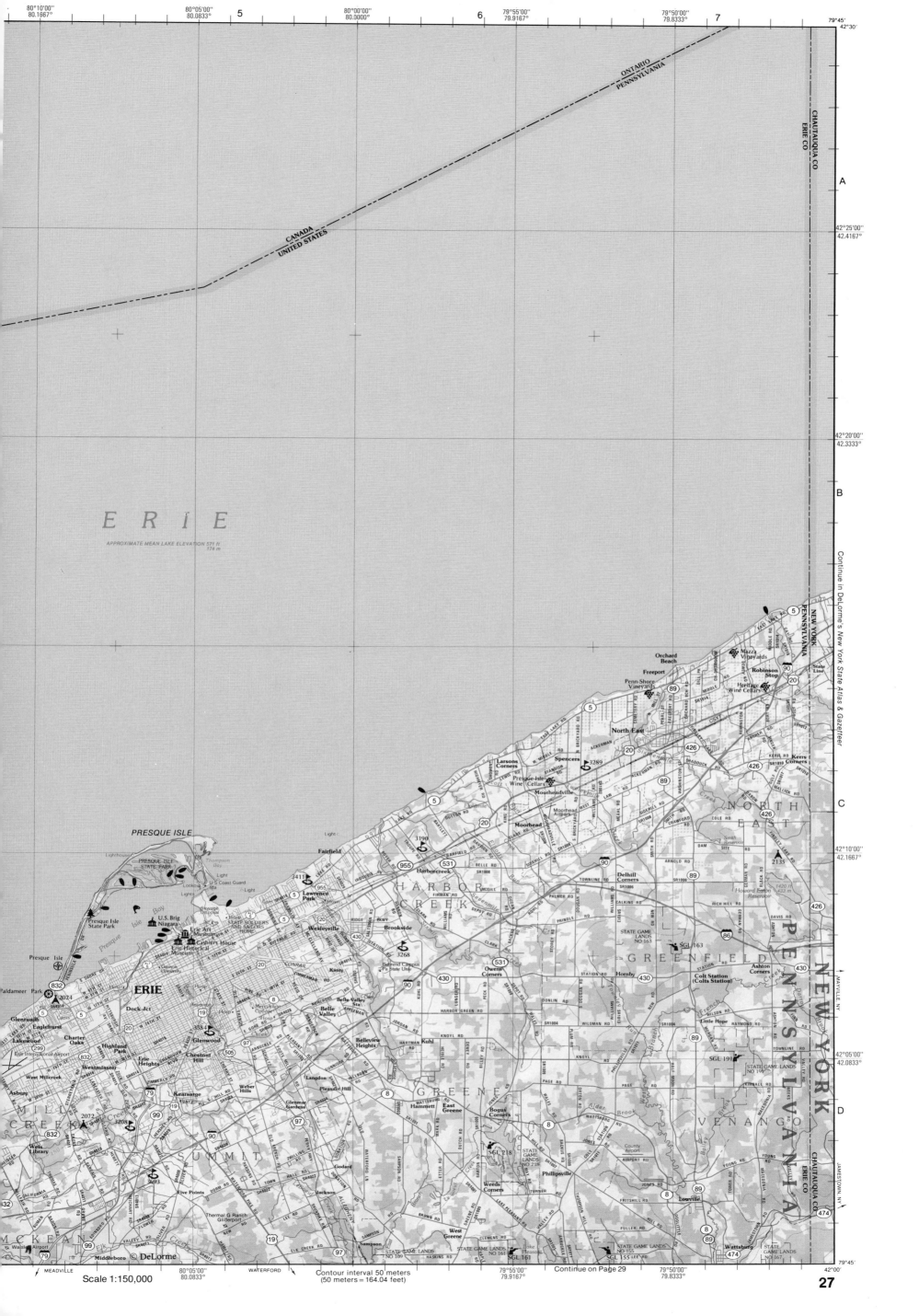

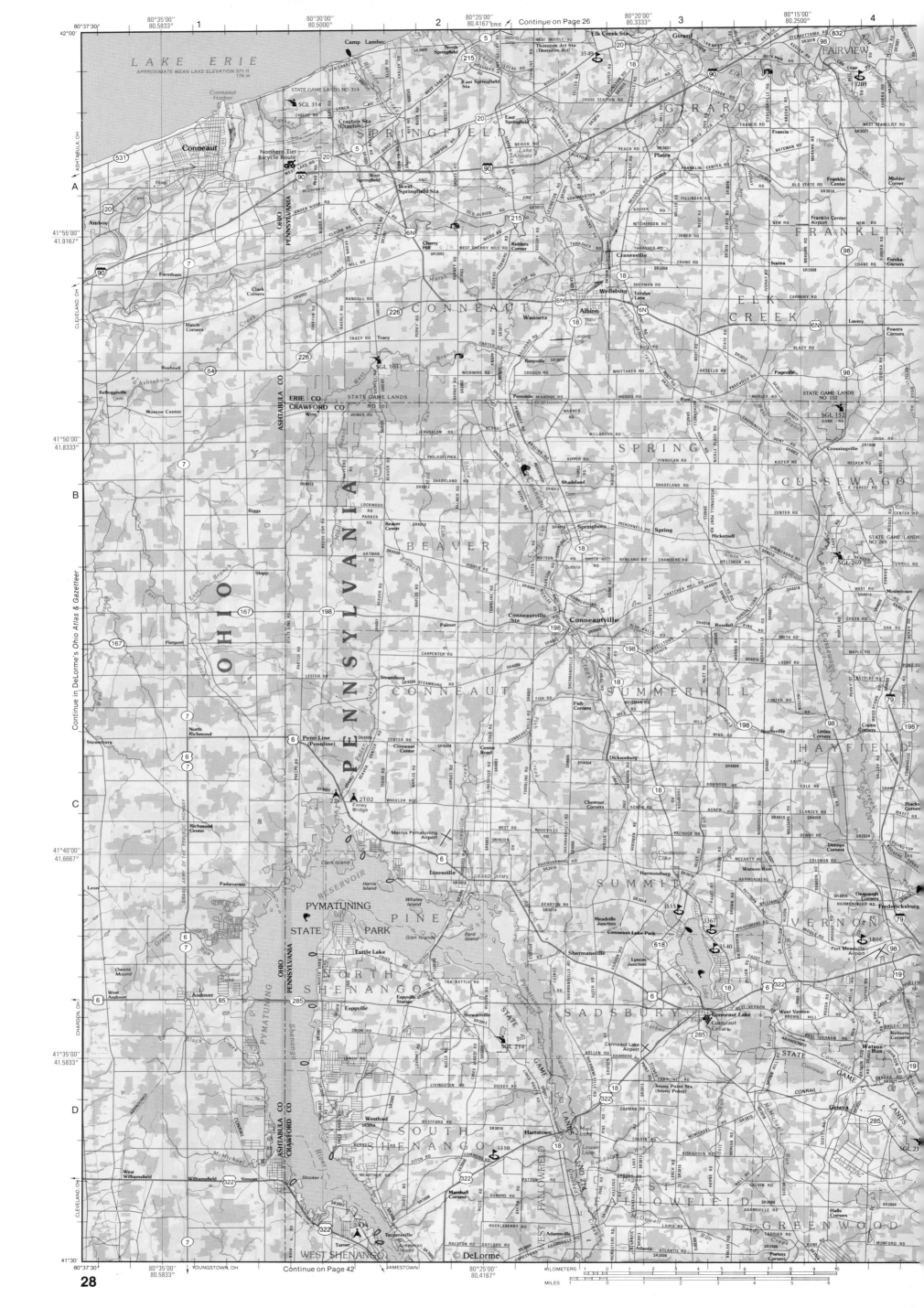

Continue in DeLorme's Ohio Atlas & Gazetteer

Continue on Page 42

© DeLorme

Continue on Page 30

Scale 1:150,000

Contour interval 50 meters
(50 meters = 164.04 feet)

© DeLorme

Continue in DeLorme's *New York State Atlas & Gazetteer*

Continue on Page 29

Continue on Page 44

© DeLorme

Continue on Page 32

Continue on Page 45

Scale 1:150,000

Contour interval 50 meters
(50 meters = 164.04 feet)

© DeLorme

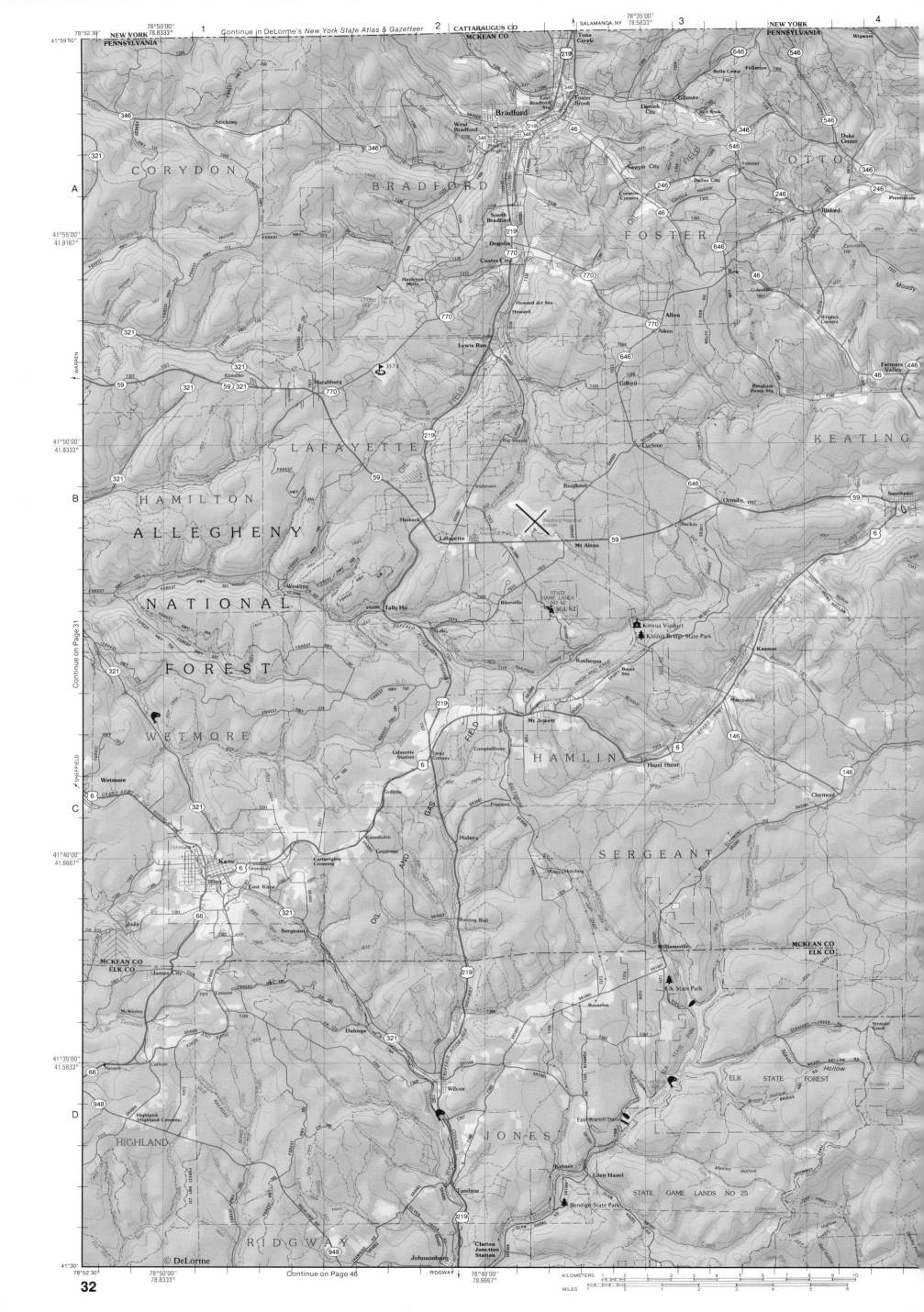

NEW YORK
PENNSYLVANIA

CATTARAUGUS CO
MCKEAN CO

NEW YORK
PENNSYLVANIA

41°59'50"

CORYDON

BRADFORD

OTTO

FOSTER

A

41°55'00"
41.9167°

Bradford

West Bradford
South Bradford

Degolia

Custer City

Hazelton Mills

Howard Jct Sta
Howard

Lewis Run

Allen
Aiken

Gifford

Bingham
Pump Sta

Farmers
Valley

B

41°50'00"
41.8333°

LAFAYETTE

Marshburg

Klondike

HAMILTON

ALLEGHENY

Big Shanty

Irishtown

Bingham

Cyclone

Ormsby

KEATING

Smethport

Lafayette

Thumbuck

Mt Alton

Bradford Regional
Airport

McKean
Memorial Park

Backus

Westline

NATIONAL

Tally Ho

Riterville

STATE GAME
LANDS NO 62
SGL 62

Kinzua Viaduct

Kinzua Bridge State Park

Kasson

Marvindale

Kushequa

Boyer Sta

Continue on Page 31

FOREST

WETMORE

Lafayette
Station

Lantz
Corners

Campbelltown

Mt Jewett

HAMLIN

Hazel Hurst

Clermont

C

41°40'00"
41.6667°

Wetmore

Griffiths

Kaneshom

Coontown

Halsey

Freeman

SERGEANT

Kane

Greendale

Cartwrights
Crossing

East Kane

JoJo

Sergeant

Burning Well

Williamsville

MCKEAN CO
ELK CO

MCKEAN CO
ELK CO

James City

Lamoni

McKinley

Dahoga

Rasselas

Elk State Park

D

41°35'00"
41.5833°

Nansen

Carlson

Wilcox

ELK STATE FOREST

Straight
Creek

HIGHLAND

Highland
(Highland Corners)

JONES

Ketner
Glen Hazel

East Branch Dam

STATE GAME LANDS NO 25

Wambine

Bendigo State Park

RIDGWAY

Clarion
Junction
Station

Johnsonburg

© DeLorme

41°30'

78°52'30"
78°50'00"
78.8333°

Continue on Page 46

RIDGWAY

78°40'00"
78.6667°

KILOMETERS

MILES

Scale 1:150,000

Contour interval 50 meters
(50 meters = 164.04 feet)

Continue on Page 47

Continue on Page 34

© DeLorme

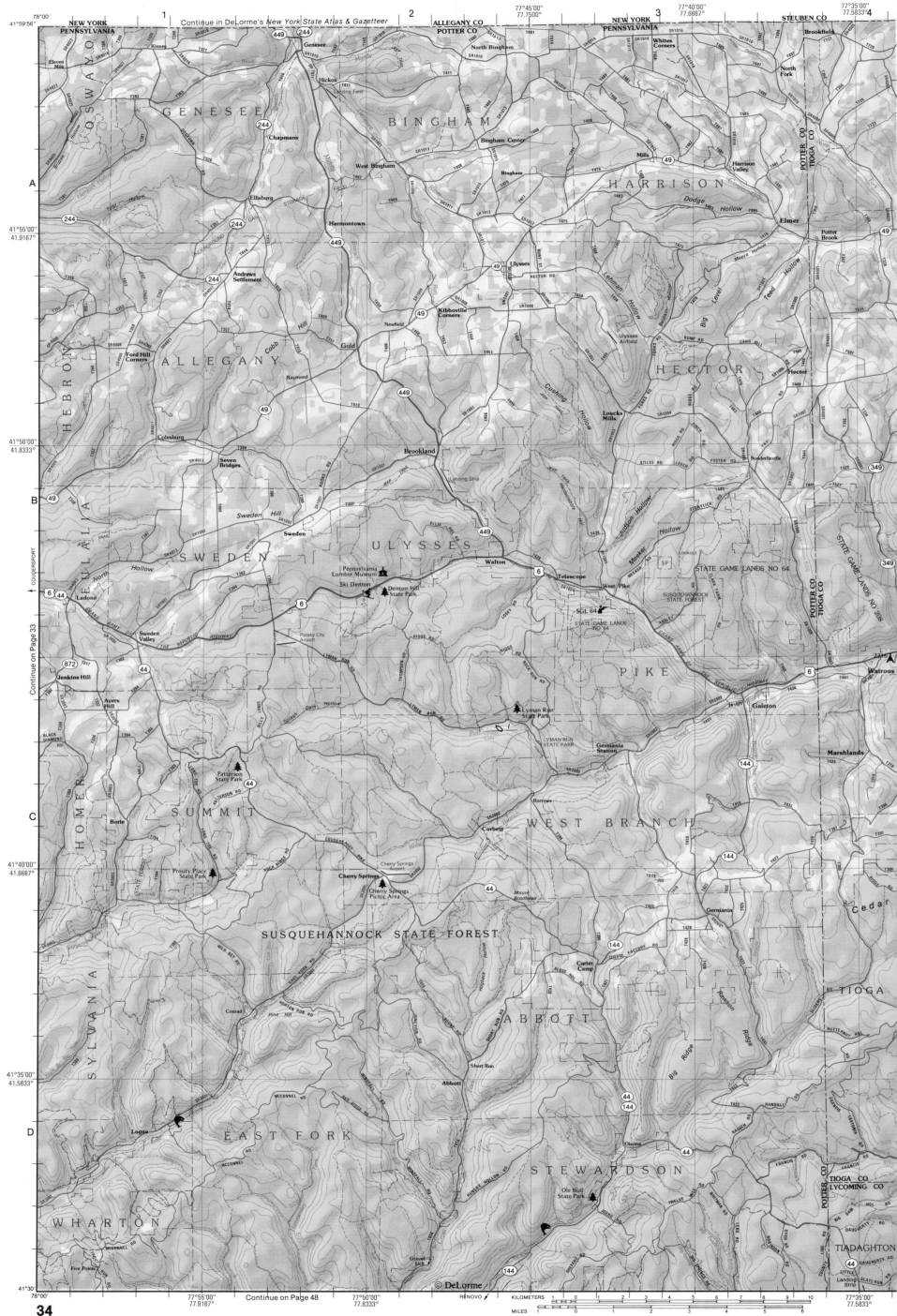

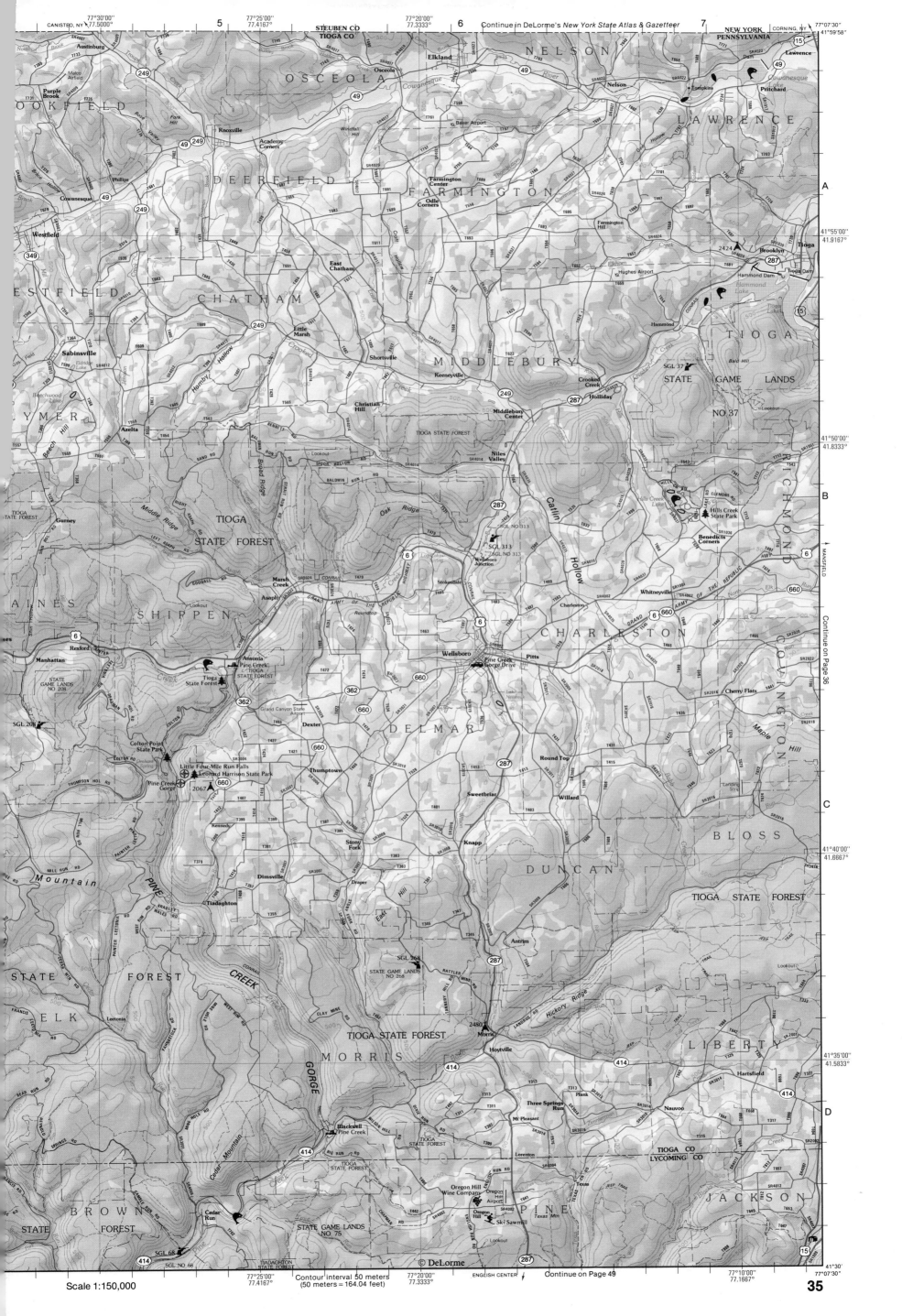

Scale 1:150,000

Contour interval 50 meters
(50 meters = 164.04 feet)

Continue on Page 49

© DeLorme

CHEMUNG CO
BRADFORD CO
76°35'00"
76.5833°
5
WAVERLY, NY
76°30'00"
76.5000°
6
Continue in DeLorme's *New York State Atlas & Gazetteer*
7
TIOGA CO
BRADFORD CO
NY 76°15'
PA 41°59'55"

Scale 1:150,000
MONTOURSVILLE
Contour interval 50 meters
(50 meters = 164.04 feet)
76°25'00"
76.4167°
Continue on Page 51
76°20'00"
76.3333°
41°30'
76°15'
37

Continue on Page 37

Continue on Page 52

© DeLorme

Scale 1:150,000

Contour interval 50 meters
(50 meters = 164.04 feet)

Continue on Page 53

© DeLorme

39

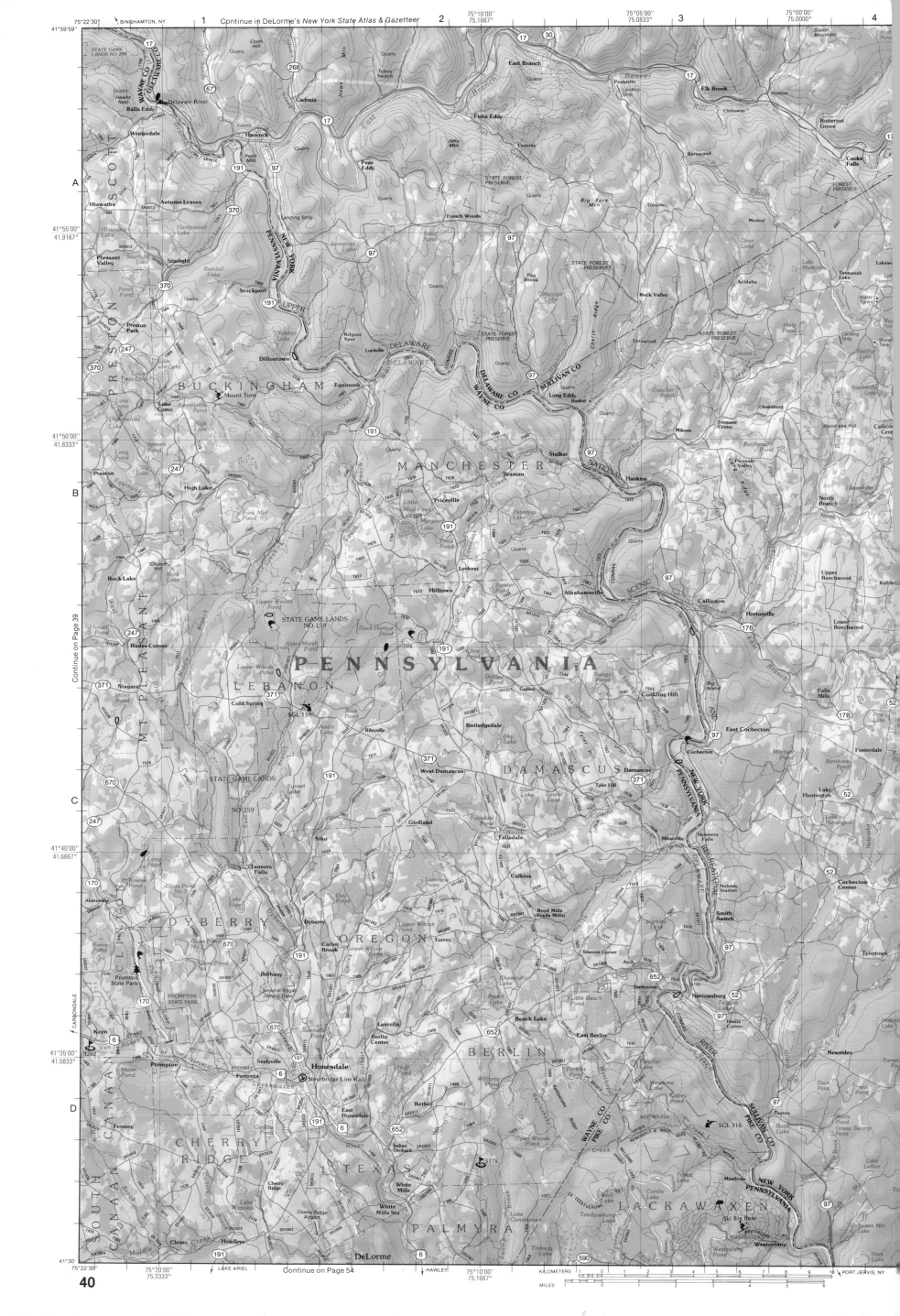

Continue on Page 39

Continue on Page 54

© DeLorme

PORT JERVIS, NY

KILOMETERS

MILES

LAKE ARIEL   HAWLEY

PENNSYLVANIA

Scale 1:150,000

Contour interval 50 meters
(50 meters = 164.04 feet)

Continue on Page 55

© DeLorme

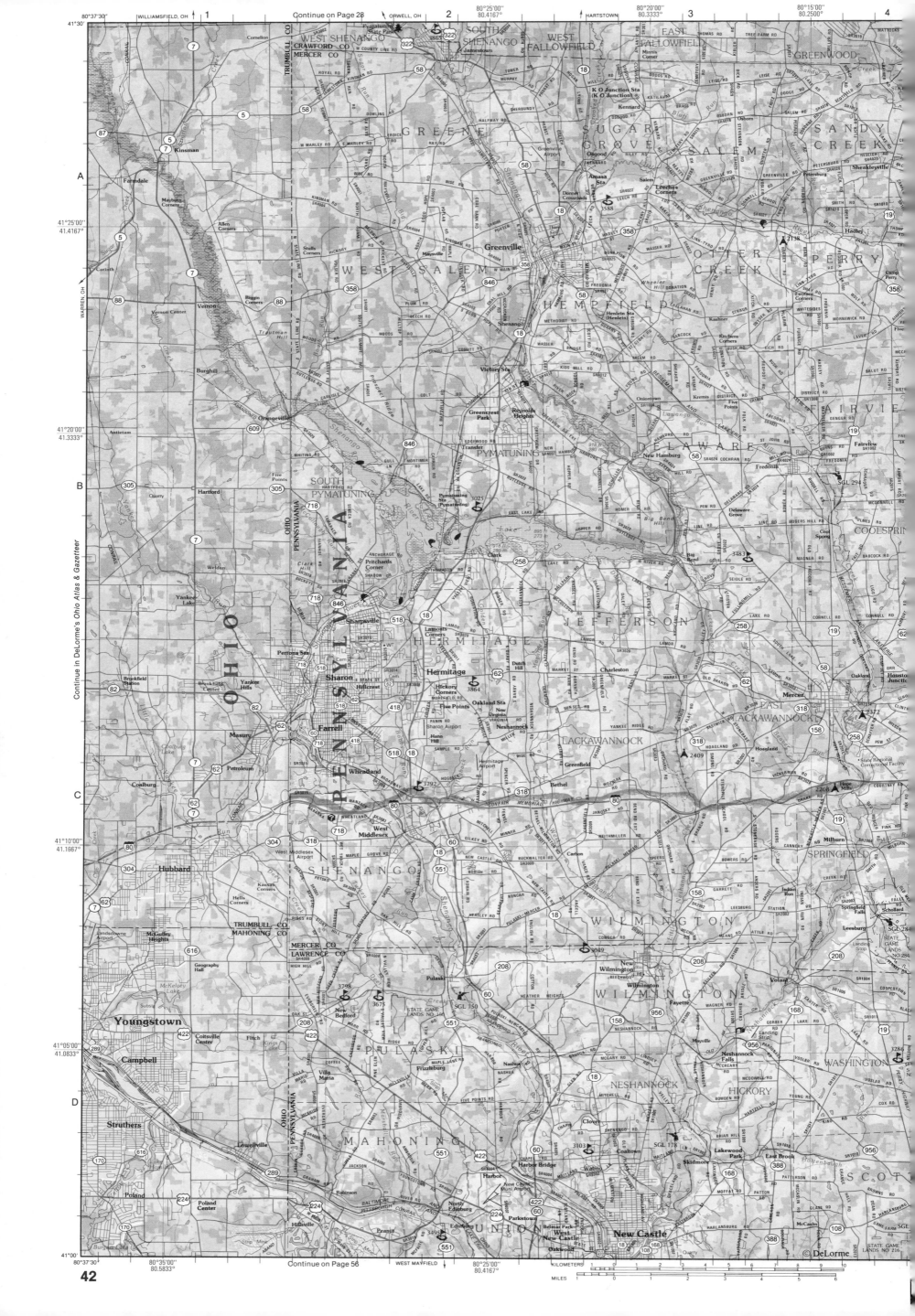

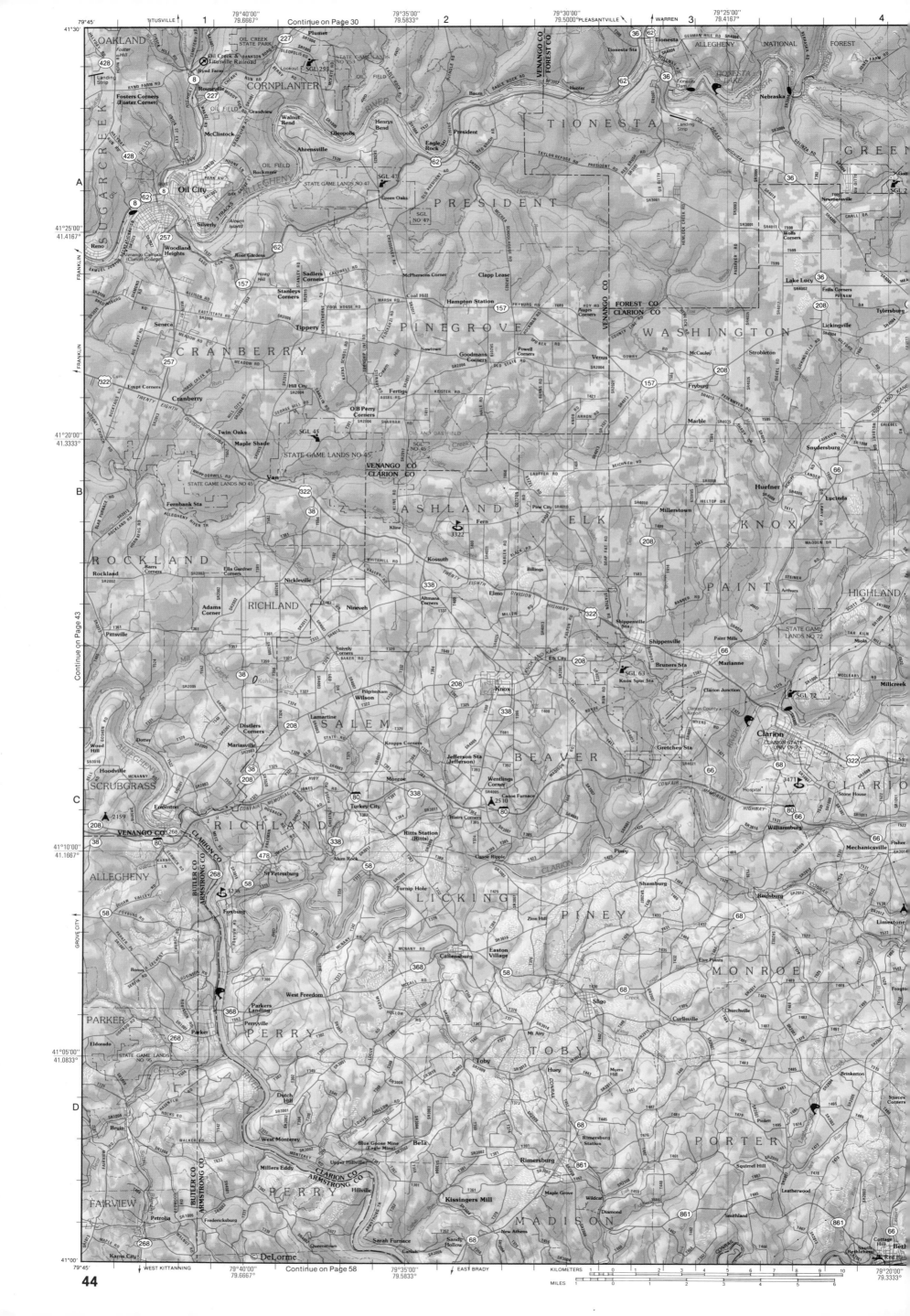

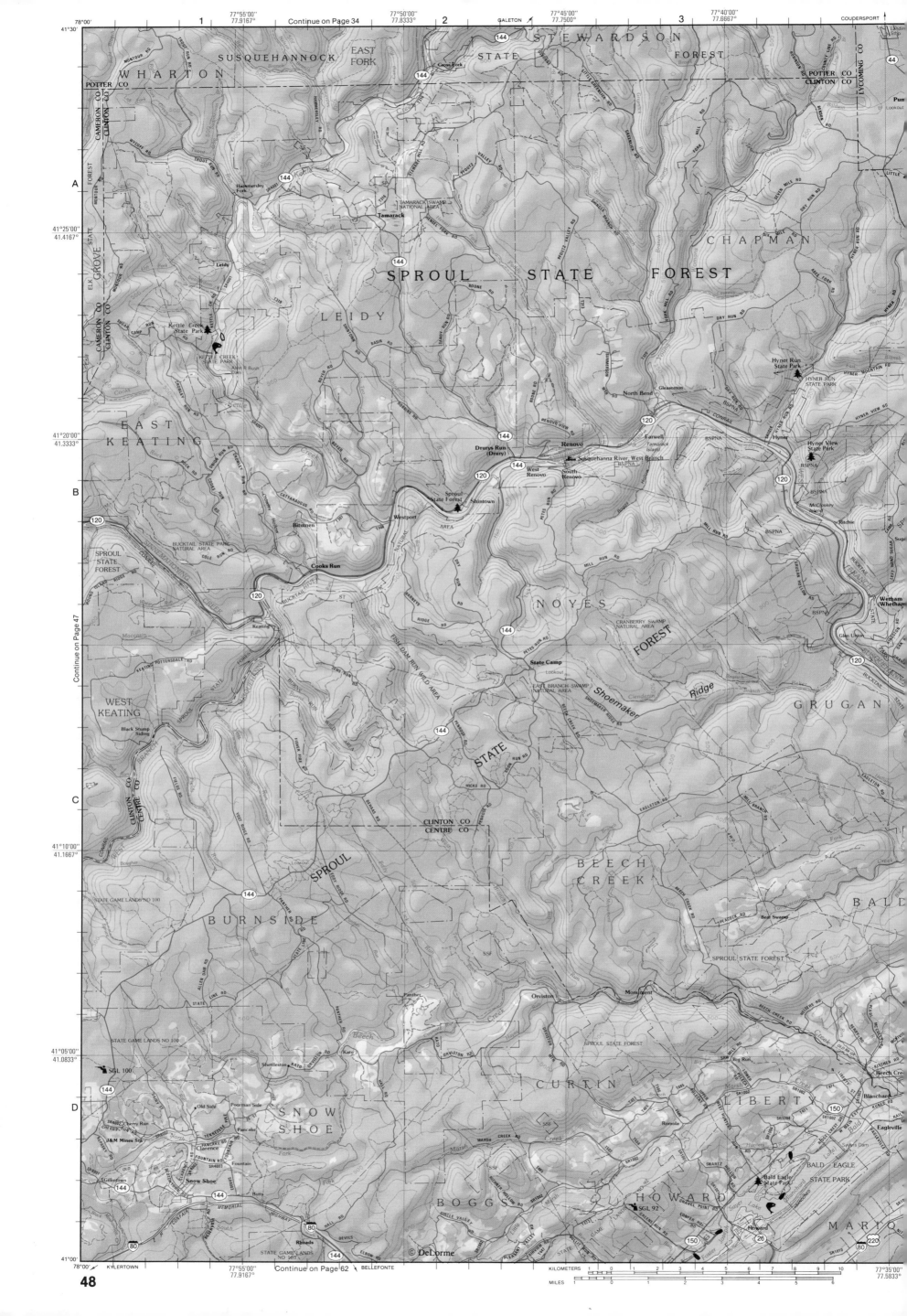

Continue on Page 47

© DeLorme

KILOMETERS
MILES

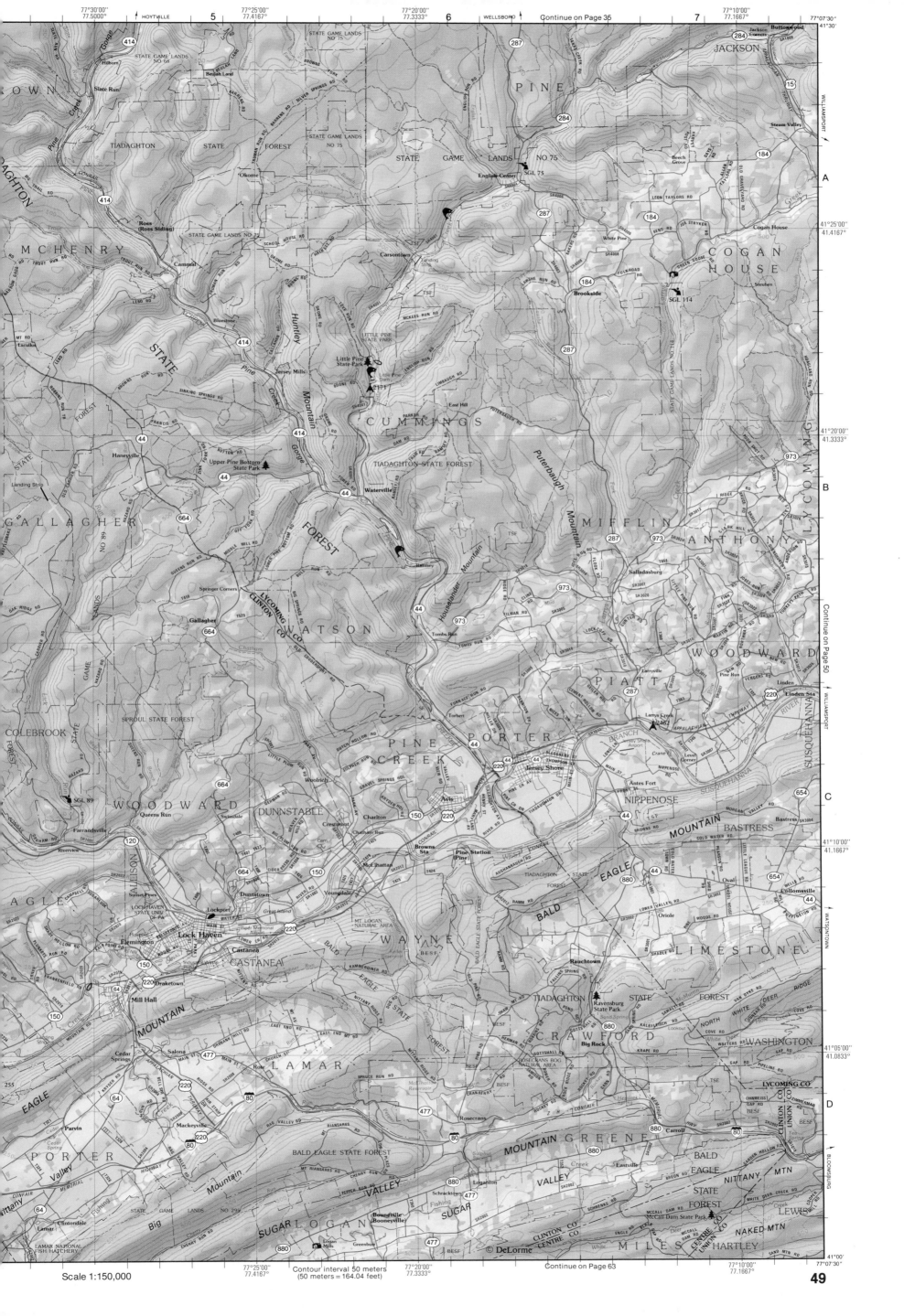

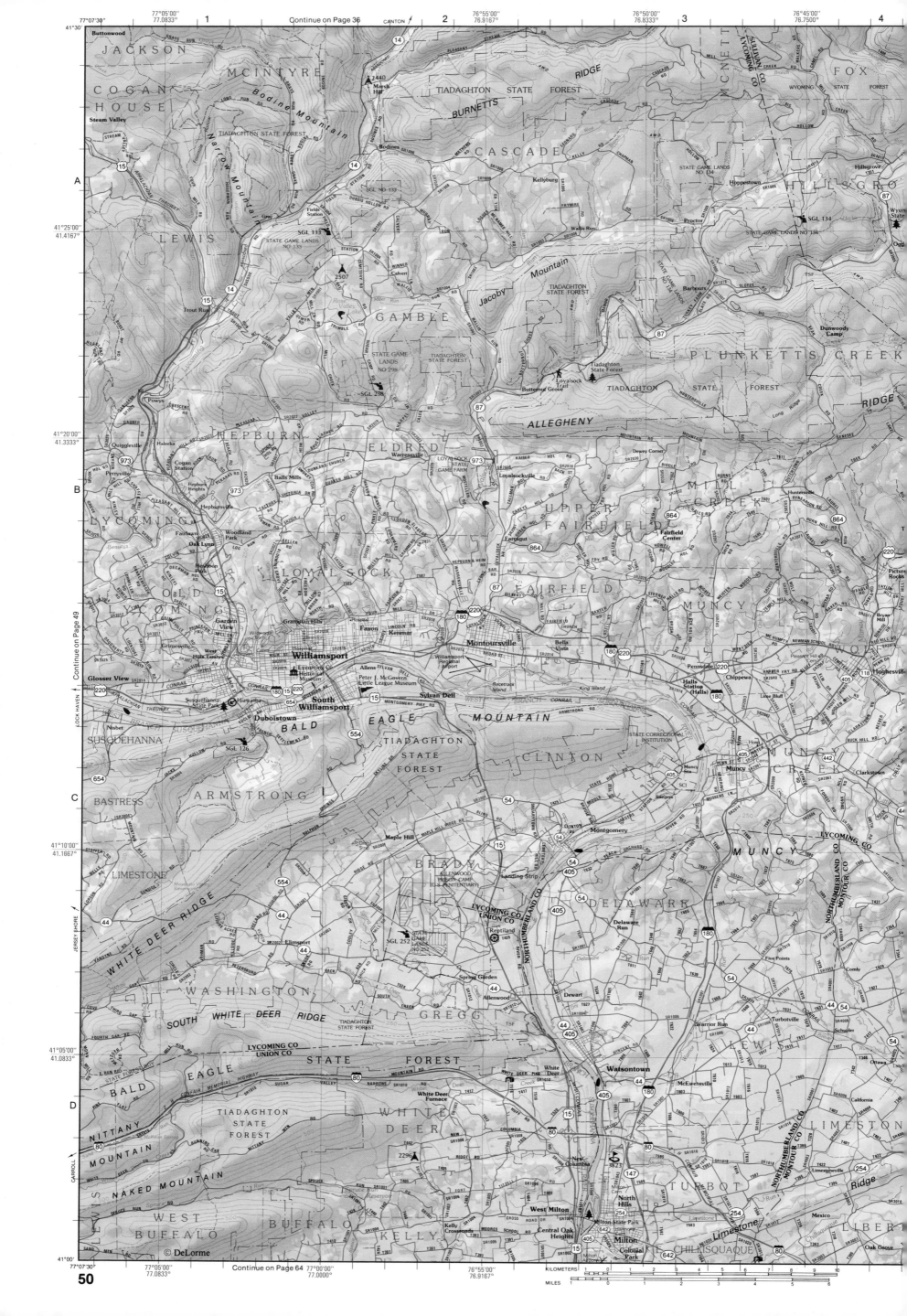

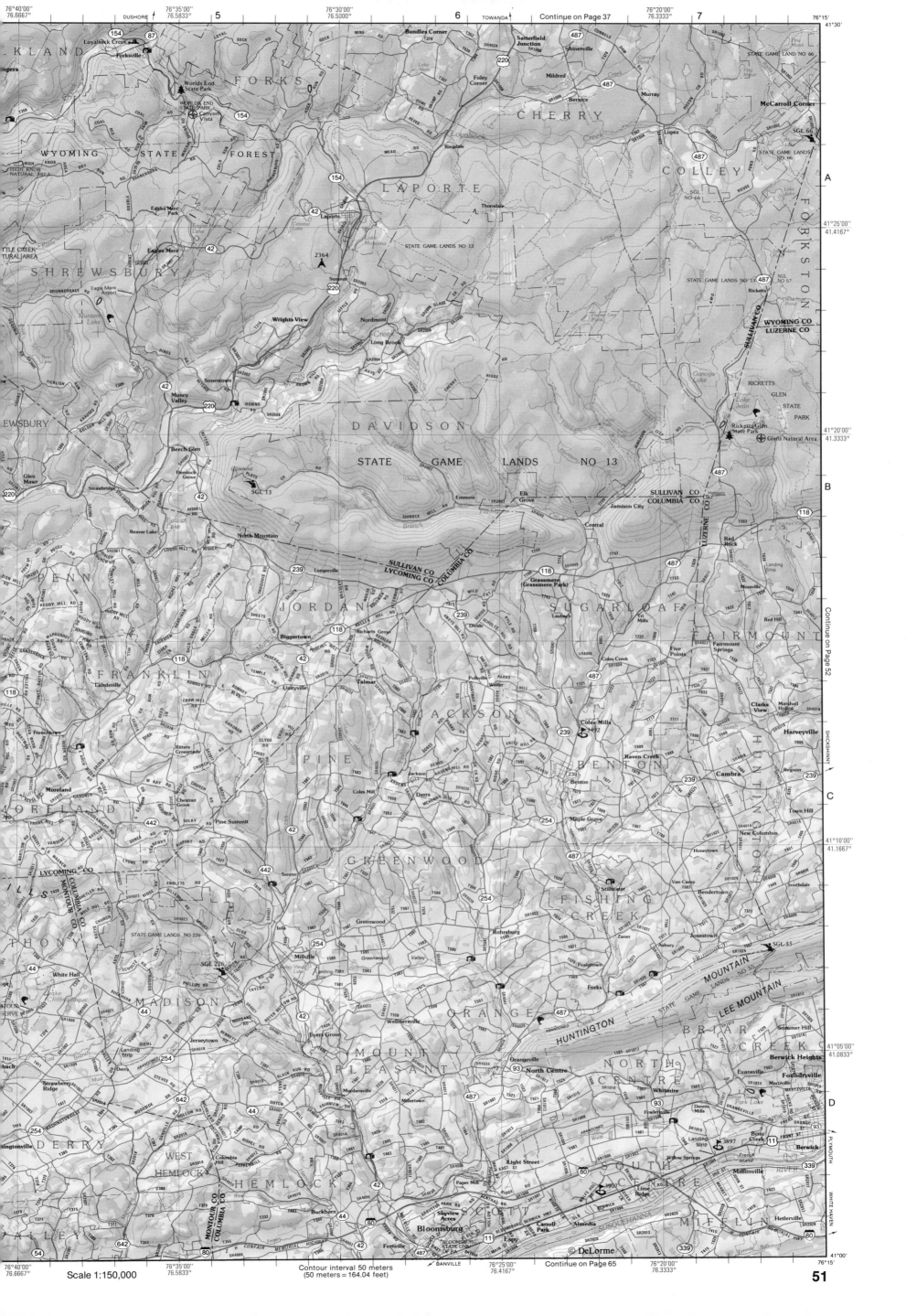

75°45'00"
75.7500°

5 NEW MILFORD

CARBONDALE 6 Continue on Page 39 7 WAYMART

75°22'30"
41°30'

Scale 1:150,000

Contour interval 50 meters
(50 meters = 164.04 feet)

75°40'00"
75.6667°

75°35'00"
75.5833°

Continue on Page 67

75°25'00"
75.4167°

BRODHEADSVILLE

75°22'30"
41°00'

53

© DeLorme

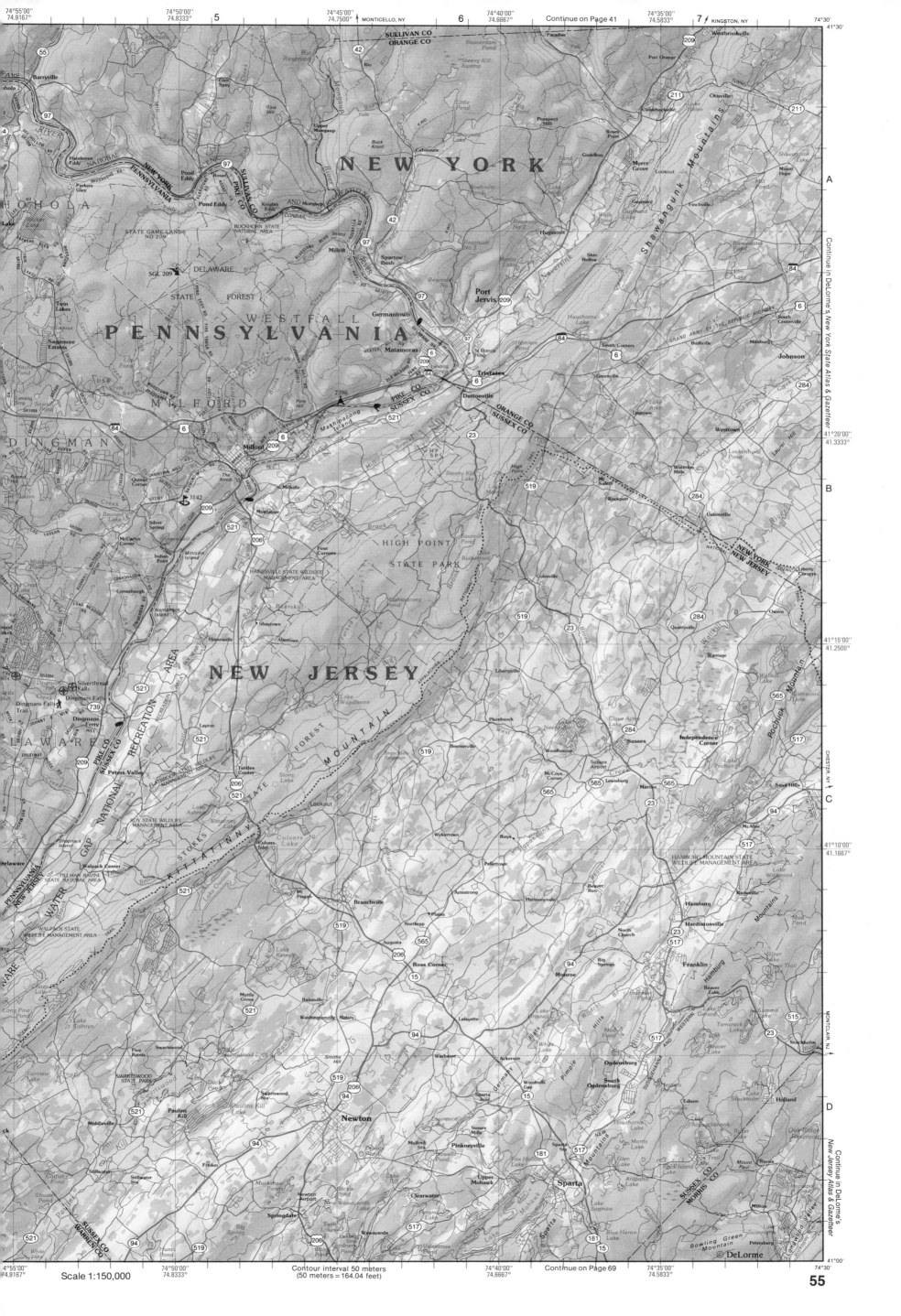

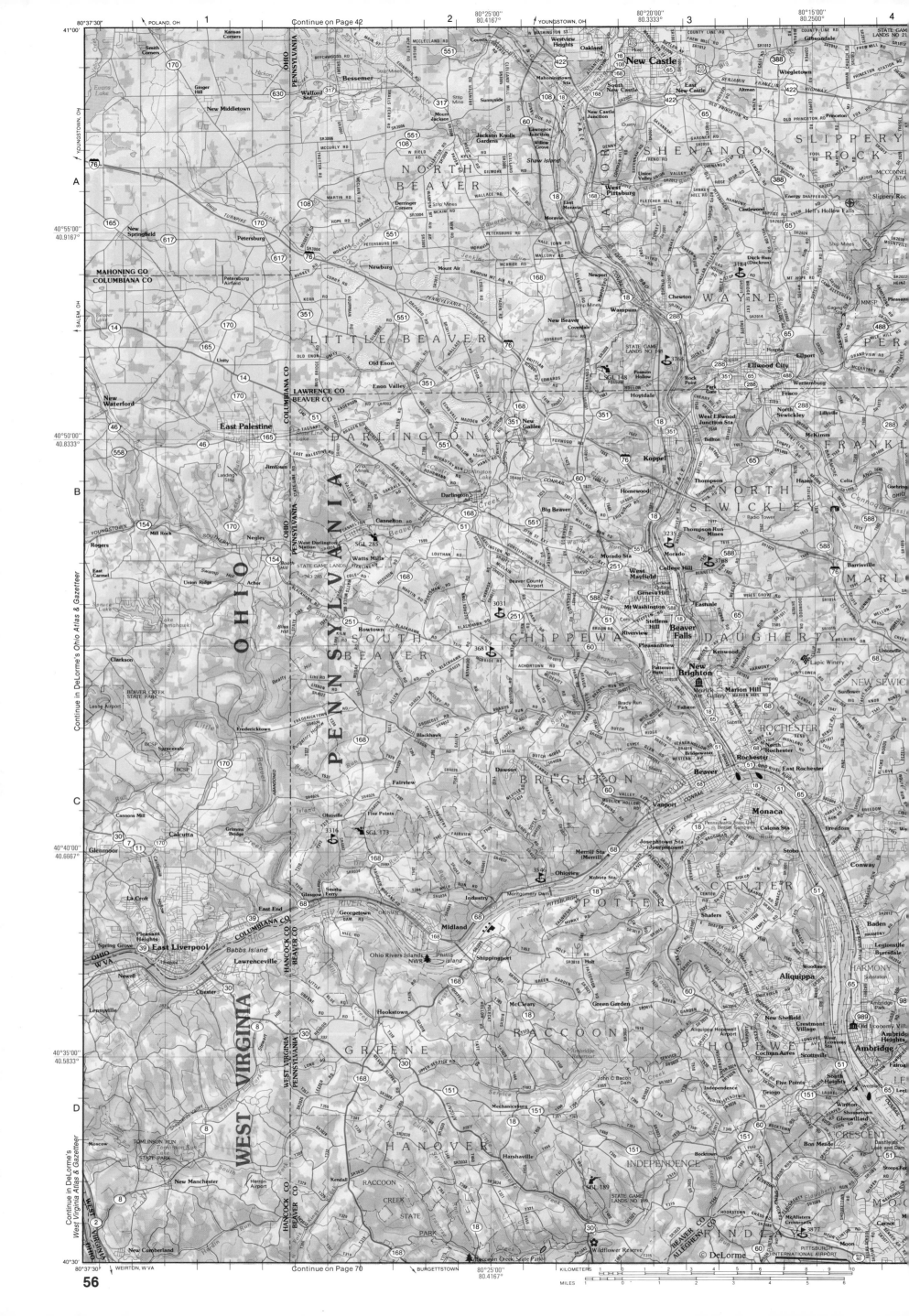

Continue on Page 43
Continue on Page 58
Continue on Page 71

Scale 1:150,000   Contour interval 50 meters   Continue on Page 71   WESTMORELAND CITY   79°45'
(50 meters = 164.04 feet)   WILKINSBURG   79°55'00"   79°50'00"   40°30'
80°10'00"   80°05'00"   79.9167°   79.8333°
80.1667°   80.0833°

57

© DeLorme

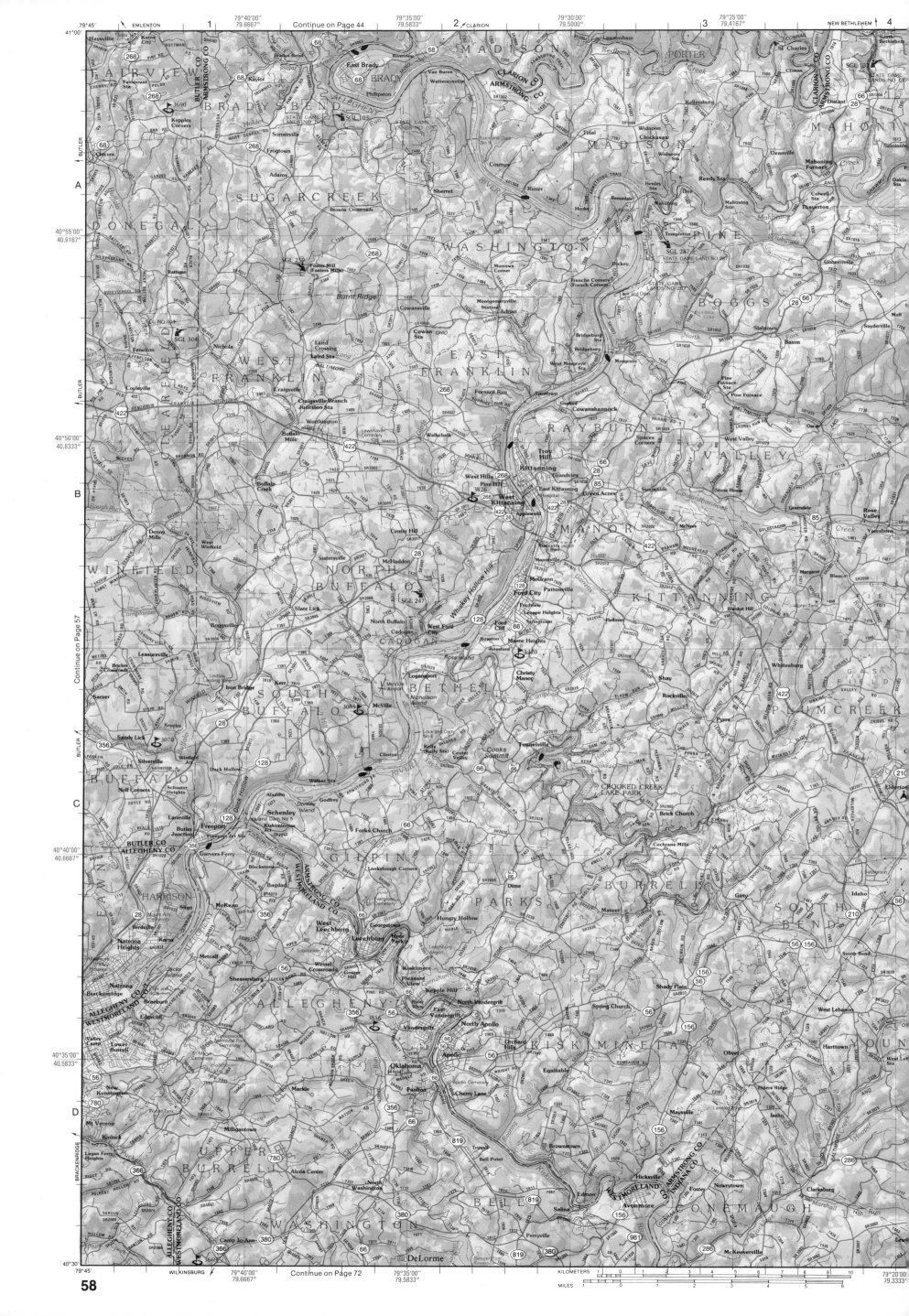

Contour interval 50 meters
(50 meters = 164.04 feet)

Continue on Page 73

© DeLorme

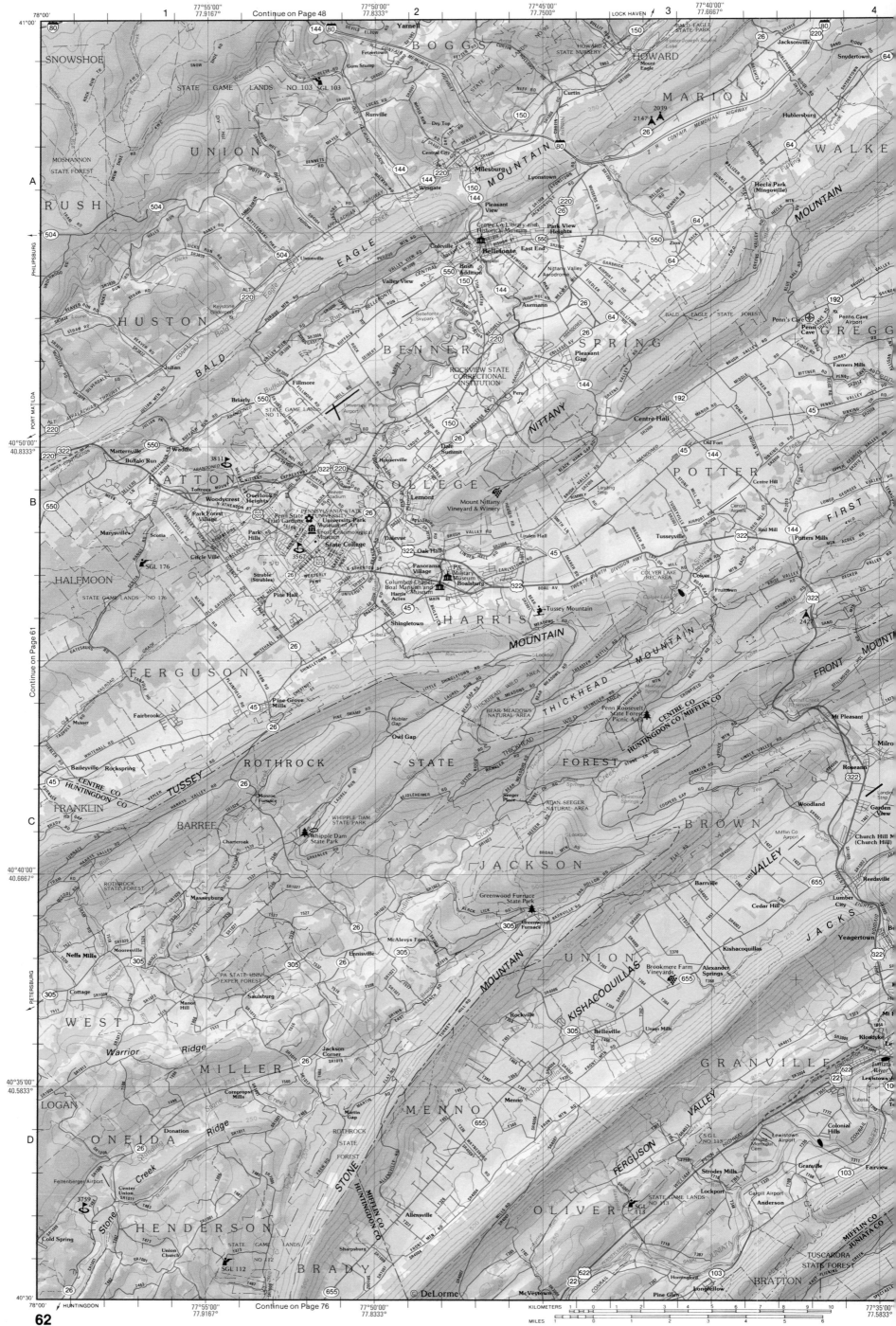

Continue on Page 61

©DeLorme

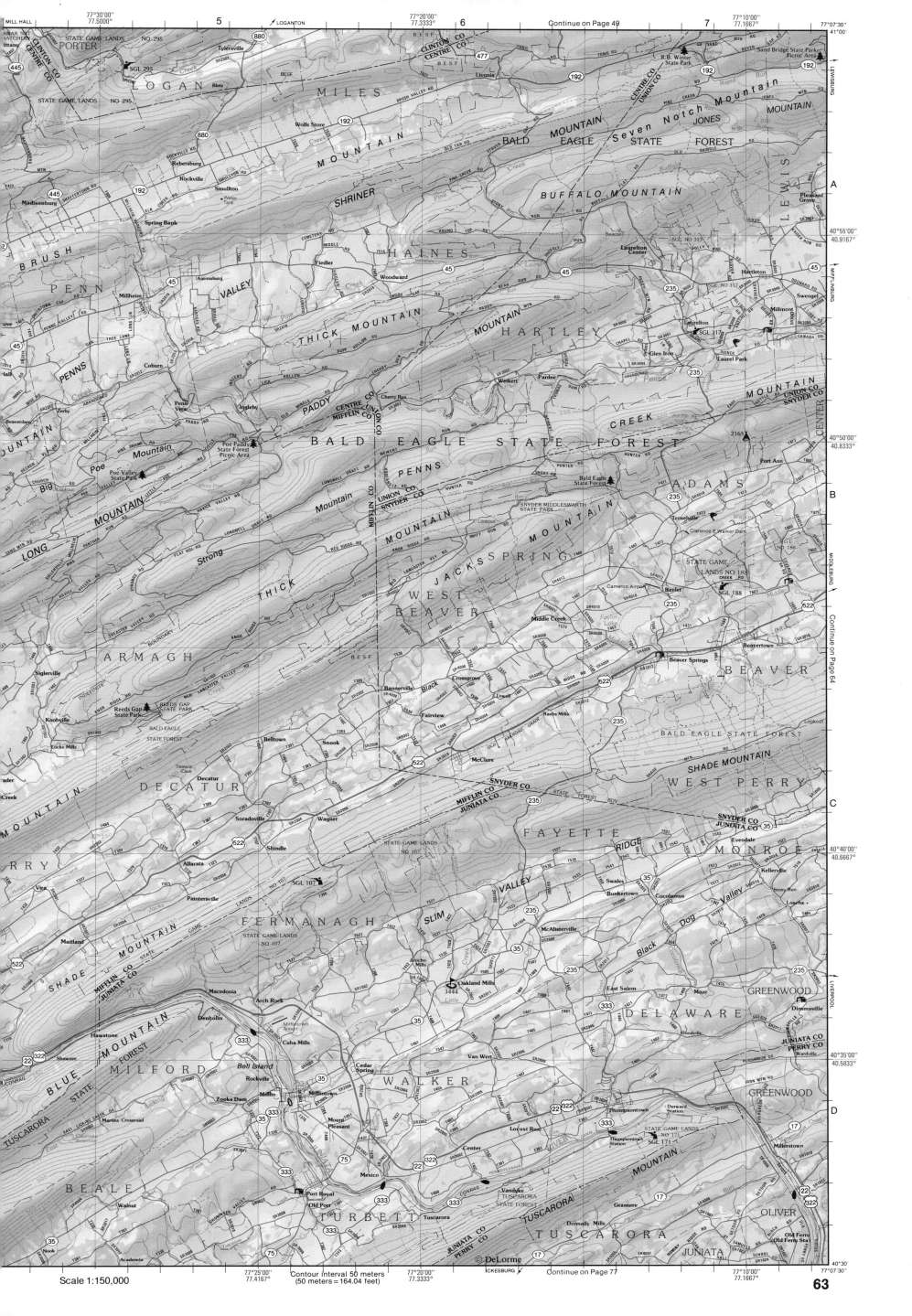

Continue on Page 64

Continue on Page 77

Scale 1:150,000

Contour interval 50 meters
(50 meters = 164.04 feet)

© DeLorme

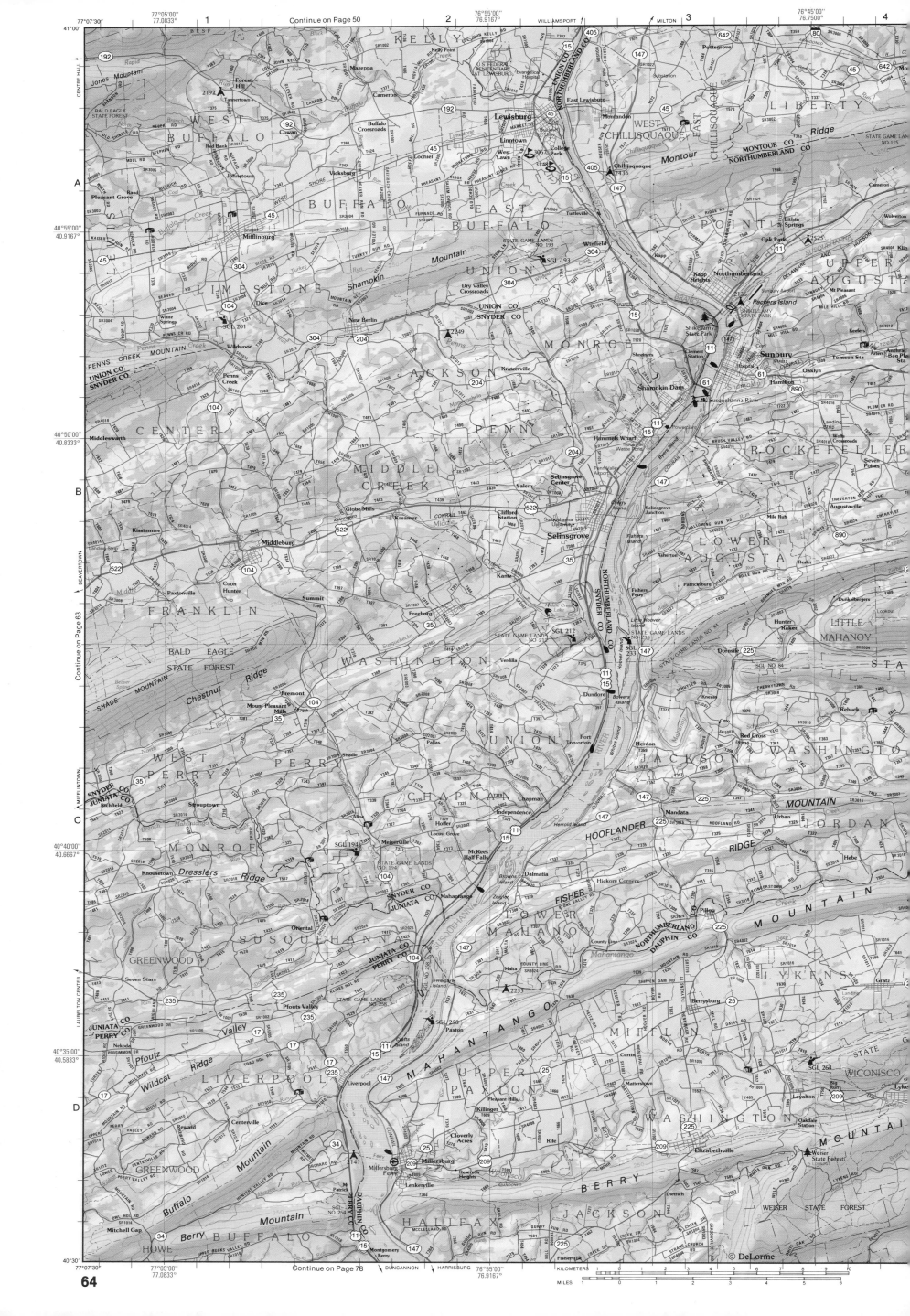

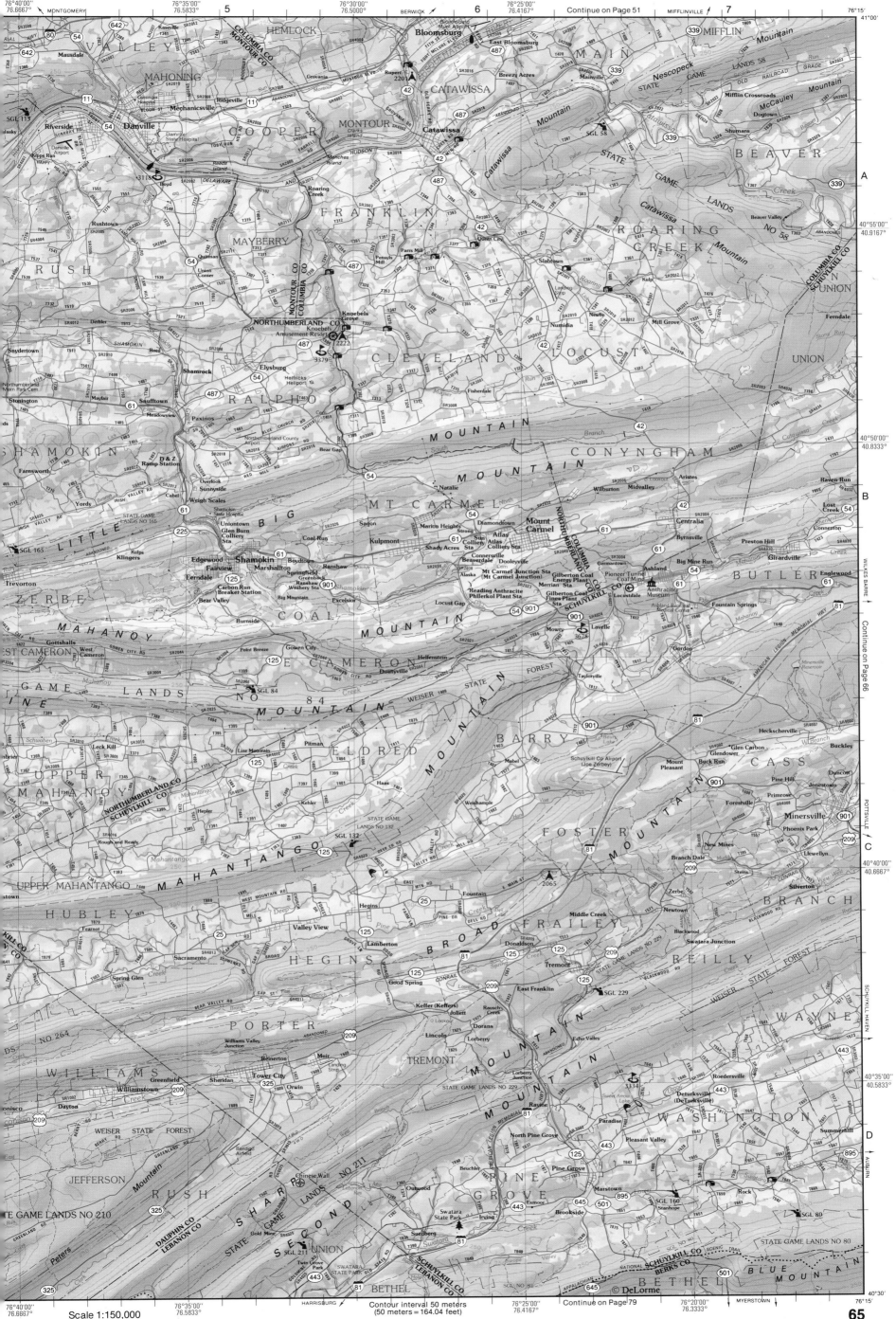

Continue on Page 66

Continue on Page 79

Scale 1:150,000

Contour interval 50 meters
(50 meters = 164.04 feet)

© DeLorme

65

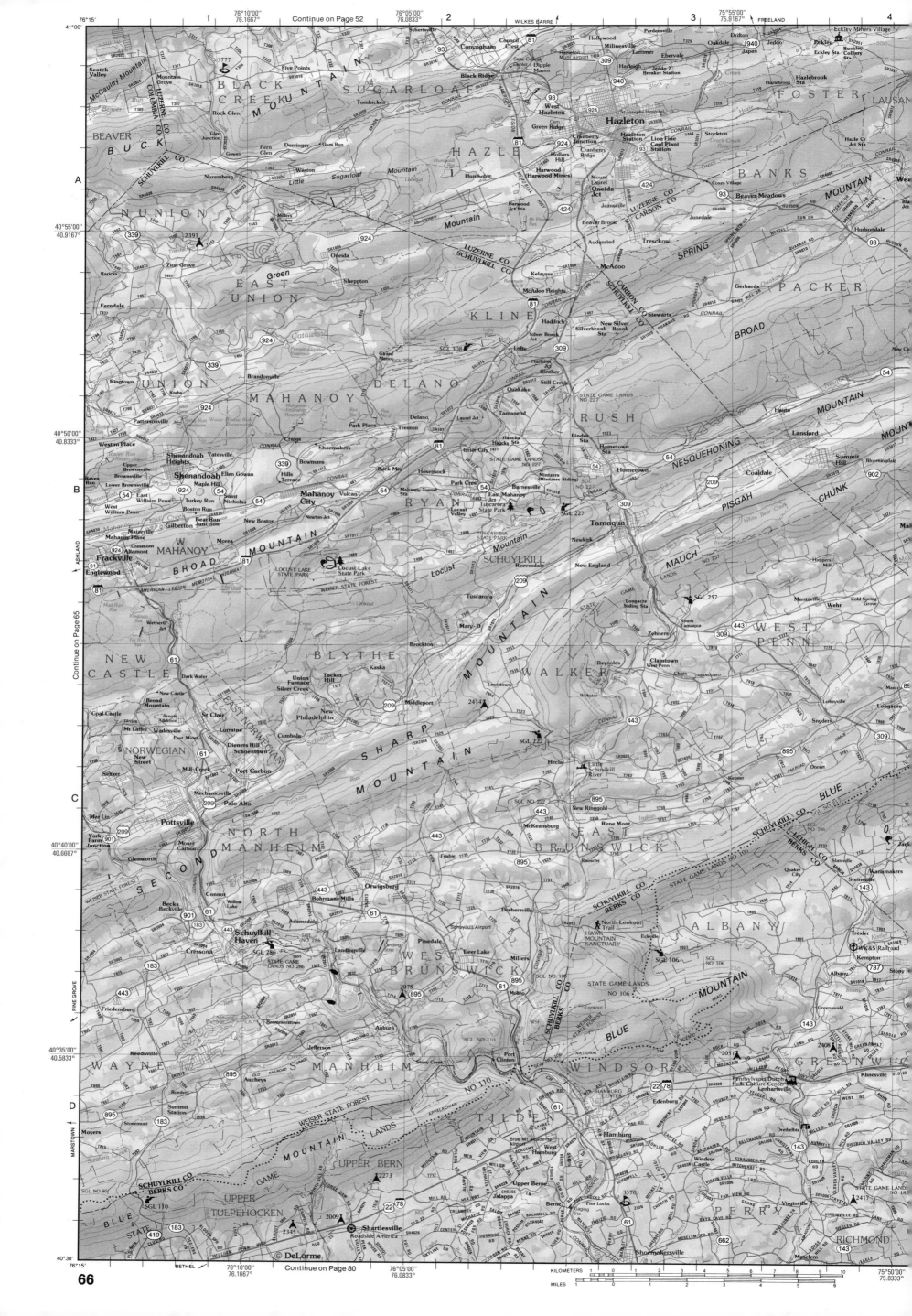

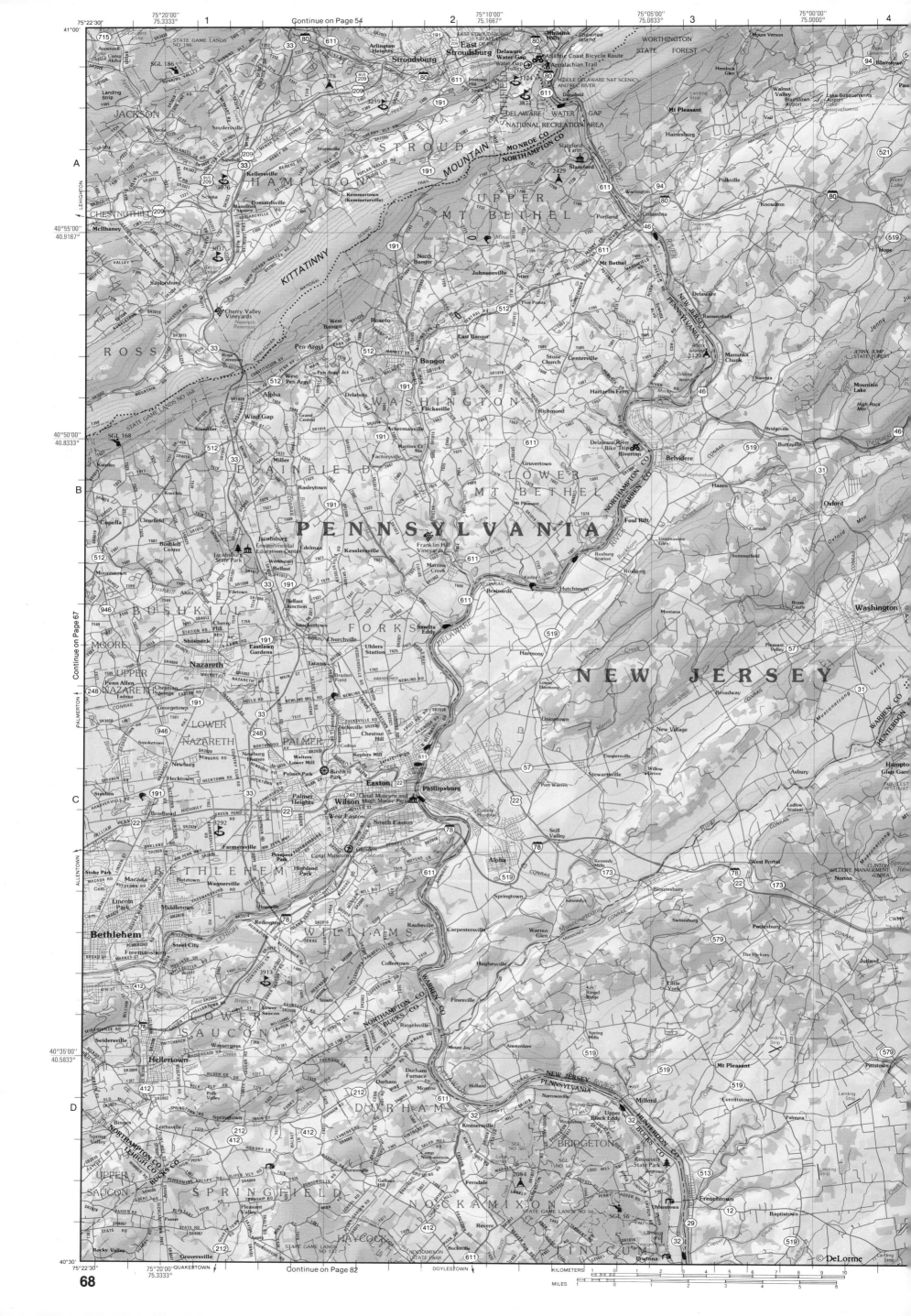

Continue on Page 54

Continue on Page 67

Continue on Page 82

© DeLorme

74°55'00''
74.9167°

74°40'00''
74.6667°

74°35'00''
74.5833°

74°30'

41°00'

40°55'00''
40.9167°

40°50'00''
40.8333°

40°45'00''

40°40'00''
40.6667°

40°35'00''
40.5833°

40°30'

A

B

C

D

Continue in DeLorme's New Jersey Atlas & Gazetteer

PATERSON, NJ

NEWARK, NJ

Scale 1:150,000

Contour interval 50 meters
(50 meters = 164.04 feet)

74°50'00''
74.8333°

74°35'00''
74.5833°

© DeLorme

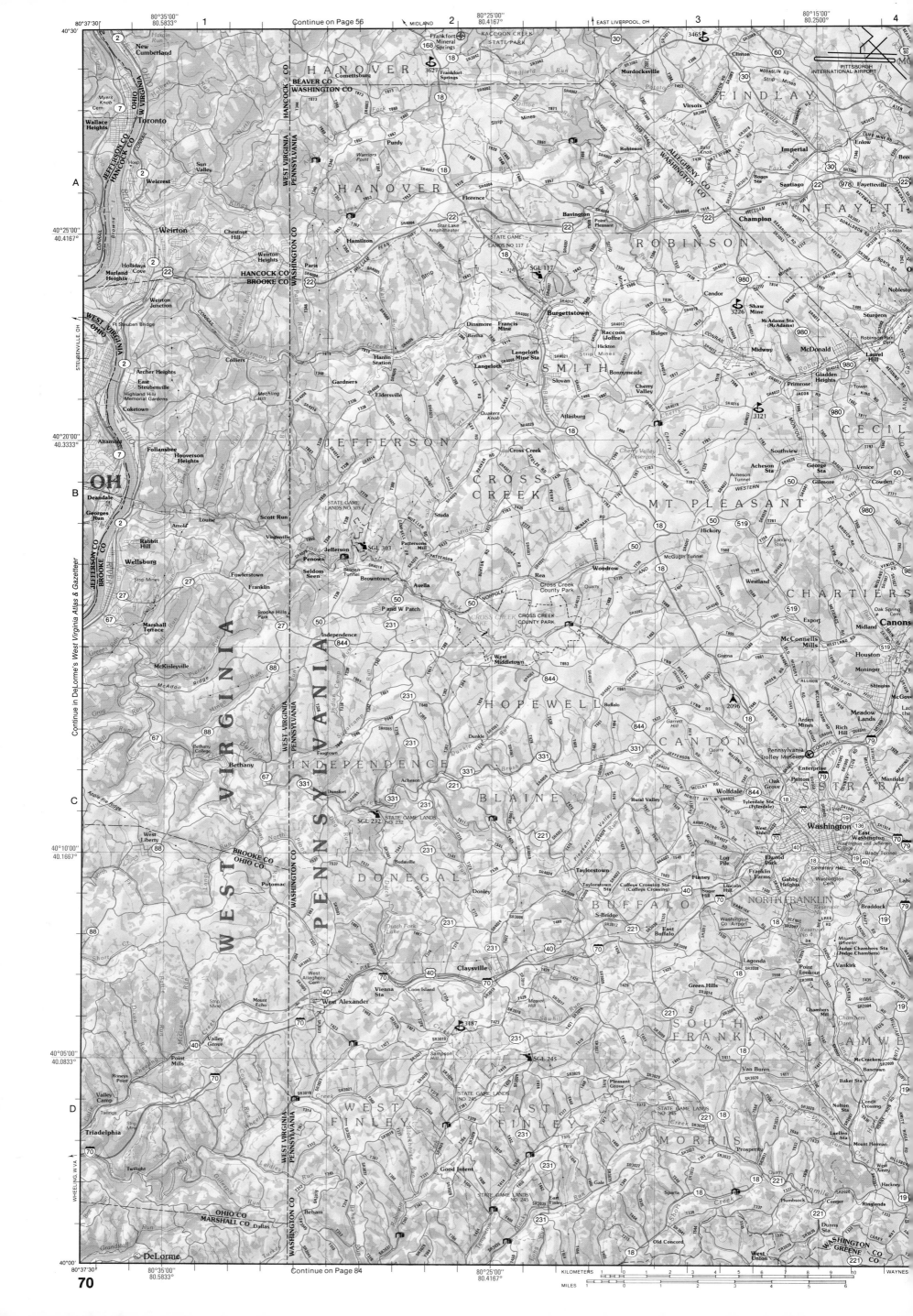

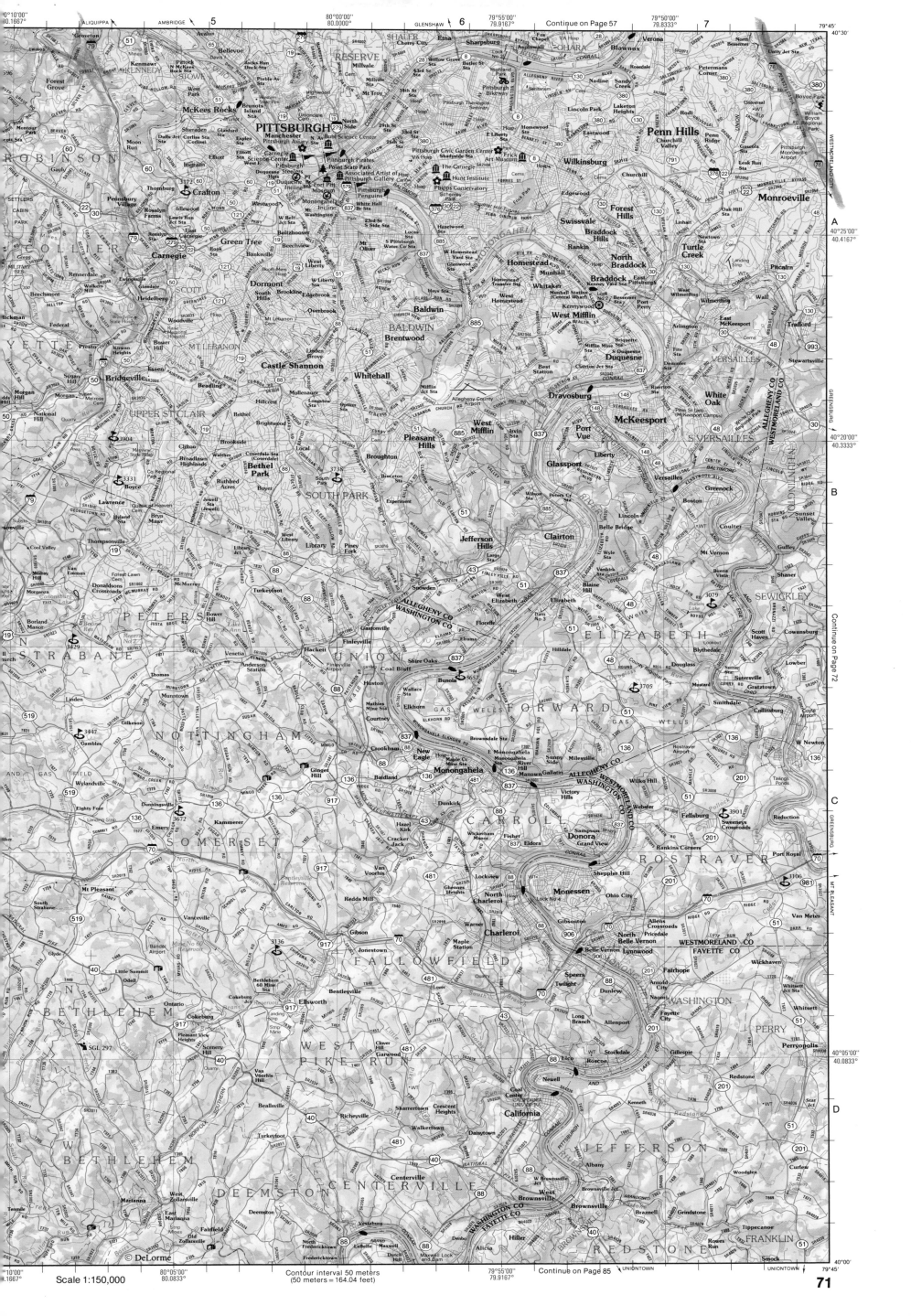

Continue on Page 72

© DeLorme

Scale 1:150,000

Contour interval 50 meters
(50 meters = 164.04 feet)

71

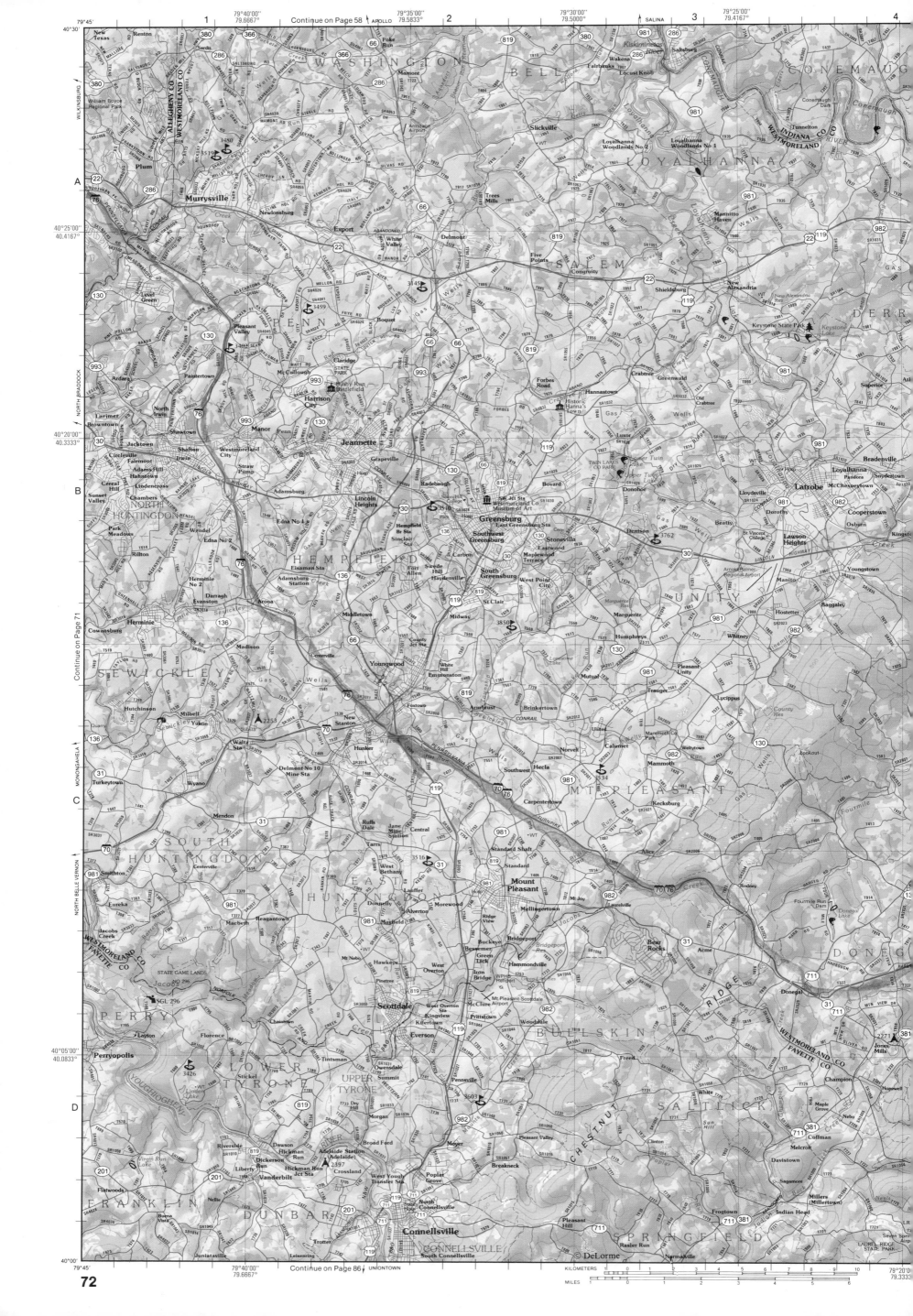

Continue on Page 58

Continue on Page 71

Continue on Page 86

© DeLorme

KILOMETERS
MILES

Continue on Page 59

Continue on Page 74

Continue on Page 87

Scale 1:150,000

Contour interval 50 meters
(50 meters = 164.04 feet)

© DeLorme

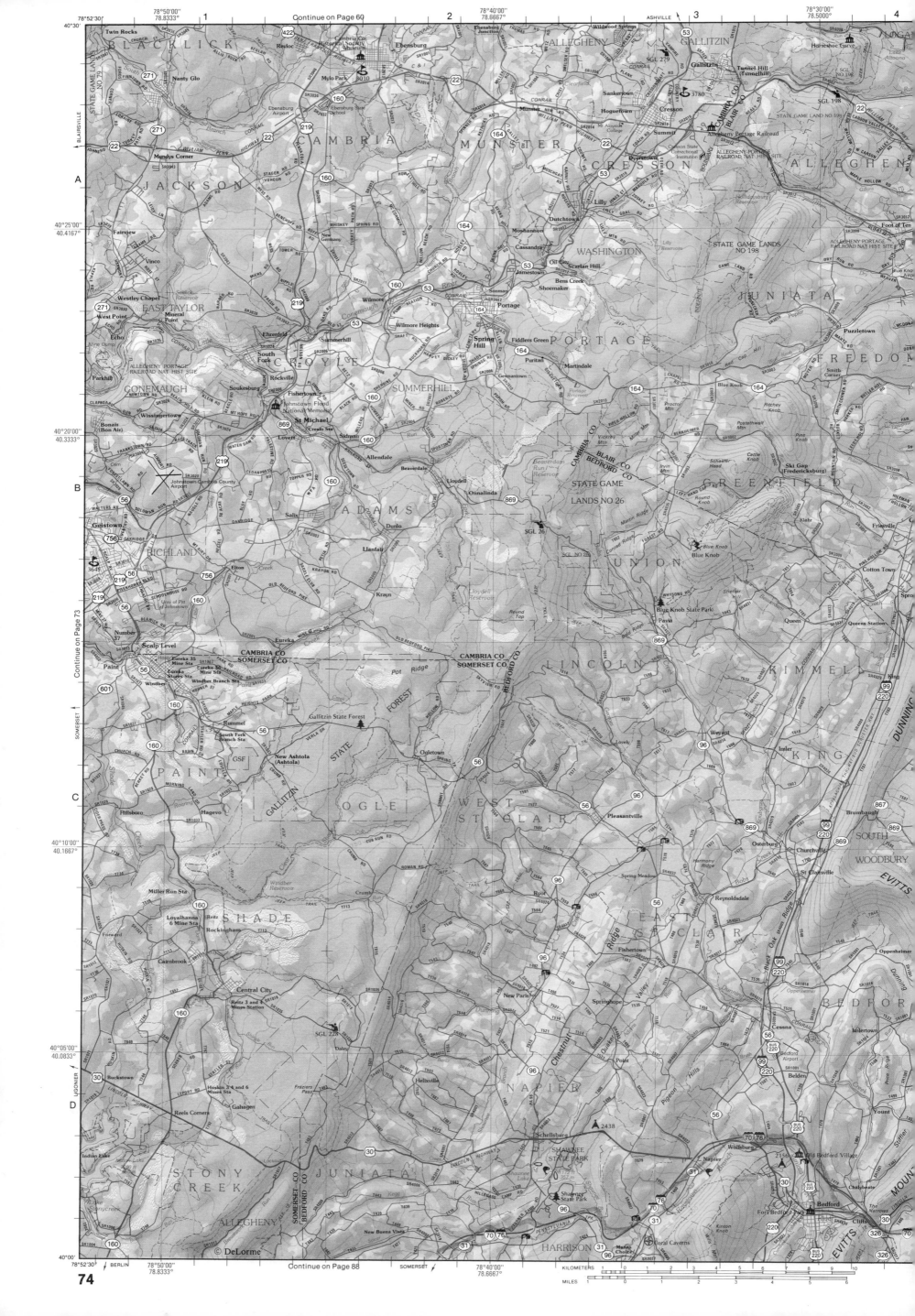

Continue on Page 60
Continue on Page 73
Continue on Page 88

© DeLorme

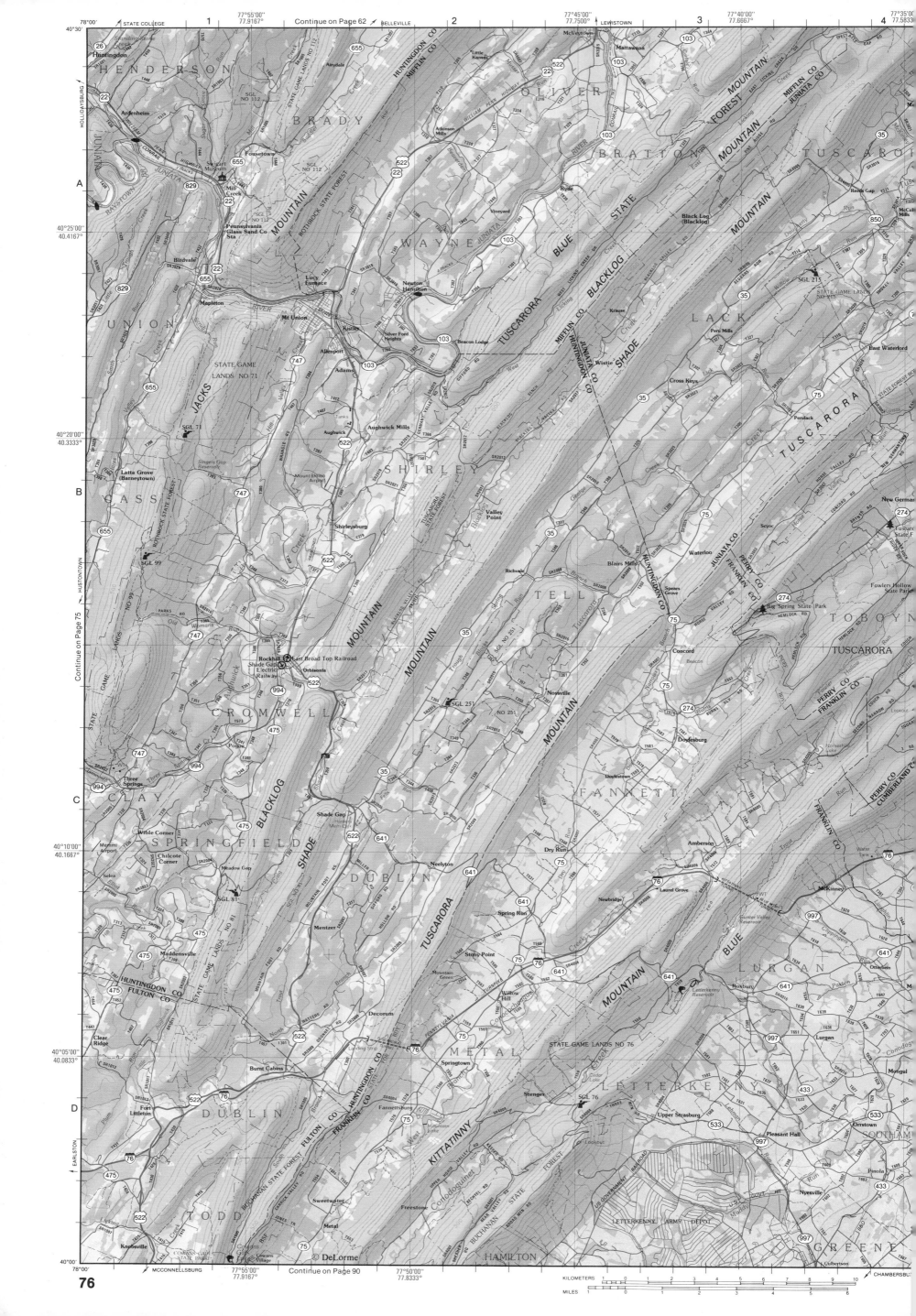

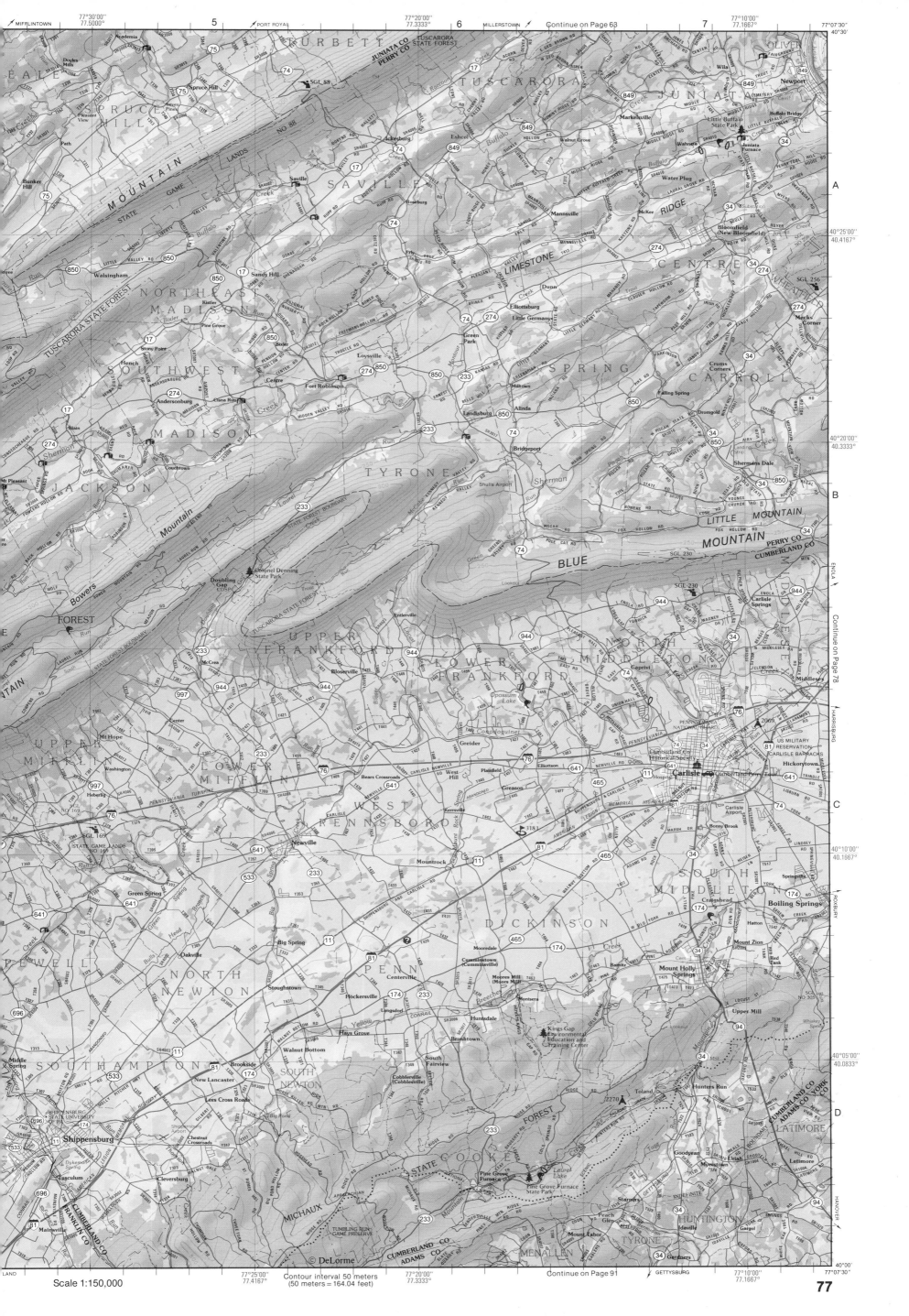

Continue on Page 68

Scale 1:150,000

Contour interval 50 meters
(50 meters = 164.04 feet)

© DeLorme

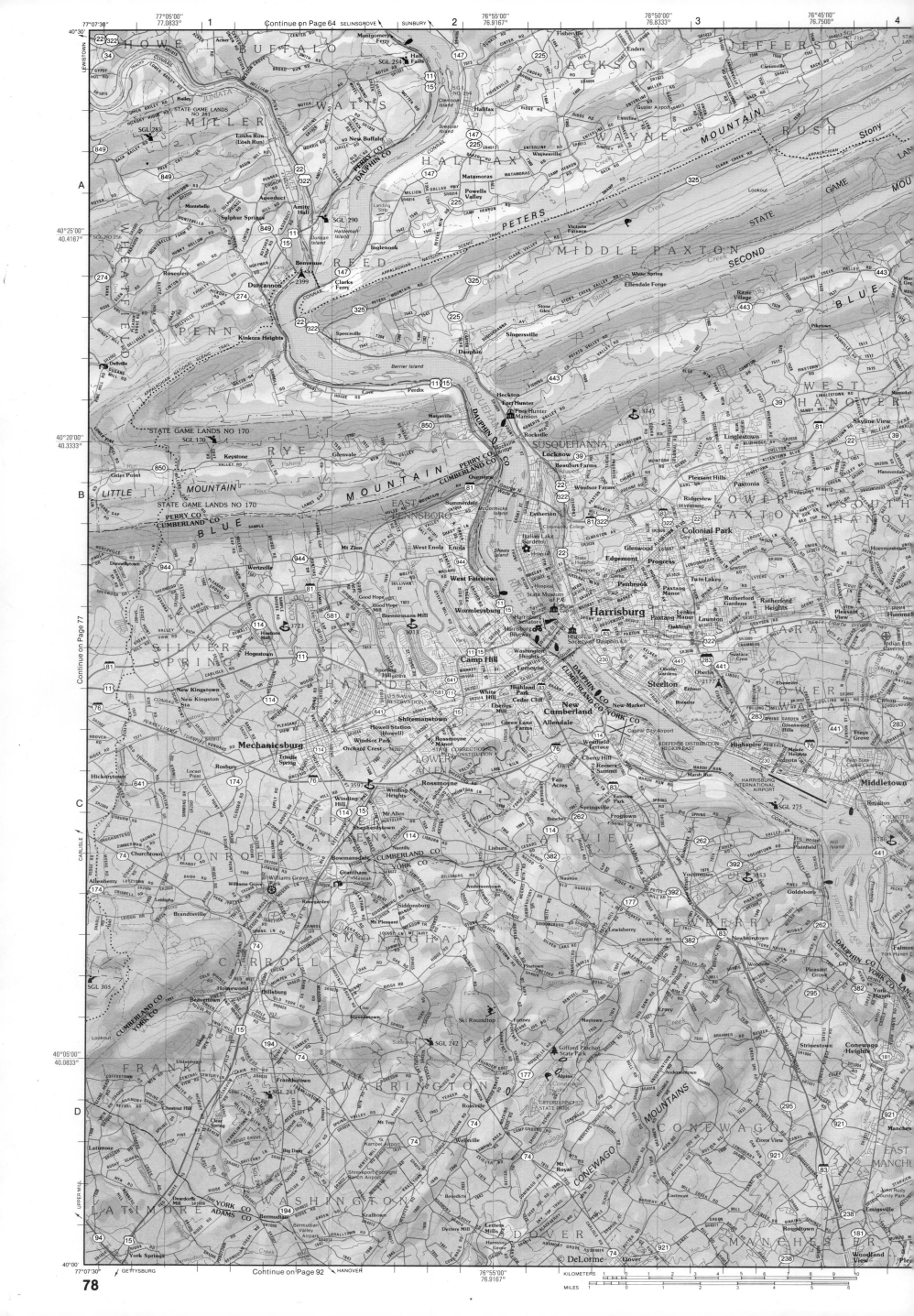

© DeLorme

Continue on Page 80

©DeLorme

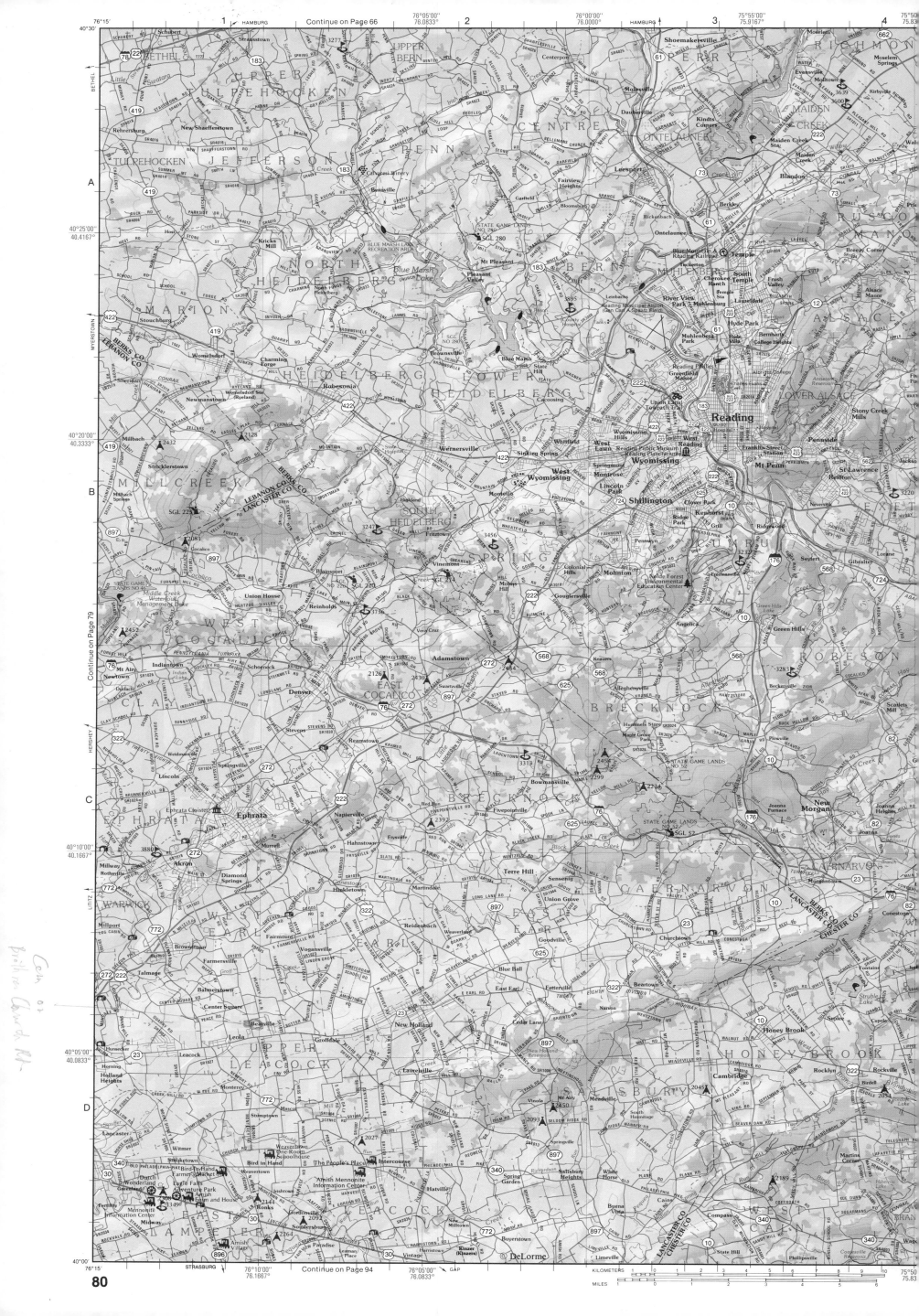

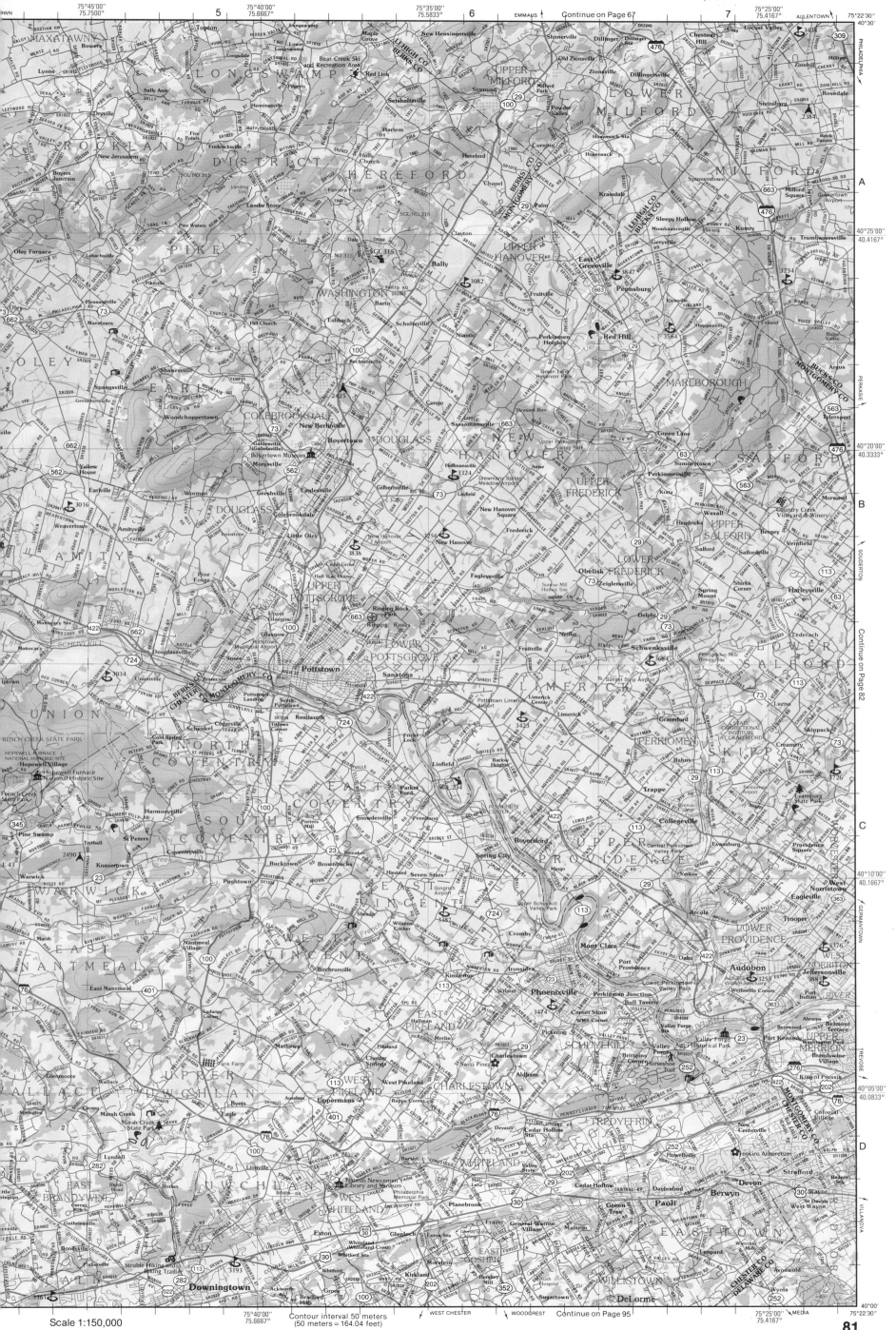

Continue on Page 82

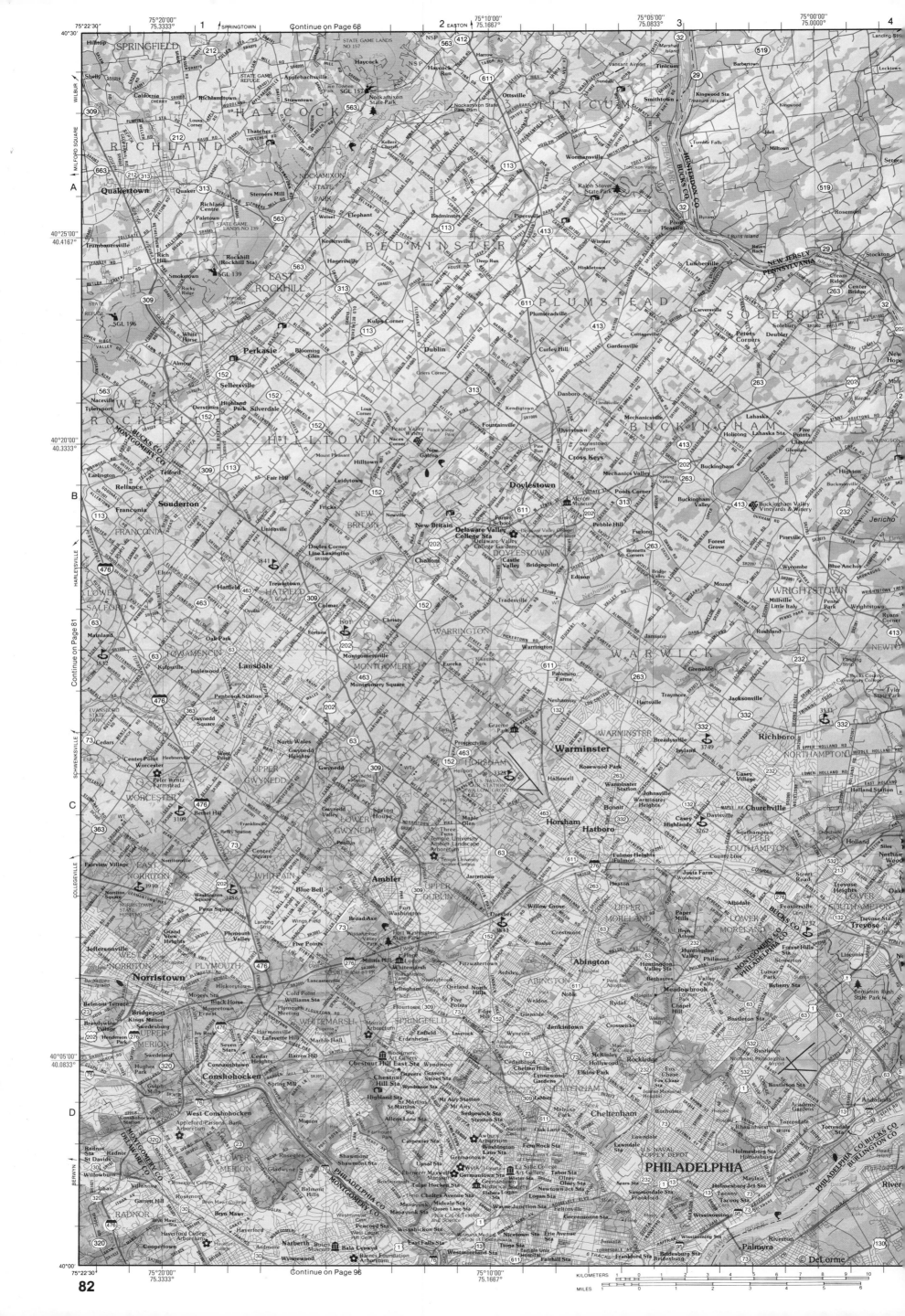

MANVILLE, NJ ↑ Continue on Page 69

Continue in DeLorme's New Jersey Atlas & Gazetteer

© DeLorme

Scale 1:150,000

Contour interval 50 meters
(50 meters = 164.04 feet)

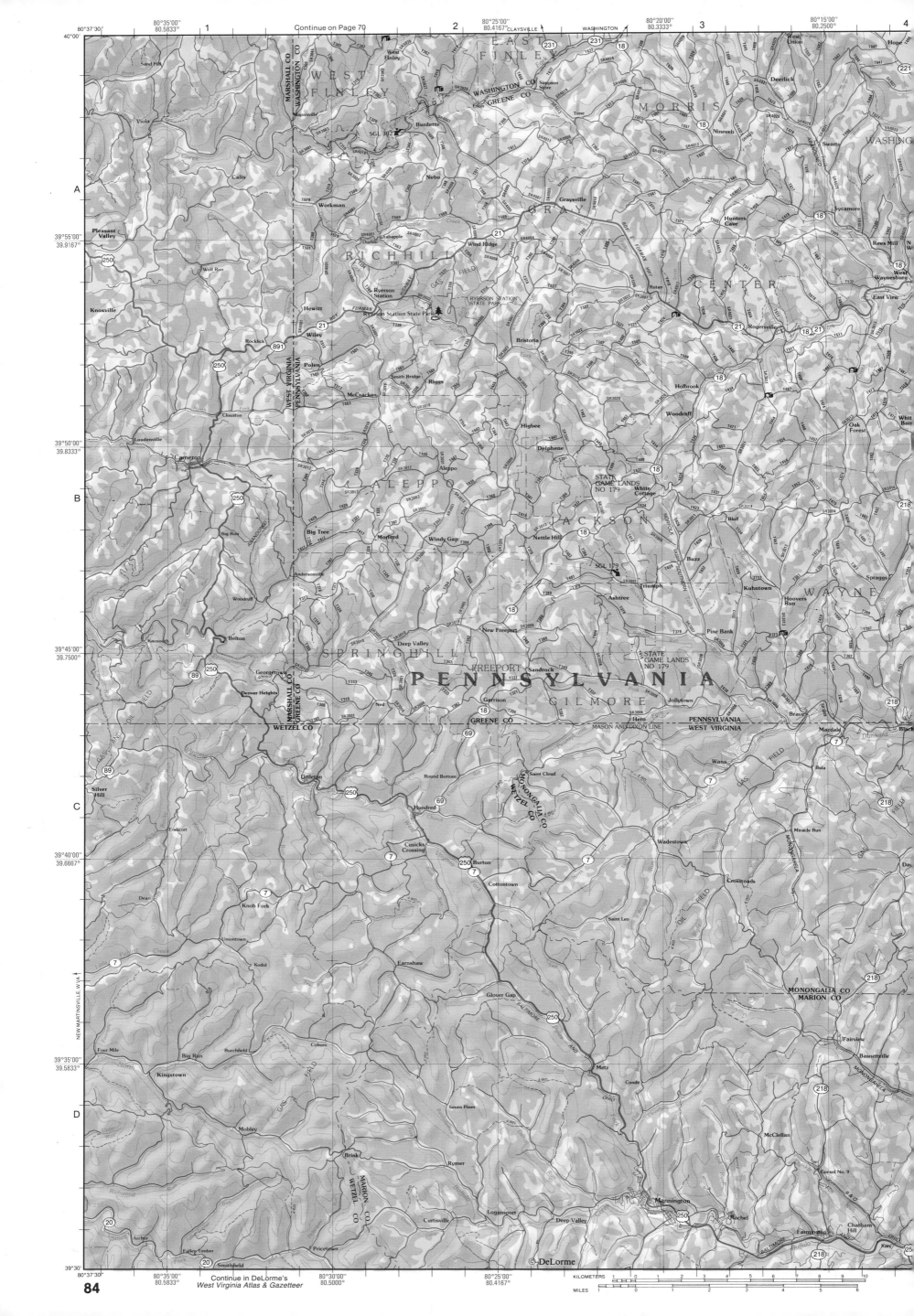

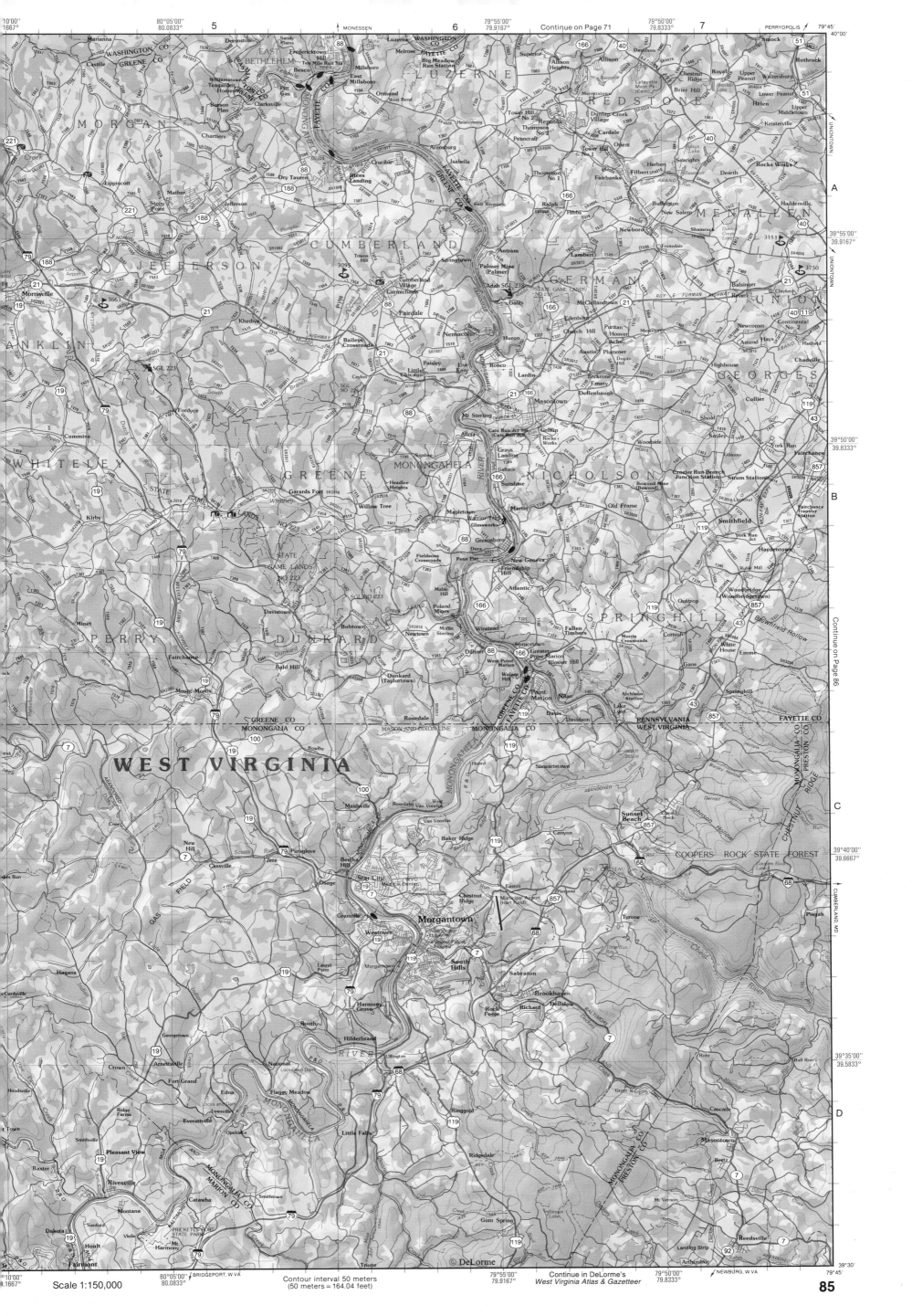

Scale 1:150,000   Contour interval 50 meters   Continue in DeLorme's
(50 meters = 164.04 feet)   West Virginia Atlas & Gazetteer
BRIDGEPORT, W.VA   NEWBURG, W.VA   85

© DeLorme

WEST VIRGINIA

Morgantown

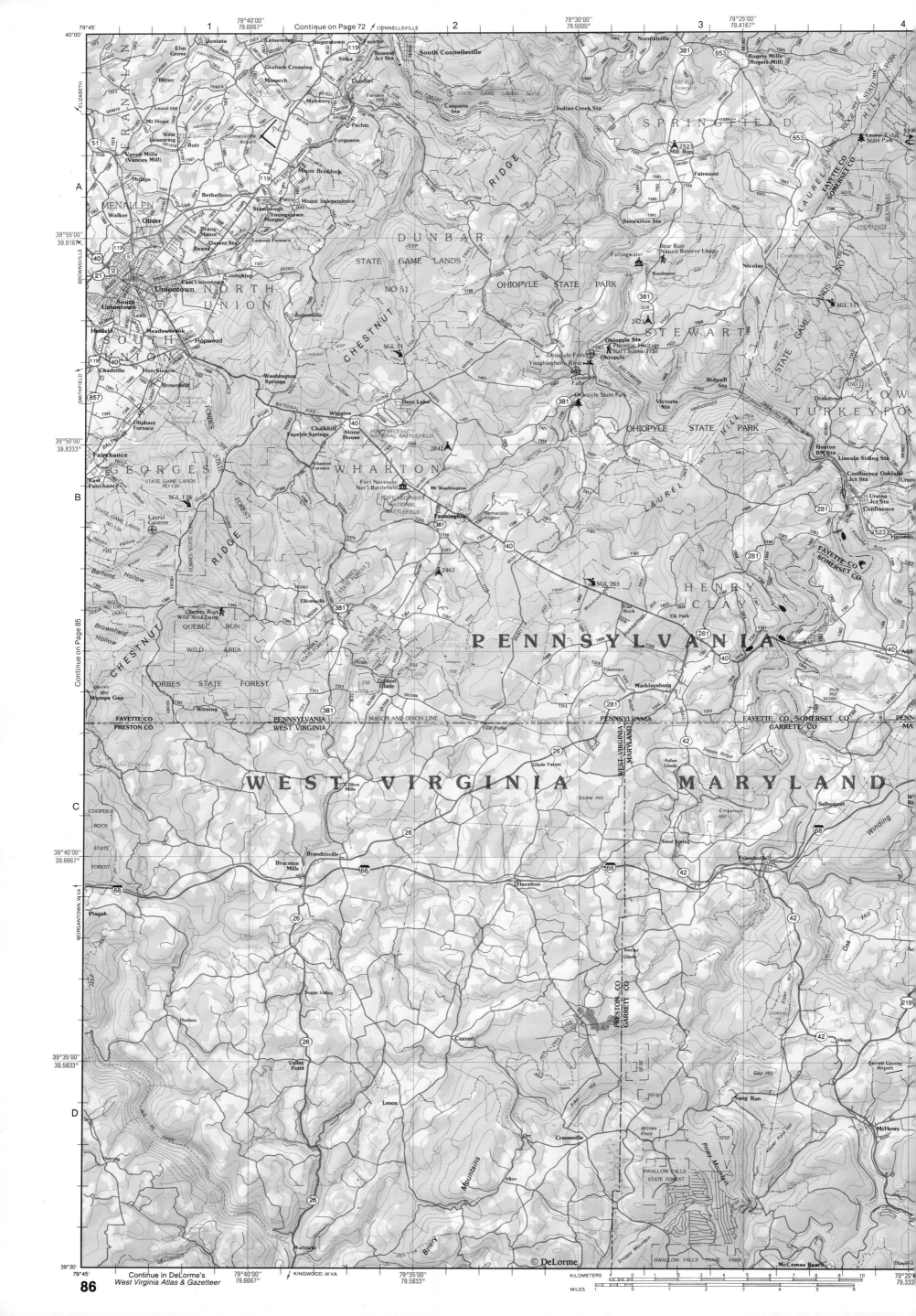

© DeLorme

Continue on Page 88

Scale 1:150,000

Contour interval 50 meters
(50 meters = 164.04 feet)

© DeLorme

Continue in DeLorme's
Maryland/Delaware Atlas & Gazetteer

87

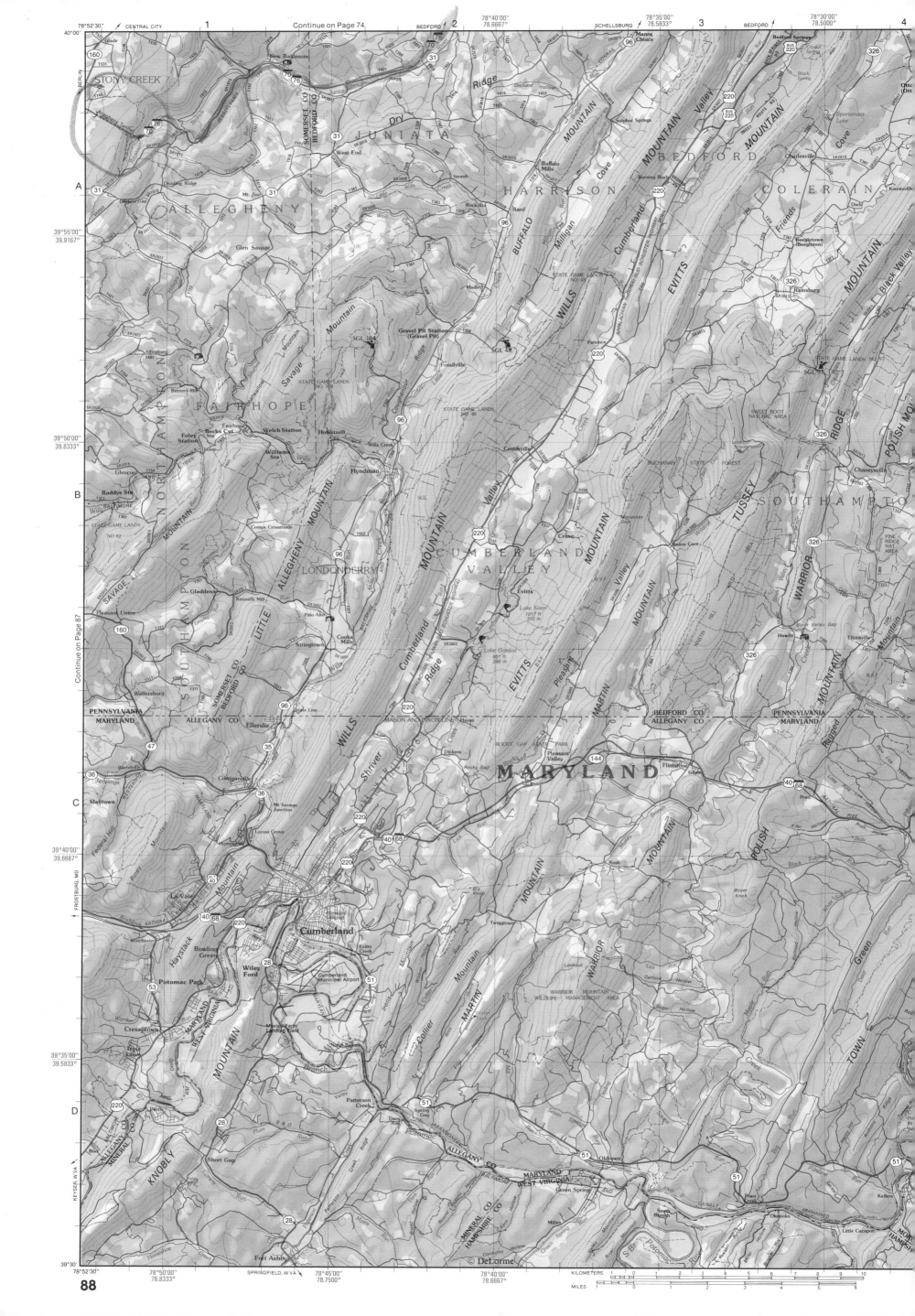

Continue on Page 87

MARYLAND

© DeLorme

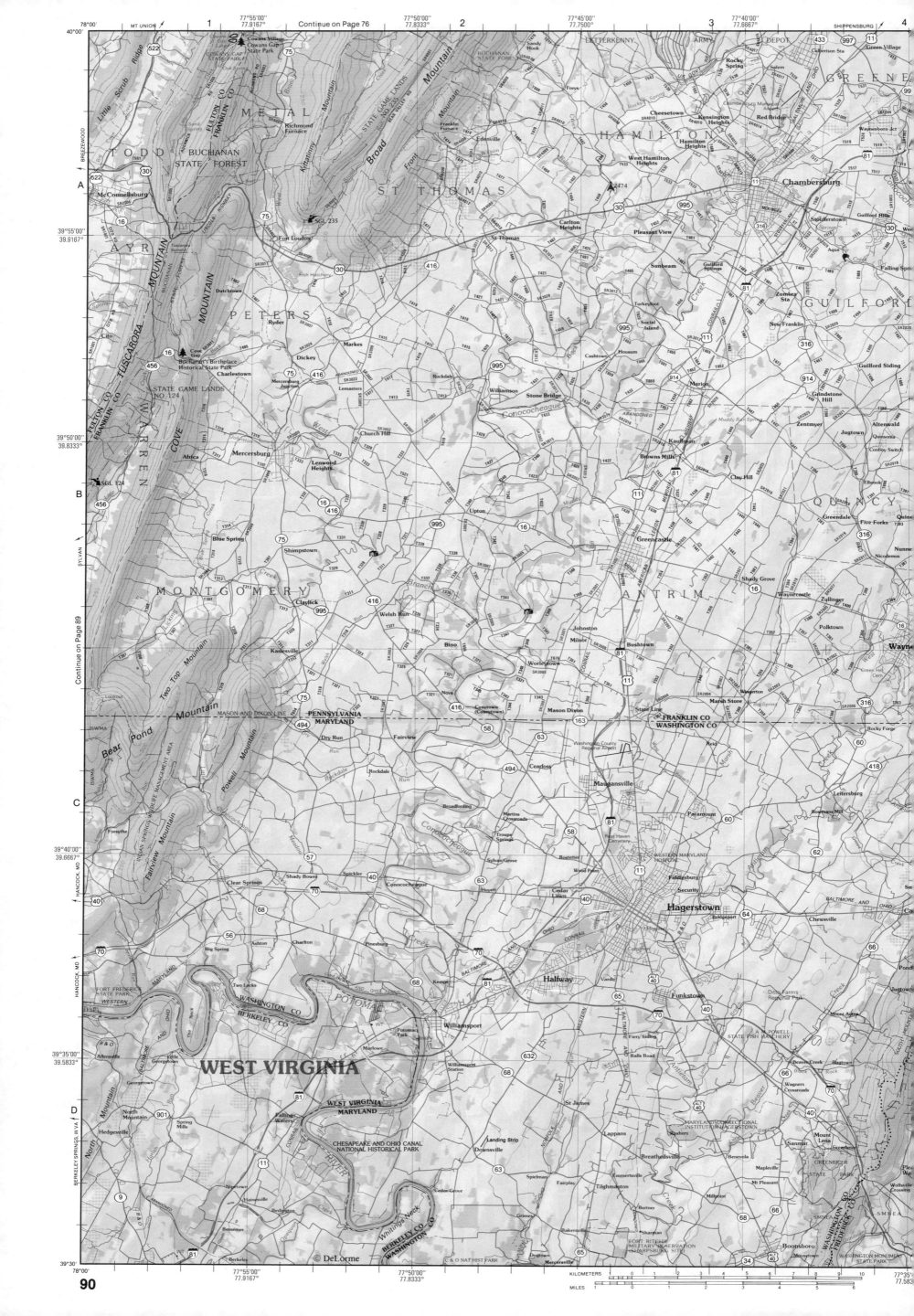

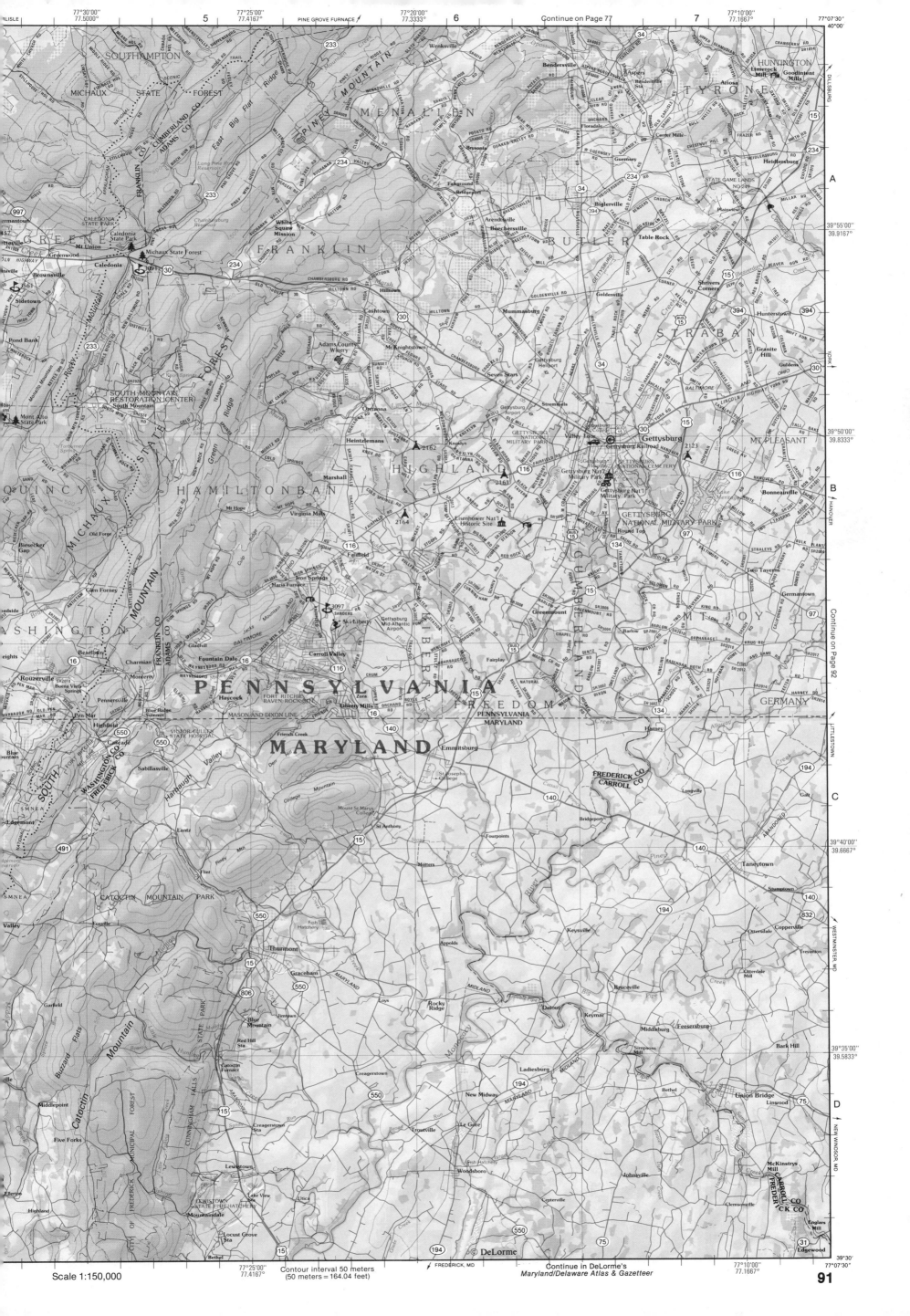

© DeLorme

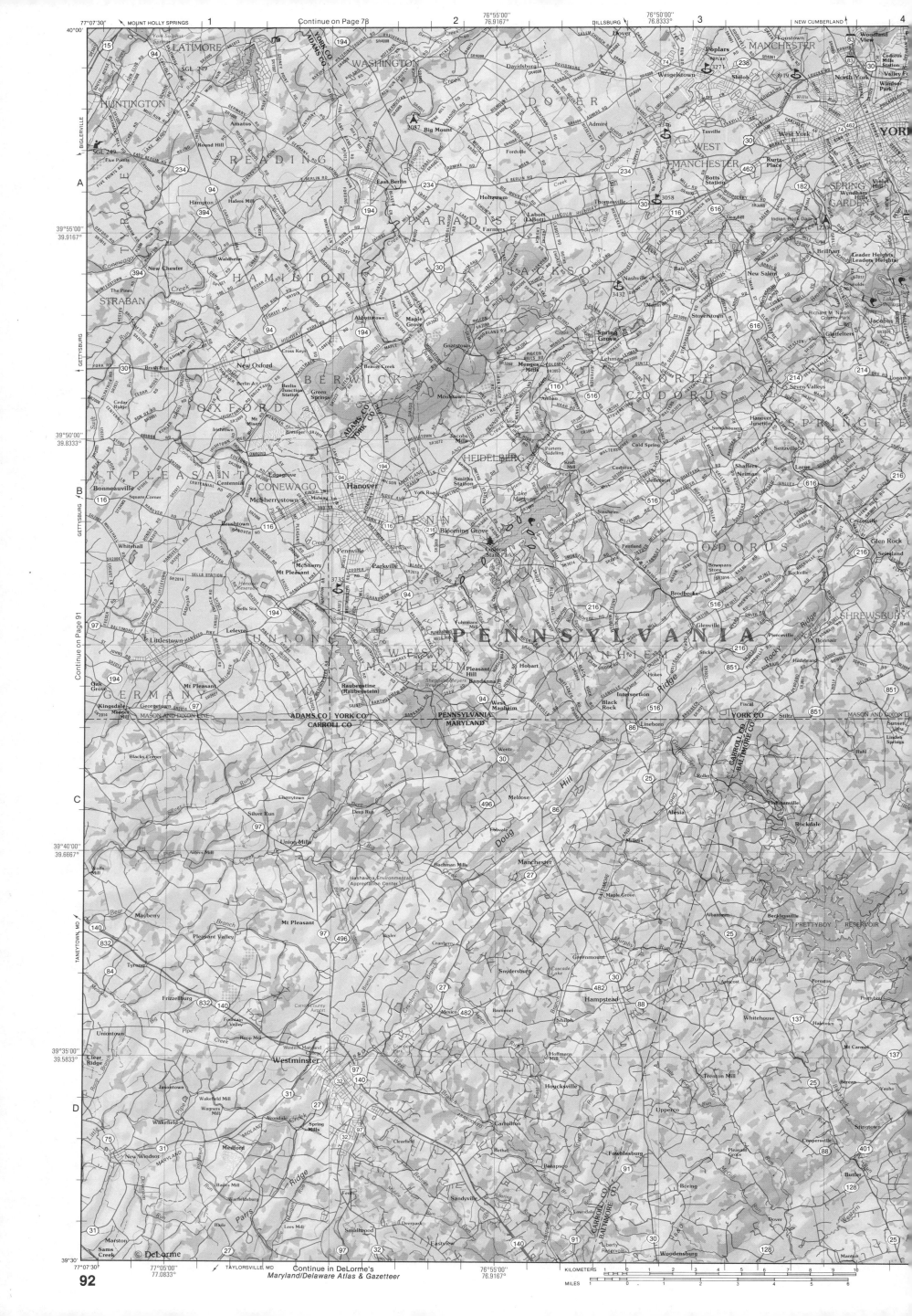

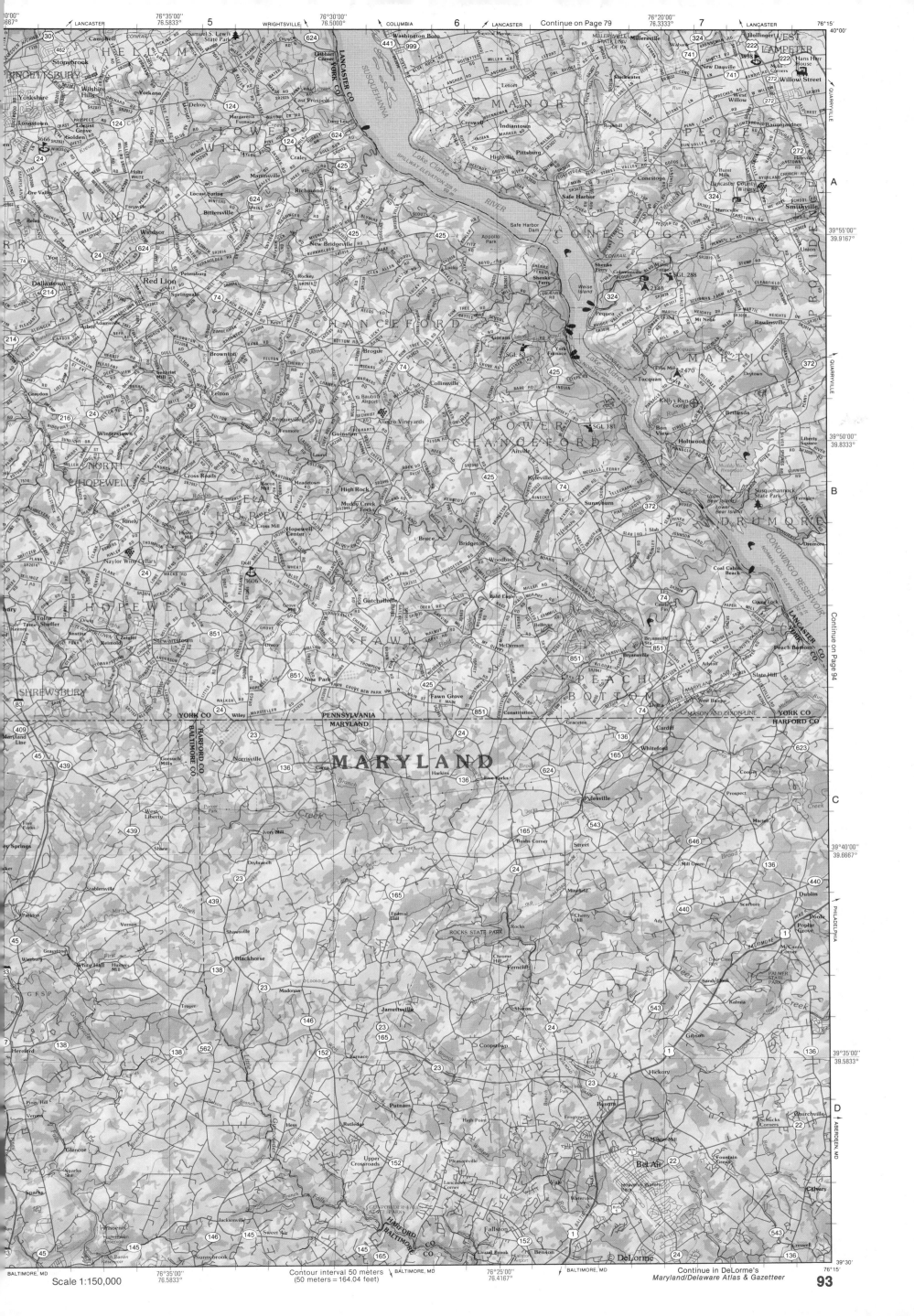

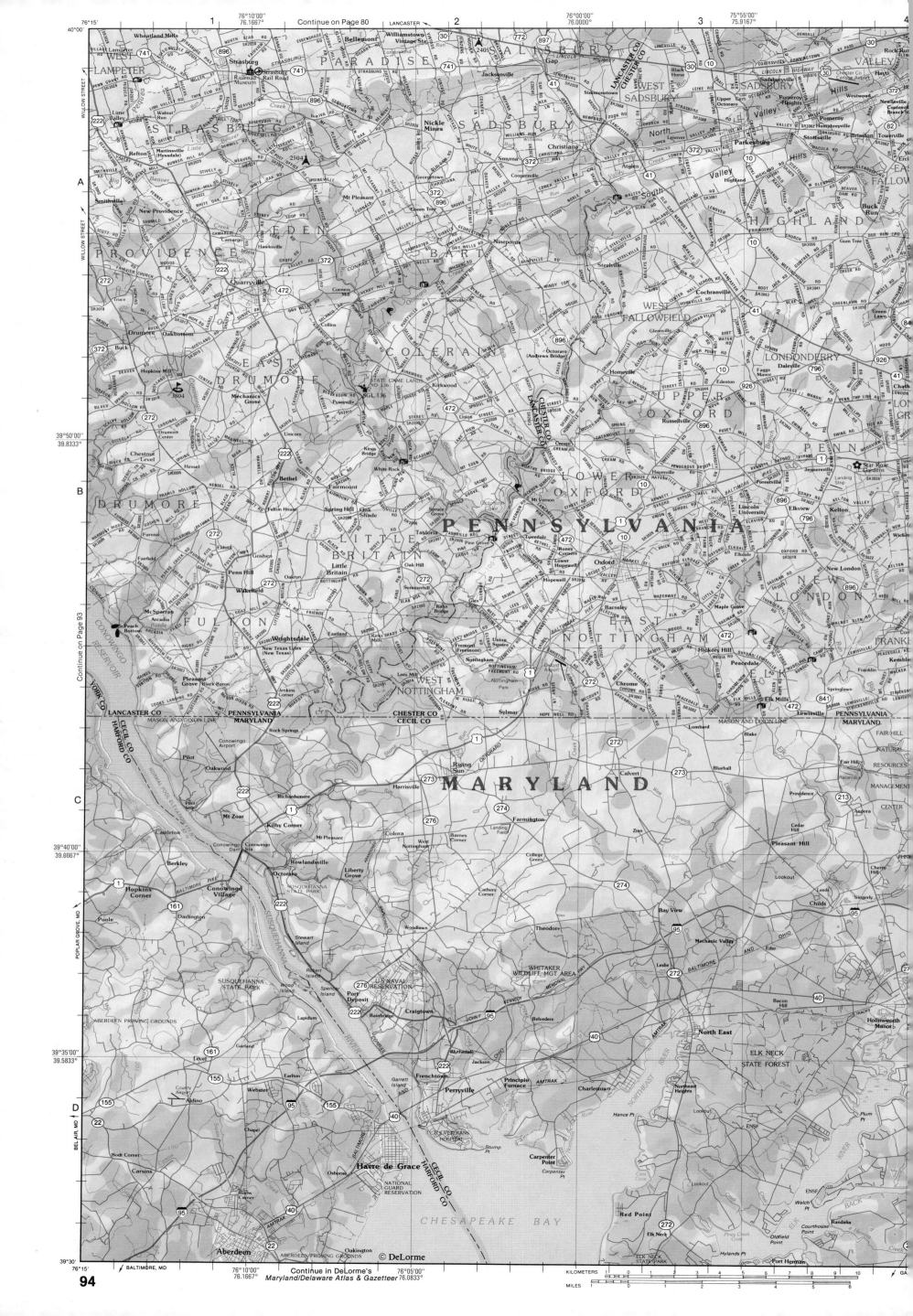

Continue on Page 93

Continue in DeLorme's
Maryland/Delaware Atlas & Gazetteer

© DeLorme

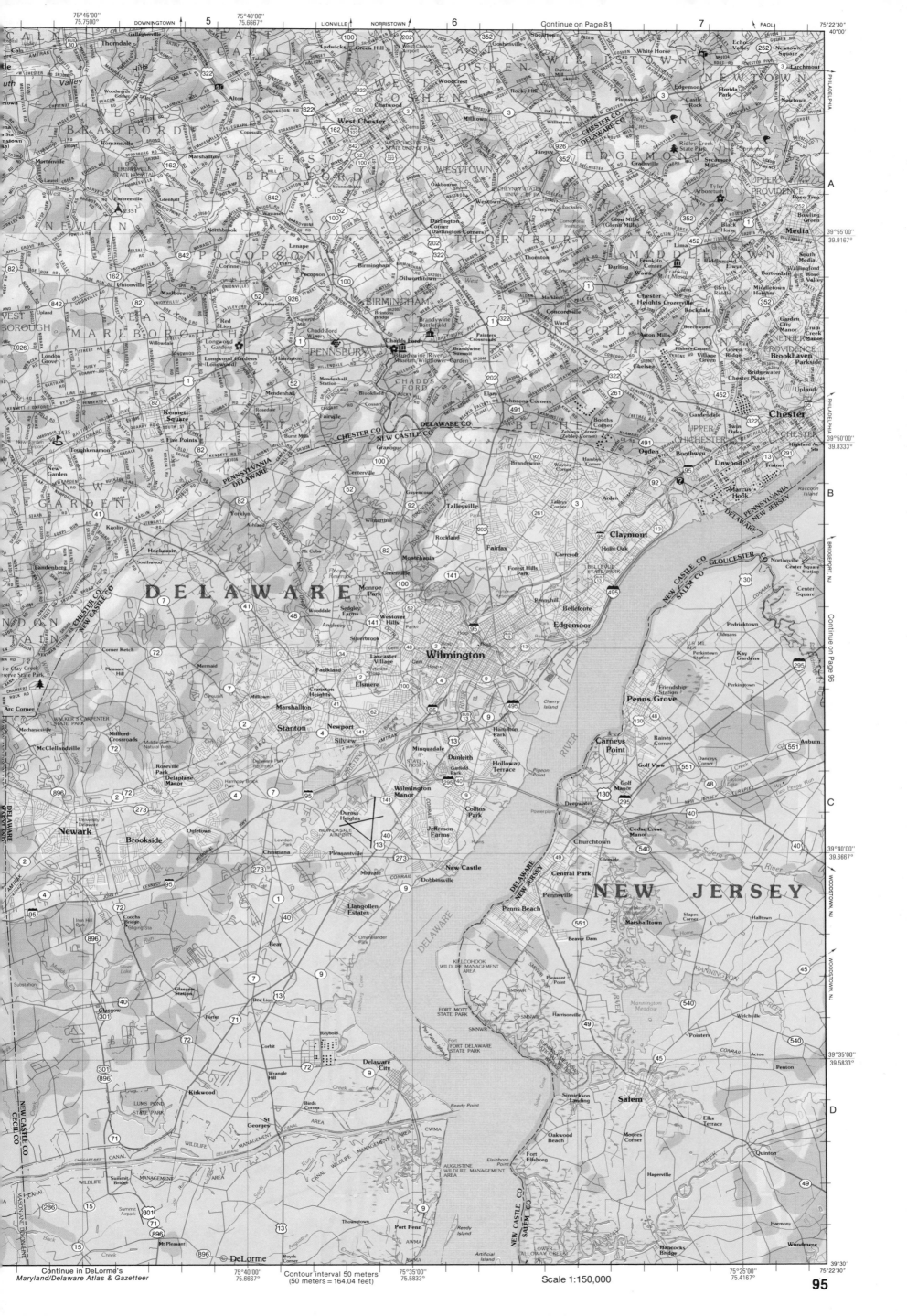

Contour interval 50 meters
(50 meters = 164.04 feet)

Scale 1:150,000